Contents

Introduction	vii
The Lure of the Orient	1
The Adventuring Cabots	4
Martin Frobisher	20
Jacques Cartier	34
Samuel de Champlain	60
Étienne Brûlé	88
Henry Hudson	104
The Quest for Furs	135

Radisson and Groseilliers	138
Henry Kelsey	164
Samuel Hearne	179
Peter Pond	210
David Thompson	225
Captain George Vancouver	261
Bibliography	283

Introduction

The land now called Canada is the second largest nation in the world, exceeded in geographic vastness only by Russia. It occupies more than half of the North American continent, stretching from the Atlantic Ocean to the Pacific, and from the Arctic Archipelago to the forty-ninth parallel. Canada has more miles of coastline than any other nation on Earth. One of the world's great rivers, the St. Lawrence, flows from the heart of the continent, with all but a short stretch of its course entirely in Canadian territory. This is a land of great geographic diversity, some of it extreme: the low, rugged, time-scoured Appalachian Mountains; the wide, rolling blanket of the prairies; the towering peaks of the Rocky Mountains; and the windswept barrens of the high Arctic. It is a land that was completely unknown to the first European explorers who set foot on what are now Canadian shores in the fifteenth century. Over the next four hundred years the adventurers who explored Canada would encounter almost every kind of geographic barrier nature could throw in their way.

Most Canadians learn in their school years about at least a few of the explorers who "discovered" a certain place or "opened up" a new territory. Names like Cabot, Cartier, Champlain and Hudson are familiar. Maps in high school history textbooks trace the routes these explorers took. The names of geographic features like Hudson Bay, Lake Champlain and the Thompson River honour some of the adventurers.

But chapters in schoolbooks and names on maps do not tell the whole story. Behind those brief academic accounts and coloured lines on the maps lie incredible tales of courage, privation and determination; sometimes darkened by greed, bigotry, jealousy and even murder. Most of the men who braved the uncharted Canadian wilderness were not altruists, nor were they seeking knowledge for its own sake. A few, like David Thompson, had training as geographers and possessed a strong desire to fill in the empty spaces on the map. But for many others the prime motivator was profit. They wanted to make their fortunes by finding a western route to China or by opening up new country for the fur trade. Having one's name bestowed on a lake or a mountain would have meant nothing to most of these men.

Canada's great explorers were certainly remarkable men. But they were also subject to the whole gamut of human faults and weaknesses. Many of them held the racially prejudiced attitudes of their time, and considered the Native people of Canada "savages," even though their expeditions were often dependent on their help. Martin Frobisher was a former pirate. Henry Hudson was a remarkably poor leader. Jacques Cartier thought nothing of kidnapping Natives and taking them back to France. Peter Pond may have been guilty of murder. But whatever their motives and whatever their means, these men made their marks on history. We may deplore their shortcomings, but we still acknowledge their remarkable achievements in the annals of exploration history.

Due to space limitations, this book does not include chapters on all of the notable explorers of Canada. In choosing from among the many chronicles of Canadian explorers, I have tried to include the most interesting and dramatic stories from across this country's various regions. I have, therefore, unfortunately and reluctantly, not included chapters on such deserving people as Alexander Mackenzie and Simon Fraser. I hope that this book will inspire readers to delve further into the rich sagas of the Canadian explorers.

Acknowledgements

There have been many accounts describing the exploits of the men who explored Canada. These have been in book length biographical form, textbook format, magazine articles, encyclopedia entries and articles on the Internet. In addition to those authors whose books are listed in the bibliography at the end of this volume, I would like to thank all of those writers whose work I have been exposed to in a lifetime of studying Canadian history. I would also like to thank Paula Sloss and Jordan Fenn for once again entrusting me with a most interesting project. My thanks, as always, to the staff of the Guelph, Ontario Public Library.

For those who continue to explore
From outer space, to the ocean floor

The Lure of the Orient

When Christopher Columbus sailed west from Spain in 1492, he was not setting forth to prove the world is round. Educated Europeans had known since ancient times that the world is a globe. However, the learned men of antiquity and the scientists who succeeded them throughout the centuries erred badly in their calculations as to the size of the Earth. Their mathematics came up short, and they believed the Earth to be much smaller than it actually is. Moreover, they had no idea that on the other side of the Atlantic Ocean lay two continental masses and beyond them another even greater expanse of ocean. Thus, Columbus and men like him believed that the same salt waters that lapped the shores of western Europe also washed the eastern shores of the fabled Orient. All that was required, they believed, was the nerve to sail westward on that unexplored ocean, until they reached Cathay (China), Cipangu (Japan) or the Indies (generally meaning islands off the eastern or southern coasts of Asia). All of these lands were shrouded in myth and legend, and Europeans had very little factual knowledge about them.

Optimists like Columbus believed the journey would take but a few weeks.

Nonetheless, the idea of venturing out onto the Atlantic terrified many European mariners of the time—even though few of them actually believed they would sail over the edge of the world. They were a superstitious lot who believed in sea monsters, giant whirlpools that swallowed ships, and strange lands prowled by man-eating demons. Exploration was also an expensive financial proposition for the sponsors who had to put up the money to pay for ships, provisions and crews.

In those days, ships rarely sailed out of the sight of land. Shipmasters tended to hug the shoreline, sailing by daylight and anchoring at night in a port or some sheltered cove where they could replenish food and fresh water supplies. When they did venture out on a sea like the Mediterranean, it was only because they knew that safe harbours lay just over the horizon. Even if they had wanted to explore farther out, the ships were not built for long ocean voyages.

We like to think that Columbus and men of his ilk were driven by the need to explore uncharted regions. While that might have been a part of their motivation, what actually drove them was the desire to get rich. A practical sea route from Europe to the Orient would mean a fortune to the man who found it.

The seeds for this great quest had been sown a few centuries earlier during the Crusades. During the Middle Ages armies from Christian Europe had gone east to battle with Muslim armies over control of the territory the Crusaders called the Holy Land—the Middle East. In the end, the Crusaders failed but their ventures into the East had acquainted them with a magnificent array of commodities that had previously been unknown in Europe: spices, sugar, medicinal herbs, silks, scented woods, unique jewellery, and intricately woven carpets that the Europeans hung on their walls because they thought them too beautiful to walk on.

Europeans wanted these luxury items, but because the goods had to travel so far to reach the eastern end of the Mediterranean, the cost was enormous. A small box of pepper was virtually worth its weight in gold. Italian ports like Venice became great commercial centres, and merchants became wealthier than kings. When the mighty city of Constantinople (Istanbul) fell to the Ottoman Turks in 1453, trade with the East was seriously compromised.

So Columbus made his first epic voyage in 1492. That expedition was soon followed by the first recorded exploratory European venture to what is now Canada.

The Adventuring Cabots

Across the Cold, Dark Sea

There was a time when almost any Canadian schoolchild could have told you that John Cabot was the man who "discovered" Newfoundland, and that his son Sebastian carried on after him as an explorer. History books credited Cabot with finding the rich fishing grounds on the Grand Banks off Newfoundland; a resource that would eventually be exploited by every maritime nation in Europe, and would be fought over by the armed forces of England and France. There is a statue honouring Cabot at Bonavista, Newfoundland, and a scenic highway, the Cabot Trail, on Cape Breton Island, Nova Scotia, is named for him. But outside Atlantic Canada the Cabot name is barely known. Yet this remarkable navigator was the first European on record (since the time of the Vikings) to set foot on what is now Canadian soil.

John Cabot's early life is shrouded in mystery. None of his letters or journals, nor even a sample of his signature, has ever been found. There is no authenticated portrait of him, and no one knows for certain where or when he was born. There is some evidence, however, that Giovanni Caboto ("John Cabot" is simply the Anglicized form of his name) was born in Genoa, Italy, in 1450.

The earliest historical mention of Cabot's name is on a document granting him citizenship in Venice in 1476. At that time, a foreigner had to be a resident of Venice for at least fifteen years before full citizenship was bestowed. His name does not appear again in Venetian archives until January 1484, when his wife's family transferred a dowry of seventy-five ducats to his name. By 1496 Cabot had three sons: Lewis, Sancio and Sebastian. Of the three, only Sebastian would follow in his father's footsteps.

During his time in Venice, Cabot was a merchant. Venice was one of the trading capitals of the world at that time. It was also a centre of finance and culture, and one of the leading cities of the Renaissance. Venetian ships carried every commodity under the sun, from spices and silks to white slaves who were captured in the Caucasus Mountains and sold in Muslim ports. Venetian mariners were on the leading edge of the science of navigation.

People who knew Cabot later in London wrote that as a Venetian merchant he had been involved in the spice trade in the Levant, a region that roughly included the lands now occupied by Syria, Lebanon, Israel, Jordan and Palestine. He had sailed all over the Mediterranean, had been to the Black Sea, and had visited Alexandria, Egypt, several times. Cabot had even travelled to Mecca, the holy city of Islam. This would have been an especially dangerous undertaking, and Cabot must have travelled in disguise, because Mecca was off-limits to non-Muslims. He did much of his travelling as an agent for a Venetian mercantile firm, trying to discover the source of the spices and other fabulous goods that Arab traders sold to the Europeans at high prices. If someone could find out where the Arabs acquired these items, it was reasoned, then, perhaps Europeans would be able to cut out the middlemen and increase their profits.

Cabot had a reputation as "a most expert mariner" and was also known as a maker of maps and globes. He was familiar with the stories of Marco Polo (a native of Venice), and in his travels he learned of the great caravans that took years to transport the wonderful products of Cathay and Cipango overland to the ports of the Near East. He became intrigued with the idea of a western sea route to the Orient at about the same time that another Italian, Christopher Columbus, was entertaining similar notions.

It is not certain just when Cabot left Venice to search for someone to sponsor a western voyage. Like Columbus, he would have already known that the city states of Italy, which were hundreds of miles from the Atlantic, had no interest in such an expedition. There is a record of a John Cabot in Valencia, Spain, from 1490 to 1493. Although it has not been established with absolute certainty that this was the same John Cabot who had formerly resided in Venice, in all likelihood it was the same person. This John Cabot had two interviews with King Ferdinand, and drew up plans for improving Valencia's harbour. He may even have been there when Columbus passed through the city after his famous voyage.

Columbus passed through many Spanish communities on his way to Barcelona, displaying the goods he had brought back with him, including four naked "Indians" from the newly discovered land. If Cabot did in fact see any of the artifacts Columbus was showing off, he would have recognized that they were different from the eastern products he had seen in the Levant and in Arabia. He would have known, too, that the Caribbean natives Columbus was parading before the amazed Spaniards did not look like any of the Asian people he had encountered in his travels. He may have also questioned why Columbus had not seen any of the fabulous cities Marco Polo had written about.

Cabot had spent years talking to mariners who had sailed all over the known world. He had heard stories about uncharted islands in the western seas. Like most people of that time, Cabot thought the Atlantic Ocean was all that lay between Europe and Asia. Given his knowledge of the Orient, Cabot probably concluded that Columbus had not reached Asia at all, but had run into some previously unknown islands. Cabot speculated that Columbus, in wanting to take advantage of the prevailing winds, had chosen the long route—one that took him across the ocean at the place where the earth was widest. For his own journey, Cabot believed that a northern ocean voyage, where the meridians of longitude were much closer together, would be the quickest way to the Orient. He calculated the trip would take a month; two months at the most.

Cabot, however, could find no backers in Spain. The Spanish Crown was already investing in another expedition to be commanded by Columbus. He tried the Portuguese, but they were already committed to finding a sea route to Asia by sailing around Africa. Cabot's last hope lay with Western Europe's other major seafaring nation: England.

Several years earlier King Henry VII had turned Christopher Columbus away when the navigator sought his sponsorship for a western voyage. Henry was known as a tight-fisted monarch, and he wasn't willing to fritter money away on ocean voyages that might not bear any profit. When it appeared that Spain and Portugal had begun outstripping England in their quest for a sea route to Cathay, Henry began having second thoughts. He was therefore very receptive when, sometime before the end of 1495,

John Cabot arrived in England with a plan to reach the Orient by a northern sea route; a sea route that England, by virtue of its geographic location, could command.

Though we know very little about John Cabot the man, the fact that Henry VII was willing to be his patron is significant. Henry was a shrewd, calculating man who never made impulsive decisions. Moreover, like most Englishmen of the time, he wasn't particularly fond of "foreigners." The monarch would have had Cabot's background thoroughly investigated before committing any money to his voyage. Cabot would also have had to pass muster with the hard-nosed businessmen and jealous sea captains of Bristol, the city in which he had settled. The fact that the king, the merchants and the captains accepted Cabot for his exploratory journey indicates that he must have been a man of considerable standing in the English maritime community.

It was no accident that Cabot chose Bristol as his new home and base of operations. Located at the confluence of the Avon and the Frome rivers, 8 miles upstream from the Bristol Channel, Bristol was the second busiest port in England, surpassed only by London in the volume of merchandise it handled. The Bristol men had watched with envy as Italian merchants grew wealthy from the spice trade. Now they rubbed their hands together in eager anticipation of Cabot's voyage. They believed his exploring success would not only provide them with an entry into that business, but might also put them in control of it.

But there was something else that drew Cabot to Bristol; a secret that most other Europeans were unaware of. Many people of the time believed that somewhere to the west of Ireland lay a legendary island called Brasilia. Bristol sailors, in search of new fishing grounds that would lessen their dependence on Icelandic cod, claimed to have seen it. It is almost certain that Bristol fishermen were making regular trips to the Grand Banks before Cabot ever sailed west. However, nobody had charted or recorded Newfoundland's location. Nobody could point to a map and show where this land was, or prove that it existed at all. Was it part of Asia? Cabot thought it could be. And even if it was just a remote island, he thought it could be an important way station for ships sailing to China. It would therefore be in England's best interest to locate it and take possession.

Bristol merchants put up the money for Cabot to undertake a voyage of exploration. Henry VII, as parsimonious as ever, did not help financially, but he gave Cabot his official and political support. On March 5, 1496, Henry signed the following declaration:

> Be it known and made manifest that we have given and granted … to our well-beloved John Cabot, citizen of Venice, and to Lewis, Sebastian and Sancio, sons of the said John, and to their heirs … full and free authority … to sayle to all partes, countreyes and seas … to seeke out, discover and finde whatsoever iles, countreyes, regions or provinces of the heathen or infidelles … whiche before this time have been unknowen to all Christians.

Though Henry had not invested financially in the voyage, the Crown would profit from any trade that resulted to the tune of "the fifth part of the Capitall gaine so gotten."

Henry had to tread cautiously, however. Spain and Portugal had recently signed the Treaty of Tordesillas, which gave them exclusive rights to all undiscovered lands from the North Pole to the South Pole. As the ruler of a country the Spanish and

Portuguese generally considered to be backwards, poor, and militarily unimportant, Henry had not been consulted on the treaty. He therefore did not believe he was legally bound by it. As far as Henry was concerned, if Cabot discovered new lands at England's latitudes, those lands were England's. But he took care to instruct Cabot not to venture south. He didn't want to provoke a war with Spain or Portugal. It has even been speculated that Spanish or Portuguese agents sabotaged Cabot's first voyage once they found out about it.

For over four hundred years, historians thought Cabot made his first voyage in 1497, and they wondered why he waited so long after receiving the king's permission to go. Then, in 1956, a letter turned up in Spain's national archives that solved the riddle. The letter was written by a Bristol merchant named John Day in December 1497, or January 1498, and may have been intended for Christopher Columbus in Spain. In the letter Day mentions Cabot's 1497 voyage, and makes reference to an aborted voyage in 1496: "Since your Lordship wants information relating to the first voyage, here is what happened: he (Cabot) went with one ship, his crew confused him, he was short of supplies and he ran into bad weather, and he decided to turn back."

This is the only documentation ever found concerning Cabot's 1496 voyage. Historians are not certain what Day meant by "his crew confused him." It is known that Cabot expected to hire Bristol sailors who were familiar with northern waters. Were the men he took aboard not as knowledgeable as he had hoped, causing him to get lost? Was there a mutiny? Did his crew include spies for the Spanish or Portuguese, who had instructions to make sure the voyage was a failure? Spies and informers were always skulking around seaports, watching and listening for information that could be of interest to foreign powers. The Spanish and Portuguese did not like the idea of England making territorial claims across the Atlantic; the king of Portugal had even sent a delegation to London, warning Henry not to support any trans-Atlantic expeditions.

King Henry VII's charter allowed Cabot to sail with as many as five ships, but the Bristol merchants, for all their high hopes, would risk only enough money for one. This was the bark *Matthew,* a small ship of 55 to 60 tons with a crew of eighteen or twenty men, which may have been specially constructed for the voyage.

Cabot sailed from Bristol late in May. He set his course for Dursey Head, a promontory on the south coast of Ireland. Once he put the coast of Ireland behind him, Cabot would be in uncharted waters. His principle navigational aids were a compass and a cross-staff and astrolabe for measuring latitude. The astrolabe was more accurate than the cross-staff, but was difficult to use if the ship was rolling. There was not yet an instrument with which to determine longitude, so navigators had to rely on dead-reckoning, a system that combined celestial observations and an estimation of the distance the vessel had drifted in a specific length of time.

No record of that epic voyage has survived. Historians aren't certain if Cabot took a direct route across the Atlantic—which would have been very difficult because of the contrary winds and the North Atlantic Drift—or if he sailed northwest from Ireland and then took advantage of the East Greenland and Labrador Currents, a more likely route. Cabot would have had to contend with icebergs, fog and perhaps even a problem that Columbus had experienced—a crew that became very uneasy once they left familiar waters.

Conditions on board the *Matthew* would have been uncomfortable at the best of times. To begin with, they were sailing in chilly latitudes. Fresh fruit and vegetables would have been consumed during the first few days. After that, it was a monotonous diet of salt beef, salt cod, hardtack biscuits and beer, which kept better than fresh water. Over time the biscuits would become wormy, and sailors sometimes waited until after dark to eat them, so they wouldn't have to see the maggots. Whenever the weather permitted, crewmen slept on deck wrapped in blankets or old sails. Below deck, the air smelled of tar and rotting food, and like every other wooden sailing ship, the *Matthew* was crawling with rats. Though Cabot's own log has never been found, we do have two contemporary references to his voyage, although some of the information may be inaccurate. In his letter to Spain, John Day wrote:

> They left England toward the end of May, and must have been on the way 35 days before sighting land; the wind was east-north-east and the sea calm going and coming back, except for one day when he ran into a storm two or three days before finding land; and going so far out, his compass needle failed to point north and marked two rhumbs [a line or course on a single bearing; any of the points on a mariner's compass] below.

Raimondo di Soncino, a personal friend of Cabot, wrote to the Duke of Milan in December 1497 about the voyage:

> He started from Bristol, a port on the west of this kingdom, passed Ireland, which is still further west, and then

> bore towards the north, in order to sail to the east [Orient], leaving the north [Pole Star] on his right hand after some days. After having wandered for some time he at length arrived at the mainland.

By the Julian calendar, in use at the time, Cabot made his landfall on June 24. That would be July 3 on our Gregorian calendar. Exactly where Cabot first set foot on North American soil is still a matter of considerable debate. Although today Newfoundland and Cape Breton Island both claim the honour, historians have speculated that he could have landed in places as far apart as Baffin Island and the state of Maine. Mainland Nova Scotians believe he landed on their peninsula, and later sailed past Cape Breton and the island he called the "new founde launde." Others believe the landing site was probably somewhere on the coast of Labrador.

Cabot and his men went ashore, probably bearing the coat of arms of Henry VII. Since Cabot and all of his crew were Catholic, they might also have carried the banner of Pope Alexander VI. Cabot later reported seeing tall trees "of the kind masts are made," as well as signs of human habitation; the remains of a campfire, snares used in capturing small animals, needles for making nets and an eighteen-inch-long stick pierced at both ends, carved and painted red. Not knowing what sort of reception they might get from the local people, Cabot and his men did not wander far, nor did they remain ashore for very long.

After returning to his ship, Cabot apparently spent some time exploring the coasts of Newfoundland and Nova Scotia. He saw dense, beautiful forests, and what he thought were small villages. One day he and his men saw the shadows of two forms running along the shore, but they could not tell if they were men or animals.

Most importantly, they noted an abundance of fish, particularly cod, which the English at that time called stockfish. As Soncino would later report in his letter, "They assert that the sea there is swarming with fish, which can be taken not only with the net, but in baskets let down with a stone, so that it sinks in the water."

It took the *Matthew* only fifteen days to re-cross the Atlantic. Once again "confused" by his crew, Cabot missed England and landed on the coast of Brittany, France. He turned back for England and arrived in Bristol about August 6. A few days later he was in London to make his report to the king. Like Columbus, Cabot thought he had reached Asia. Henry was immensely pleased. He gave Cabot a present of ten pounds—a lot of money at the time, especially coming from a skinflint like Henry—and promised Cabot an annual pension of twenty pounds. Soon Cabot was walking the streets of London dressed in silk, with admiring crowds following him. The ambassadors of various nations quickly wrote to their lords and sovereigns, telling them of Cabot's discoveries on behalf of England. Pedro de Ayala, representing King Ferdinand and Queen Isabella of Spain, told King Henry that the lands Cabot had discovered were rightfully Spain's. De Ayala wrote to the Spanish monarchs:

> I find that what they have discovered or are in search of is possessed by Your Highnesses because it is at the cape[1] which fell to Your Highnesses by the convention with Portugal. ... The king has spoken to me several times on the subject. ... I told him that I believed the islands were

[1] De Ayala thought Cabot had made his landfall at Cuba, which Columbus had already claimed for Spain. Columbus thought Cuba was a cape or peninsula attached to China.

> those found by Your Highnesses, and although I gave him the main reason, he would not have it. Since I believe Your Highnesses will already have notice of all this and also of the chart or mappermonde which this man has made, I do not send it now, although it is here, and so far as I can see exceedingly false, in order to make believe that these are not part of the said islands.

In February, 1498, King HenryVII signed a new charter for Cabot. This time the explorer would have five armed ships, supplies to last a year, and instructions to follow the coast southwest from the "new founde launde" until he reached the land of the Great Khan, the emperor of China. Cabot was also given a large number of convicts who were to be "colonists" in the new land. This was a direct challenge to Spanish claims. It is very possible, though as yet no solid evidence has been uncovered, that the Spanish decided to thwart Henry's plans by means of a hired killer.

The expedition sailed from Bristol in early May. In July, news came that one of the ships had been damaged in a storm and put into an Irish port. From that point nothing is certain, and John Cabot vanishes from history. Historians have suggested several possible explanations.

Perhaps Cabot's expedition failed and he returned to England in disgrace, and then either died or went home to Italy. There has been no documentation to prove this, but his pension was drawn for the years 1498 and 1499. Although it's possible, the pension could have been paid to his wife. Cabot would have been in his late forties, which was considered old age at that time.

It might also be that all of Cabot's ships went down in a storm. An Italian chronicler writing about the event around 1512 stated:

> John [Cabot] set out in this same year and sailed first to Ireland. Then he set sail towards the west. In the event he is believed to have found the new lands nowhere but on the bottom of the ocean, to which he is thought to have descended together with his boat … since after that voyage he was never seen again anywhere.

However, if Cabot's entire fleet was lost, it would be the only time in all the great age of exploration that a disaster of such magnitude occurred. There is evidence, too, that at least some of Cabot's ships made it to North America. In the summer of 1501 the Portuguese explorer Gaspar Corte-Real made a landing at a location historians believe was either Nova Scotia or Quebec. He found the natives there in possession of a piece of a broken gilt sword that had been made in Italy, and two silver earrings that were clearly from Venice. These artifacts could not have come from anyone else but Cabot's crew. It was known that Cabot had taken along such goods for use in trade. Had the natives killed the Europeans? Possibly, but not likely, as the natives showed no hostility toward the Corte-Real party. It is not out of the question, though, that a sinister fate did befall the men of Cabot's 1498 expedition.

The Spanish were not at all happy about Henry of England sending explorers into what they considered their domain. The Spanish government had also become disillusioned with Christopher Columbus, who still had not brought back the mountains of gold and silver he'd promised. They also felt that he was mismanaging their affairs in the New World. Ferdinand and Isabella believed they had the answer to both problems in the person of Alonso de Ojeda. This man was the prototype for the ruthless conquistadores who would carve out an empire through violence and treachery. De Ojeda was a soldier of fortune, who had been captain of a ship in Columbus' second expedition. He was a cutthroat who treated the Natives with brutality and committed acts of piracy whenever he could get away with it.

The Spanish government gave de Ojeda three ships and copies of Columbus' charts, and sent him off in 1499 to look for the gold Columbus had failed to find. It is very possible that de Ojeda had instructions to watch for the Cabot expedition. Knowing the sort of man de Ojeda was, the king and queen would have a good idea of how he would deal with the interlopers.

De Ojeda landed in South America, and then rampaged up and down the coast, robbing, raping and killing Natives he encountered. He named one region Venezuela (Little Venice) when he saw Natives living in houses that were built over the water on stilts. Then, according to one Spanish historian, "It is certain that Hojeda in his first voyage [1499] encountered certain Englishmen in the vicinity of Coquibacoa."

The only Englishmen they could possibly have been would be Cabot's men, making their way south from Newfoundland in their search for the land of the Great Khan. Unfortunately there is no record saying just what happened. We can only assume that if de Ojeda encountered the English, he and his men killed them. There is evidence that this may have, in fact, been the case. When de Ojeda returned to Spain, he was rewarded with property on the island of Hispaniola (now the Dominican Republic and Haiti) "for the stopping of the English."

On that expedition with de Ojeda was a cartographer named Juan de la Cosa. In 1832, a map made by de la Cosa in 1500 was discovered. It showed geographic features that the Spanish had not yet discovered by that time, including one place labelled *mar descubierto par inglese* ("sea discovered by the English"). De la Cosa could only have discovered such information from charts and notes made by Cabot or his men. If so, the English had made a remarkable journey of 5,500 miles, only to be murdered by the vicious de Ojeda. Fittingly, in 1510, de Ojeda died of wounds he received in a battle with the Natives.

The English were slow to exploit John Cabot's discoveries. More than a century passed before they made any serious effort to stake their claims to North America, and by then they would find themselves engaged in a series of bloody conflicts with the French. Meanwhile, another Cabot took to the sea as an explorer.

John Cabot's name was not as exalted as that of Christopher Columbus, and this was largely because his son Sebastian tried to steal his father's glory. It's possible that Sebastian was with his father on the *Matthew,* though there is no record of it. Sebastian would have been thirteen or fourteen years old, not an uncommon age for boys to be sent to sea. In 1508, Sebastian, sponsored by the same Bristol merchants who had backed his father, sailed off in search of a Northwest Passage. No record of that voyage has survived. However, according to chroniclers who wrote of it later—based on information that supposedly came from Sebastian Cabot himself—the explorer set out with two ships and three hundred men. The geography the younger Cabot described indicated that he might have actually made it to Hudson's Bay. If he did, all records of the accomplishment were lost, leaving the bay to be "discovered" again more than a century later.

After that one voyage to the Arctic, Cabot could find no more backing in England. Henry VII died, and the new king, Henry VIII, was not interested in Arctic voyages, though he did employ

Cabot as a cartographer. In 1512, Sebastian went to work for the Spanish. He decided to embellish his personal resumé by claiming his father's accomplishments as his own. As a result, for generations, historians credited Sebastian Cabot with explorations done by John.

In 1525, Cabot led a Spanish expedition of three ships and 150 men to Brazil. He was to explore the east coast of South America to its southern extremity and then continue up the Pacific coast. Instead, he went looking for gold in the vicinity of Rio de la Plata, where he lost men in battles with the natives. When Cabot returned to Spain in 1530 with only one ship and twenty-four men, he faced criminal charges for mismanaging the expedition and disobeying orders. A court ordered him banished to Africa, but he appealed his exile and won.

Cabot worked for the Spanish until about 1547, when he returned to England. He was one of the founders of the Muscovy Company of Merchant Adventurers, which engaged in trade with Russia. On his recommendation, the company financed further explorations, looking for the Northwest Passage, which were all disastrous. Sebastian Cabot is believed to have died in London in 1557. Eventually his claims to his father's accomplishments were proven false, and John Cabot was restored to his rightful place in Canadian history.

Martin Frobisher

Fool's Gold

If Captain Martin Frobisher had any second thoughts about pursuing his quest for the Northwest Passage that stormy July 13, 1576, he did not show it. His small bark, the *Gabrielle,* was being tossed around like a cork in the icy seas off Greenland and his crew was panic-stricken. A few days earlier one of the *Gabrielle*'s companion vessels, a small pinnace, had gone down with all hands in just such a storm. Then the *Gabrielle's* sister ship, the *Michael,* had turned tail for England, where the skipper reported the *Gabrielle* lost.

But the *Gabrielle* was not lost. Bellowing orders over the shrieking of the wind and the crash of green water on his decks, Frobisher was as determined to beat the storm as he was to find the Northwest Passage. As the vessel shipped water and was almost on her beam, he clambered along her side and told the terrified sailors to cut away the mizzen-mast to lighten the drag. The men wanted to cast away the main mast, too, but Frobisher wouldn't allow it. Instead he ordered the men to heave on the weather leech of the foresail to rock the *Gabrielle* and empty her of water. This worked, and the small ship righted herself on the huge swells. The next day Frobisher's confidence emerged unshaken from his battle with the Atlantic. The storm died down, and the battered *Gabrielle* continued on her quest. The eighteen crewmen, relieved though they were that the captain had saved them from a watery grave, wanted to turn back for England. Frobisher would have none of it.

Martin Frobisher was a man of his times, cut from the same cloth as the sea dogs John Hawkins and Francis Drake. He was born in the Yorkshire village of Altofts around 1539 and had little formal education. But he went to sea as a youth and became a mariner and navigator. As a young man he engaged in the African slave trade. In this Frobisher was no worse than most of his European contemporaries. The enslavement of non-white, non-Christian people was considered a perfectly legitimate business, however reprehensible it seems now.

Ironically, the slave trade was a dangerous profession for the white men who went to Africa's Guinea Coast to obtain their human merchandise. Violence was the hallmark of the trade. Slavers from England, France, Spain and Portugal fought each other over the best hunting grounds and slaving stations. African chiefs in coastal regions joined in the fray, fighting each other for the right to raid inland and sell their fellow Africans to the whites. Tropical diseases, to which the whites had no immunity, swept through the crews of slave ships. Thousands of European sailors died far from home and were buried on the African coast, or were simply dropped overboard into shark-infested waters. Frobisher endured more than the usual hardships that were part and parcel of the slaving business. He was once taken prisoner by a tribal chief and turned over to the Portuguese, who held him hostage for nine months. According to one contemporary, the young man was able to survive such an ordeal because of his "great spirit and bould courage and, naturall hardnes of body."

Frobisher's misadventures in commercial trade—even something as exotic as slaving—seem to have soured him on the prospects of being a merchant seaman. Like other rising young Englishmen of the time, Frobisher wanted to make his fortune. He saw his opportunity not in legitimate trade, but in privateering and even outright piracy. By the age of thirty, he was captain of a ship, and was pillaging the vessels of France and Spain, nations with which England was not at war. Frobisher was a big man—probably over six feet tall—and muscular. He was known for his great physical strength and his explosive temper. It's hardly surprising that in Frobisher's best-known portrait, he is holding a pistol. His "divers and sundrye pyracies" angered the king of Spain and were an embarrassment to England's Queen Elizabeth I.

Frobisher was arrested four times for piracy, and was once imprisoned. But Queen Elizabeth had a soft spot for English freebooters who harassed England's main rivals. Instead of being punished for his roguish ways, Frobisher was given command of a ship that was supplying the English army fighting rebels in Ireland. Once he had delivered his cargo, Frobisher went right back to plundering French vessels. Another warrant for his arrest was issued, and once again Frobisher managed to avoid prosecution.

The English still believed that their path to wealth and glory lay in the discovery of a Northwest Passage through John Cabot's "new founde launde," which would lead to the fabulous Orient. Such a shortcut would put England ahead of Spain and Portugal,

At first glance Frobisher, a former slaver and an unrepentant pirate, seems an unlikely candidate for the position of Arctic explorer. But he had qualities that were essential to such an undertaking; he was utterly fearless, he let nothing stand in the way of his quest for riches, he was an energetic and inspirational leader, and when he got hold of an idea he held onto it with unshakeable determination. George Best, a soldier of fortune who sailed with Frobisher, wrote of the captain's obsession with the Northwest Passage:

> He began first with himselfe to devise, and then with his friends to conferre, and layde a playne platte unto them, that that voyage was not onely possible by the Northwest, but also as he coulde prove, easie to be performed. And further, he determined and resolved with himselfe, to go make full proofe therof, & to accomplishe, or bring true certificate of the truth, or else never to returne againe, knowing this to be the onely thing of the Worlde that was left undone, whereby a notable mind mighte be made famous and fortunate.

Frobisher biographer James McDermott considers Best's observations somewhat exaggerated. In his opinion, Frobisher would have been willing to undertake any project that might make him "famous and fortunate." Nonetheless, Frobisher presented himself as the man who could find the Northwest Passage for England.

A major problem for Frobisher was the Muscovy Company, a powerful firm that monopolized all northern exploration and trade. The Muscovites, as the company men were called, had been seeking a Northeast Passage via the White Sea and Russia, but had developed a lucrative trade with the Russians, and neglected their search.

Frobisher persuaded the company, through a director named Michael Lok, to permit him to search for the passage. Lok was a remarkable man, who came from an influential family (his great-grandfather had been sheriff of London and a member of King Edward IV's honour guard, and his father had been mercer to King Henry VIII), and had a strong interest in cosmography and cartography. He had travelled widely and spoke Spanish, French, Italian, Latin, Greek and possibly even Arabic. He was a patriot with a great desire to see England emerge from its position as a backwater nation to take a leading role as one of Europe's foremost commercial powers. Lok was impressed with the robust, swaggering Frobisher. Some historians have speculated — though there is no solid evidence — that Lok was the man who secured Frobisher's release from his Portuguese captors years earlier. Lok wrote the following about his close relationship with Frobisher:

> And hereupon I used M(aster) Furbusher as my fellow and frinde, and opened unto him all myne own private studies and labores passed in twenty yeares continuans befor, for knowledge of the state of the worlde, and shewed him all my bookes, cartes, mappes, instruments … and writings, and my notes collected thereof … And to be short, dalye increased my good will towards him, making my howse his howse, and my purse his purse at his neede.

The director believed that if a search for the Northwest Passage should prove unsuccessful, "the Cuntries … Canada, & the new fownd Lands thereto adjoining" were full of commodities, such as furs, that were highly profitable. Lok talked other men into supporting the venture, and he himself put up half the money, about 550 pounds, for Frobisher's voyage.

On June 7, 1576, the *Gabrielle* and the *Michael* were ready to sail. Both were barks of 25 to 30 tons, three-masted and about forty feet in length and twelve feet in the beam. These were small crafts in which to brave the forbidding Arctic. The *Gabrielle* had a cabin for Frobisher's use, while the rest of the men had to work, eat and sleep on deck or in the hold in conditions modern sailors would find appalling. Frobisher also had a 7-ton pinnace that could be used for in-shore exploration. The captain sailed with thirty-five men and the queen's blessing, as well as letters from Elizabeth recommending him to the Oriental princes he expected to meet.

Frobisher was uncomfortable with some of the new navigational aids available to him. Instead, he relied heavily on maps, charts and sheer instinct. Since many of the maps were inaccurate, Frobisher made mistakes when judging his fleet's position, including mistaking Greenland for the mythical island of Friesland. In late July, after his heroic battle with the storm, Frobisher sighted land, which he named Queen Elizabeth's Foreland. Later, what he took for a part of Greenland was actually Resolution Island, off the southern tip of Baffin Island. Turning north, Frobisher sailed into "a great gutte, bay or passage dividing as it were two mayne lands or continents asunder."

The land Frobisher and his men saw was completely alien to them. It was treeless, ice-bound and surrounded by high, barren peaks. Cold winds blew relentlessly and the sky was continually overcast and grey. The men could not have imagined a more forbidding place.

They decided to land on a tiny island to reconnoiter the area from a high point. A sailor named Robert Garrard picked up a black rock, "as great as a halfe pennye loaf," which he thought was coal. He took it back to the ship, where they were short on fuel for cooking and heat. The finding of that rock was to have dramatic consequences in the near future.

Frobisher believed he had found the Strait of Anian, the channel that supposedly separated America from Asia. He decided to rename it Frobisher's Straits. He made repairs to the *Gabrielle,* and then continued on into the "straits," steering around icebergs that would have sunk his ship with the slightest brush. At any moment he expected to see the great western ocean that would take him to the Orient.

Nineteen miles short of the head of what is now Frobisher Bay, where he realized his error, Frobisher landed on another small island. There he had his first encounter with the Inuit, whom he described as "strange and beastly." The features of the Natives, which Frobisher likened to those of "Tartars," further convinced him that he had reached a northern extremity of Asia.

The first meeting of Inuit and Englishmen was peaceful. The sailors traded knives and mirrors for sealskins and bear hides. The awestruck Natives examined the *Gabrielle* from top to bottom. They marvelled at the guns and rigging, but spat out the strangers' offerings of salt meat and beer.

One hunter agreed, through signs, to guide the ship up the coast. After that, everything went sour. A landing party of five men, including Garrard, disappeared, along with the ship's only boat. Cut off from shore, and suspecting that the Natives were holding his men hostage, Frobisher decided to take prisoners himself and arrange a trade. He lured an Inuit in a kayak to the ship by ringing a bell then "plucked him with maine force boate and al into his bark and out of the sea." There was a brief struggle in which the terrified Inuit bit off his own tongue.

Frobisher waited for three days, but there was no sign of life along the bleak shore. Short of provisions and manpower, lacking a ship's boat, and with the season running late, Frobisher had to sail for England. He had no choice but to leave the missing men behind. Their fate remains a mystery to this day.

Frobisher arrived in London on October 9 to a hero's welcome. He was hailed as the new Columbus. He had brought home the *Gabrielle,* which was presumed lost, and he had evidence of a Northwest Passage. Samples of flora Frobisher had gathered intrigued scientists, and people were thrilled by the captain's story of a "mighty deere" (a musk ox) that had nearly gored him. The captured Inuit and his "bote" were displayed for the curious throngs. Then the unfortunate man died from a "cold" he had developed during the voyage. Oddly enough, this "savage" was given a Christian burial in a London churchyard.

But thrilling stories and deceased captives did not put money into the coffers of the men who had financed the expedition. Michael Lok was anxious to see some return on his considerable investment. He looked closely at the black rock Robert Garrard had picked up.

The men on the *Gabrielle* were disappointed to find that the rock was not coal. If someone had just tossed it over the side, the history of the Canadian Arctic would be quite different. But Frobisher decided to keep it and give it to Lok as a souvenir. Hoping the rock might have some mineral value, Lok sent pieces of it to several assayers. They all declared it worthless. Then an Italian alchemist, Giovanni Agnello, determined the stone was gold ore, because it glittered when it was placed in fire.

Lok took Agnello at his word. He tried to keep the news of the "gold strike" quiet as he began to look into the possibility of a new voyage, but soon the news was all over London. People said Frobisher had found a treasure trove to rival the fortune Spain had stolen from the Aztecs in Mexico and the Incas in Peru. When the Spanish got word of all this, they were skeptical. They thought the Arctic was too cold to be a likely place for a gold mine.

English speculators did not agree. Men with money rushed to invest in another expedition led by Frobisher, who now bore the title High Admiral of Cathay. The queen ventured a thousand pounds of her own money, loaned Frobisher the 200-ton *Aid,* and named his newly discovered country Meta Incognita (Land Unknown). She granted a license to the new Cathay Company and made Lok its governor. On May 31, 1577, Frobisher sailed for the Arctic with the *Aid,* the *Gabrielle,* the *Michael* and a company of 120 men. This was, in effect, Canada's first gold rush.

Frobisher had never claimed the black rock had gold in it. But once Lok told him of Agnello's findings, he was as anxious as anyone else to get more. The Northwest Passage could wait!

By mid-July, Frobisher arrived in the "straits" again. Still hoping to rescue the men he had lost the previous year, he decided to take native hostages. He captured a Native hunter, but received an arrow wound in the backside for his efforts. Several of his men were also wounded by Inuk bowmen.

Against Frobisher's orders, a party of about thirty Englishmen went in search of Native villages. The Englishmen found a village and attacked it. Six Inuit were killed and one sailor was badly wounded before the surviving villagers fled. The white men captured an elderly woman and a young mother with a baby. They stripped the old woman naked to see if she was indeed human, and then released her. The young woman and baby were kept as hostages. When the victors examined the bodies of the slain Inuit, they found that some of them were wearing articles of clothing that had belonged to the missing sailors. One doublet had numerous arrow holes in it. The site of this battle between Englishmen and northern Natives was called Bloody Point.

A few days after the battle, a number of Inuit strode boldly into the English camp, and by means of signs made it known that they wanted the three hostages back. Frobisher admired their courage, but made it clear to them that he wanted the five men who had vanished the year before. He probably believed they were already dead, but for the morale of his crew he had to be seen to be making the effort to rescue them. The Natives indicated that the five Englishmen were alive, and that if Frobisher would write a letter, they would deliver it.

That the Inuit knew about writing was proof to Frobisher that his missing men had been among them. He wrote the letter and gave it to the Natives, along with a pen, ink and paper for a reply. They left with the materials, promising to return. Frobisher did not expect to actually hear back from his men, and he was correct.

While he awaited the Natives' return, Frobisher had his men build a defensive bulwark of barrels filled with dirt, with a cliff face at their backs. The Inuit returned three days later without any of the missing sailors. They kept their distance and tried to lure the Englishmen into an ambush, probably hoping to take prisoners they could exchange for the woman and child Frobisher was holding. When the ruse failed, the Inuit demonstrated aggressively, brandishing their weapons and letting the Englishmen see their numbers.

Frobisher responded by having his men stage a mock skirmish so the Inuit could see that they, too, were prepared to fight. Then he had one of the big guns on the *Aid* fired. That stunned the Inuit. They withdrew, but they did not leave. This limited the amount of exploring Frobisher could do in that area, but his men were able to get down to the task of mining the supposedly valuable black rock. To the dismay of the "gentlemen" among the expedition's officers, Frobisher himself went to work with pick and shovel. If the admiral was putting his back to manual labour with the common men, they realized they would have to do so, too.

By late August, 200 tons of black rock were loaded into the ships and the English sailed for home. They took along the three captives, all of whom would die shortly after reaching England. Once again, Frobisher received a hero's welcome upon his return. He was entertained at Windsor Castle, where he presented Queen Elizabeth with a 6.5-foot long horn of a "sea unicorne" (a narwhal). She rewarded Frobisher with a gift of one hundred pounds.

Controversy still raged over Frobisher's ore, which was stored under heavy guard in the Tower of London and Bristol Castle. Agnello still insisted it was rich in gold. His critics challenged that if the black rock contained gold at all, it was of a very low quality. But still other assayers supported Agnello, saying the black rock contained not only gold, but also silver.

The Queen of England had invested in Frobisher's venture, so it was imperative that the black rock prove to be valuable. At that time, however, the methods for assaying the mineral value of rock were very primitive. Unable to determine the value and the content of the black rock, the Cathay Company, sponsored by the Crown, prepared for a third expedition. This would be the most ambitious one yet.

On May 31, 1578, Frobisher sailed with fifteen ships from Harwich. He was to mine 2,000 tons of gold ore and establish a settlement. This was the first English attempt to place a colony in the New World. On board the ships were 120 would-be settlers, including miners, carpenters and a minister who intended to convert the "infidels" to Christianity. By establishing a colony, the English government was asserting its claim to this new land, which the Spanish and French had been challenging. Though Frobisher was in command of this venture, he was against the whole idea of the colony. He argued that the winter weather was too extreme, and it was a dangerous place to live. Frobisher wanted to resume the search for the Northwest Passage, a quest that his sponsors seemed to have forgotten about entirely.

Once again Frobisher mistook Greenland for Friesland and, on June 20, took possession of the island in the queen's name, renaming it West England. On July 2, he sighted Meta Incognita. Kept offshore by heavy ice and strong winds, the fleet drifted into what Frobisher called Mistaken Straits, and what is now known as the Hudson Strait. Though he wanted to explore the area further, Frobisher had orders to mine gold.

Despite icebergs, fog, and unpredictable currents, good luck and Frobisher's great seamanship brought the fleet safely to the mine site. Upon their arrival, one ship deserted and fled for England. Another bark, carrying supplies and building materials, struck ice and sank, taking with her all hope of starting a colony. The other ships found themselves surrounded by deadly ice floes during a storm, and it was only Frobisher's iron will and resourcefulness that saw them emerge from the nightmare without the loss of more vessels or men. Even so, a few more captains decided they'd had enough and turned their prows toward home. The Inuit stayed away, so the Reverend Mr. Wolfall had no one to convert. He did, however, conduct the first Anglican church service on Canadian soil. In hopes of re-establishing communications with the natives, the English left a peace offering before they set sail for home. They built a small stone house in which they placed some trinkets and loaves of bread. The order came directly from Queen Elizabeth that her "new subjects" were not to be mistreated.

Frobisher weighed anchor on August 31, and was back in England by October 1. This time there was no triumphant welcome. The glitter in the black rock, which had been collected at such great cost, turned out not to be gold after all. The black rock was sandstone and the "glitter" was caused by mica. Canada's first "gold rush" had been started by a form of fool's gold! Spanish spies who had managed to steal some samples of the ore assayed it themselves and gleefully wrote to King Philip II that it was worthless.

The Cathay Company went bankrupt shortly after. Michael Lok was thrown into debtor's prison and blamed Frobisher for the calamity. Frobisher in turn blamed Lok, whom he called "a bankeroot [bankrupt] knaive." Lok would spend the rest of his life fighting creditors and trying to restore his reputation. The Queen herself was out three thousand pounds, a considerable sum at that time. The worthless ore was hauled out of vaults and dumped in Bristol Harbour or used for repairing roads in Kent.

Though his importance as an explorer was overshadowed by the disastrous gold rush, Frobisher was nonetheless the first European in recorded history to penetrate the Canadian Arctic. He was also the first Englishman to seek an answer to the riddle of the Northwest Passage, a mystery that would remain an enigma for centuries to come.

Martin Frobisher never returned to the Canadian Arctic. He rode out the storm created by the gold fiasco, and went on to have an illustrious career in Her Majesty's navy. He was a commander of one of the English ships that defeated the Spanish Armada in 1588, and was knighted for his service. Six years later he was shot in the thigh while storming an enemy castle in France. The wound became gangrenous, and on November 22, 1594, Martin Frobisher died at about fifty-nine years of age.

Frobisher's Arctic adventures were all but forgotten in England until 1861, when the American explorer Charles Francis Hall found the site of the "goldmine" in Frobisher Bay. Hall collected some relics of the expedition and sent them to London and New York, where they were subsequently lost. Hall also discovered, to his astonishment, that the old sea dog was well remembered by the Inuit, even though almost three hundred years had passed since Frobisher's last Arctic visit.

Native folk tales passed down through the generations described in detail the activities of the white men who came "in ships with wings of white," how they dug up the land, fought with the Inuit, and carried some of them away. The strange white men, the stories said, came three summers in succession, and then were never seen again. Five who had been left behind, the Inuit claim, "died in our land ... we did not harm them." The island on which Hall found the scars of mining was still known to the Inuit as Kodlunarn, The Island of the White Men.

Jacques Cartier

The Man Who Named Canada

At the turn of the sixteenth century, France had yet to send any mariners on voyages of discovery across the Atlantic. French fishermen from Normandy and Brittany were making annual trips to the rich fishing grounds off Cape Breton Island and John Cabot's "new founde launde." Basque whalers were also plying those waters and may have been doing so even before Cabot's voyages. Frenchmen had even gone ashore in the New World to hunt walrus and to barter with the natives for furs. In 1506, a fishing captain named Jean Denys cruised along the coast from the Strait of Belle Isle to Bonavista, but he made no maps. Two years later Thomas Aubert of Dieppe visited the same region and returned to France with several Natives; quite likely Micmacs.

But the French had made no territorial claims in the New World. No French ships had gone in search of a western sea route to the Far East. While Spain and Portugal had claimed vast territories across the sea, and Cabot had planted an English flag on a shore well to the north of Spanish and Portuguese claims, the

French had yet to claim an acre of new territory, and the French king, Francis I, wanted to do something about that.

From 1337 to 1453, the French had been bogged down in a struggle with England that is now called the Hundred Years War. It took France another half century to recover from a long period of warfare, plagues, famines and widespread banditry. Now, as his country was emerging as a continental power, Francis saw King Charles V of Spain as his main rival. Francis was envious that Pope Alexander VI had named Charles as Holy Roman Emperor. He also disagreed with the Papal Bull that gave all of the undiscovered territories in the world to Spain and Portugal. Like Henry VII of England, Francis did not feel he was legally bound by the ruling. He would, in fact, eventually convince Pope Clement VII to withdraw the Bull. Meanwhile, Francis wanted to get in on the race for new lands and the search for a western passage to the Orient.

The Spanish had been searching the southern latitudes, claiming territory from the Caribbean up to what is now South Carolina. The English had been probing Nova Scotia, Newfoundland and points north. But what about the vast area in between? No one yet knew what lay between Florida and Nova Scotia. In 1523, Francis hired an Italian navigator, Giovanni da Verrazano, to find a passage to the Pacific Ocean for the greater glory and profit of France.

Verrazano reached what is now North Carolina and sailed north as far as Cape Breton. He mapped the coast, traded with the natives and claimed all the previously uncharted territory for France, giving places French names. But he did not find a sea route to the East. Verrazano returned to France in 1524, only to find that Francis had been captured in battle and was now a prisoner in Spain. Verrazano could make no plans for another voyage until the French king had been ransomed. Meanwhile, a Spanish explorer named Estevan Gomez sailed up the same coast Verrazano had explored, claimed it all for Spain, and replaced the French place names with Spanish ones.

Verrazano was not ready to sail again until 1528. When he did, he sailed out of recorded history. No one is certain what happened to him. One story says he simply returned to Italy and died. Some historians think he was captured by the Spanish and hanged as a pirate. However, another account says that somewhere near Guadeloupe Verrazano went ashore with a few men and was captured by Carib Indians. Within sight of the men on the ship, he was cut to pieces and eaten. One other mystery about Verrazano has stumped historians. When he made his voyages, was a mariner named Jacques Cartier part of the crew?

Jacques Cartier was born in St. Malo, Brittany, in 1491. The fortified port town already had a strong seafaring heritage. It was a base for French privateers and pirates, and an important supply centre for French slavers.

Nothing is known of Cartier's early years, but growing up in St. Malo, he almost certainly went to sea as a lad, starting out as a lowly ship's boy (*mousse*) and working his way up through the ranks of a ship's crew as he grew older and learned the mariner's trade. By the time of Verrazano's first expedition, Cartier would have been an experienced seaman. He was also evidently a man of good reputation because, in 1520, he married into a prominent family well above his social class.

There is no documented evidence that Cartier sailed with Verrazano. Nonetheless, he could have sailed in western waters before his first recorded voyage. In 1532, Cartier was recommended to King Francis I by the very influential Jean Le Veneur, who was both bishop and count of Lisieux. Le Veneur described Cartier as a pilot who "by virtue of his voyages to Brazil and the New Land [was well able] to lead ships in the discovery of new territories in the New World." Le Veneur would not have vouched for Cartier unless he had the utmost confidence in his experience and his ability to take French ships to what he called "the blessed shores of Cathay."

In 1534, Cartier received a royal commission to sail west in search of gold, new lands and a passage to Cathay. That document has never been found, but a royal order for payment of some of the expedition's costs tells us that Cartier was instructed to "voyage to that realm of Terres Neufves [Newfoundland] to discover certain isles and countries where it is said there must be great quantities of gold and other riches." Cartier's rank of *Capitaine et Pilote pour le Roy* (captain and pilot for the king) was about as high as a mariner from a common background could aspire.

Cartier sailed from St. Malo on April 20, 1534. He had two ships, each weighing about 61 tons, with sixty-one men, all of whom had sworn "to conduct themselves well and loyally in the king's service." Cartier expected to be gone for about a year.

Cartier made the Atlantic crossing in twenty days; a record at that time. Good luck spared him from the storms that had plagued so many other voyages. He reached Cape Bonavista and sailed north along the Newfoundland coast, but was forced back south by ice. He put in at Catalina Harbour, and remained there for ten days awaiting fair weather.

Cartier then sailed to the Île des Ouaiseaulx (Isle of Birds, now Funk Island), which was known to have a huge population of great auks. While there, the sailors killed and salted down a large number of birds. They also managed to kill a polar bear. The expedition then continued north along the Newfoundland coast, where Cartier gave names to several previously unnamed locations. He sailed up the east coast of the Great Northern Peninsula, rounded the tip and sailed into the Strait of Belle Isle, which separates the island of Newfoundland from the mainland. He then went in a southwest direction along the coast of Labrador, which he called "the land God gave Cain." He thought this area did not even deserve to be called land because it appeared full of "frightful and ill-shapen stones and rocks." Cartier claimed he "saw not one cartload of land in all that northern coast." He encountered a fishing vessel from La Rochelle, and went aboard to guide her into a harbour that he called one of the finest in the world, which he named Havre Jacques Cartier (now Cumberland Harbour). Here Cartier erected a cross and claimed the land for France. This was the humble beginning of a French empire in North America.

Cartier was now sailing in uncharted waters. If any Europeans had been in this area before him, they had made no record of it. Cartier is thus credited with the European discovery of the Gulf of St. Lawrence. On June 15, he began to explore the west coast of Newfoundland, which no European had yet seen. The island was still thought to be a peninsula of Asia. Had he continued in a southeasterly direction he would have realized that Newfoundland is an island and that a strait separates it from Cape Breton. But at a place he called Cap St. Jean (probably present day Cape Anguille), he turned southwest and sailed across the Gulf of St. Lawrence.

He hoped this body of water would be the key to the Northwest Passage. He stopped at the Magdalen Islands where his men hunted more birds. On June 30, he sighted a headland and went ashore at several locations. He praised this place as "the finest land one can see, and full of beautiful trees and meadows." Cartier thought this was part of the mainland. In fact, he was the first European to set foot on Prince Edward Island. When he sailed around the northwestern tip of the island he saw the opening of the Northumberland Strait, but mistook it for a bay.

Cartier turned north, determined to probe every bay and inlet that might prove to be the entrance to the Northwest Passage. This was a systematic investigation that took him up the coast of what is now New Brunswick to the deep Baie des Chaleurs. Four days of exploration in July revealed that this was not the elusive passage. But it did bring the Frenchmen into contact with Micmacs who were eager to trade their furs. The French were initially suspicious of the Natives, and fired their guns to frighten them off. The natives were persistent, however, and on July 7 there was a ceremonial exchange of furs for cheap French trade goods. Obviously, the Micmacs had met other Europeans, and knew that white people were willing to barter for furs. But this was the first documented account of such commerce with the Natives of the Gulf of St. Lawrence.

Disappointed that Chaleur Bay was not the opening to the Northwest Passage, Cartier continued north. He reached the Gaspé Peninsula of Quebec, and there he met Native people who were very different from the Micmacs. These were the Iroquois, a powerful confederacy of tribes who had spread out from their home country south of Lake Ontario three centuries earlier to dominate much of the St. Lawrence Valley. These people would play a significant role in the story of the future colony of New France.

The Frenchmen encountered the Iroquois at what is now Gaspé Harbour, and knew immediately from their language and mannerisms that they were a different tribe. Cartier considered them "the sorriest folk there can be in the world" because they wore little or no clothing and ate their fish and meat almost raw. The Iroquois happily accepted the small trinkets the French gave them, but did not seem to know much about trade. Instead, they stole the sailors' property at every opportunity.

On July 24 Cartier raised a thirty-foot cross engraved with three fleurs-de-lys and the words *Vive le roi de France.* This angered the local chief, Donnacona. Dressed in a black bear skin, Donnacona, along with three of his sons and a brother, paddled a canoe to within shouting distance of the French ships. Through signs he made it clear to Cartier that he was displeased with the cross. All the land around them was his country, he gestured, and the French had no business putting up the cross without his permission.

Cartier held out an axe, and indicated to the chief that he wanted to trade it for the bear skin. The Natives paddled closer to the ship so Donnacona could take the axe. As soon as he reached for it, French sailors seized the canoe and bundled the "astonished" natives onto the ship.

Cartier assured the five Iroquois men that he meant them no harm. The cross, he said, was just a landmark to help them find the place again. He assured them that the French would return with many goods to trade. He also told them that he wanted to take two of Donnacona's sons to France so they could learn French. Afterwards, he would return them to their village of Stadacona (near present-day Quebec City).

The French brought out clothes for the two youths, Domagaya and Taignoagny. They happily took off the few furs they'd been wearing and allowed the white men to dress them in "shirts and ribbons and in red caps." Cartier gave the other Natives gifts of knives and axes, and promised them the pair would be well-cared for. Donnacona gave his consent, and told Cartier the cross would not be pulled down.

Europeans thought nothing of kidnapping Natives and taking them home as curiosities to be displayed like animals in a menagerie. But that's not why Cartier wanted the boys. Cartier knew that it would be a great advantage if he could use the local people as guides. That could not happen, however, until some of them learned French and could act as interpreters. The agreement he had struck with Donnacona concerning his sons, therefore, was something of a diplomatic coup.

The French ships left Gaspé Harbour on July 25. Had they taken a westward course, they would have found themselves in the St. Lawrence River. But a mirage effect convinced the mariners there was a land mass in that direction, so they turned northeast. On July 29, they sighted Anticosti Island, which Cartier took to be a peninsula. Here Cartier once again came close to discovering the St. Lawrence River, but stormy weather caused him to turn east again. On August 5, he decided to return to France. Cartier and his men reached the open Atlantic by way of the Strait of Belle Isle, and were in St. Malo by September 5.

Cartier had not found any gold, nor had he discovered the Northwest Passage. Nonetheless, he received a hero's welcome. He had found what appeared to be an inland sea beyond Newfoundland, he had claimed new lands for France, and he had not lost a single man. Moreover, as the two young Iroquois learned to speak French, they told him of a great river that flowed through their country and of a place called Saguenay, where the people had copper. Upon hearing this news, the king became very interested in supporting another expedition.

Cartier sailed again on May 19, 1535. This time he had three ships: his flagship the *Grande Hermine* of 100 to 120 tons, the *Petite Hermine* of 60 tons, and the *Emerillon* of about 40 tons. He had about 110 men, as well as Domagaya and Taignoagny, who, unlike most of their predecessors, had not died of European diseases. The expedition was to continue the search for the Northwest Passage and to "pursue the discovery of certain distant lands."

This time stormy weather battered the fleet almost all the way across the Atlantic. They were at sea for fifty days before they reached the Isle of Birds. Once again Cartier entered the Gulf of St. Lawrence through the Strait of Belle Isle. As he probed along the north shore in search of a good harbour, he found a large, beautiful bay that he named St. Lawrence. Thirty years later, the name was applied to the Gulf and then to the great river. The bay is now known as Ste. Genevieve Harbour.

On August 13, the ships headed toward the western end of Anticosti, which Cartier still thought was a peninsula. Domagaya and Taignoagny, who had been there before, told him it was an island. Two days journey from there, the Iroquois said, was the kingdom of Saguenay, and beyond that, was a place called *kanata.*

The information that Anticosti was an island gave Cartier a much greater understanding of the local geography. Here was a golden opportunity for exploration further to the west, and perhaps at last the way through to the western ocean. When Cartier heard the word *kanata,* he did not realize it was Iroquoian for "town or settlement." He thought it was the name given to the entire country. Not being very familiar with the pronunciation of Iroquoian words, he heard it as "canada," and entered it as such in his log. Thus, on August 13, 1535, the name Canada was first spoken and written on a document.

Domagaya and Taignoagny told Cartier the river was the road to their *kanata* and a place called Hochelaga (now Montreal). They said the river was "ever narrowing as far as Canada: that then there is fresh water in the said river, which goes so far that no man has ever been to the end."

Quite likely Cartier wanted to proceed west with all due speed in order to see the western ocean with his own eyes, but he was also a pragmatic man. Instead, he explored Anticosti and made sightings from its shores. When he set sail again on September 1, he followed a zigzag course, searching both shores for possible openings. He saw the mouth of a deep, fast river (the Saguenay) that flowed down from between mountains of rock. His Iroquois guides told him this river led to the kingdom of Saguenay, but because of rocks the ships could go no farther than the mouth.

They continued upstream and on September 7, reached the Île d'Orleans, which Cartier believed to be "the beginning of the land and province of Canada." The explorers anchored in the north channel and a landing party went to the island. The Iroquois there kept their distance until they realized that Domagaya and Taignoagny, who would have been wearing French clothing, were their countrymen. Then they welcomed the visitors and held a feast in their honour.

The next day Donnacona arrived. He was overjoyed to be reunited with his sons, and regaled them with questions about France. He hugged and kissed Cartier. There was more feasting, and Cartier presented the people with gifts.

The Iroquois village of Stadacona was a little further upstream, probably near Cape Diamond at the confluence of the St. Charles and St. Lawrence rivers. Here, at a place in the St. Charles River, Cartier found a good harbour for his ships.

Relations between the French and the Natives seemed very good indeed, but they were about to take a bad turn.

When Donnacona learned from his sons that Cartier wanted to go to Hochelaga, he was horrified. He had planned on himself and his people profiting as middlemen in trade between the French and other Iroquois communities. After all, he had been the first to greet the French and had sent his sons to their country. There was also a matter of inter-tribal politics. The Iroquois chief was not the "lord of Canada" as Cartier believed him to be. Stadacona was dominated by Hochelaga. Donnacona hoped that his special relationship with the French would free him from that situation.

On September 16, Donnacona, Taignoagny and a large group of Iroquois approached Cartier. Taignoagny told Cartier that Donnacona was angry because Cartier wanted to go to Hochelaga. He said his father had forbidden him to accompany Cartier upriver, as Taignoagny had promised to do, and that the river was not worth exploring. Cartier replied that he had orders from his master, the king, to go upriver. He promised Taignoagny a fine reward if he would go with them. Taignoagny refused.

The Iroquois went back to their village, but the next day they returned. This time Donnacona gave Cartier a gift of three children: a girl and two boys. Cartier accepted the gift, and right away Taignoagny told him that the gift had been given with the intent of preventing him from going to Hochelaga. Cartier replied that if the gift was given with that intent, he must return it. Now Domagaya spoke up. He said Donnacona had given the children out of sincere affection and that he (Domagaya) would accompany him to Hochelaga, if he had his father's permission.

Then the brothers argued. Cartier noted, "we were convinced, as well from this as by other bad turns we had seen him do, that

Taignoagny was a worthless fellow, who was intent on nothing but treason and malice." Cartier accepted the children, and gave Donnacona a sword and a brass bowl. The chief seemed pleased with the gifts, and he asked Cartier to fire the ships' big guns. His sons had told him about the thunder the guns made, and he wanted to hear it for himself.

Cartier gave orders for the *Grande Hermine* and the *Petite Hermine* to fire their guns into the woods opposite the ships and the crowd of Iroquois. A dozen cannons roared, sending their missiles crashing into the trees. The effect on the Natives was dramatic. "These were all so much astonished as if the heavens had fallen upon them, and began to howl and shriek in such a very loud manner that one would have thought hell had emptied itself there." The natives ran away in fear.

The following day, Donnacona made one last attempt to stop Cartier from sailing upriver. He and his two sons performed a ritual that Cartier called witchcraft, and then told the French that their god, Cudouagny, had told them everyone in Hochelaga would perish from ice and snow. The Frenchmen laughed at this. Cartier replied that the Iroquois god was a fool, and that the French had Jesus to protect them.

Finally Donnacona said he would allow one of his sons to go to Hochelaga, if Cartier would leave a hostage. By this point Cartier no longer trusted Donnacona or either of his sons. He would not leave a hostage, and if the interpreters would not come willingly, he didn't want them. Leaving the two larger ships at anchor, on September 19, Cartier started upstream with the *Emerillon* and two longboats.

Word of the Frenchmen's presence at Stadacona had obviously spread along the shore, because Natives came out in canoes to greet them and to trade for knives, mirrors and other items. On September 28, Cartier's party reached Lake St. Pierre. The *Emerillon* could go no further due to the shallowness of the river above the lake, so Cartier left the ship at anchor and continued on in the longboats with about thirty men. On the evening of October 2, they reached Hochelaga.

The Iroquois community was a fortified town of about fifty longhouses on the island of Montreal, at the foot of the mountain that Cartier named Mont Real (Mount Royal). It was clear the people had been expecting the French visitors, because they came out in a great crowd to greet the strangers and brought them fish and corn bread. Cartier passed out gifts, and the Natives danced and sang all night.

The next day Cartier was given a tour of the town and was taken to the top of the mountain, from which he could see for miles around. In his journal he wrote of the people's habitations, food, defences and clothing—or rather, the lack of it. He was the first European to see *esnoguy,* the little white shell they valued the way Europeans valued gold, and with which they made wampum. The Natives seemed to believe that Cartier had curative powers, because their chief, a man of about fifty named Agouhanna, wanted Cartier to heal his crippled legs. Cartier massaged the old man's legs, then recited from the Gospel of St. John and made the sign of the cross. He read the Passion of Christ aloud while the people listened in profound silence. When Cartier passed out the usual gifts of knives and axes, he added rosaries and Agnus Dei medals.

Cartier learned that the river above Hochelaga was impassable due to a series of rapids, and that another great river (the Ottawa) joined it farther up. The people who lived on this river, he was told, had gold and silver. Past the rapids, the Natives said, the river was navigable again for a very long distance. But in that country, they warned, were their enemies, people who were "armed to the teeth" and who made war constantly.

All of this was communicated by signs. Having no interpreter, Cartier decided there was no more to be learned just then at Hochelaga, so he and his men got into their boats for the trip back downriver. The disappointed Iroquois followed in their canoes for a long way.

Cartier was back at Stadacona by October 11. Donnacona and his sons were all smiles as they greeted him, but Cartier saw immediately that tension had increased. In front of the place where the ships were anchored on the other side of the St. Charles River, about a mile and a half from the village, his men had built a fort of heavy timbers and armed it with artillery. He learned that Donnacona was still angry about the trip to Hochelaga. Moreover, Domagaya and Taignoagny, having learned something about the real value of the white man's trade goods while they were in France, had been telling their people to demand more for the provisions they bartered to the French. Donnacona also demanded the return of the children he had given to Cartier. Cartier would not release the children, though the little girl was eventually able to run away and rejoin her people. Concerned about security, Cartier strengthened the fort, dug a wide ditch around it, and posted sentries at night.

After a while Donnacona expressed regret at having lost favour with Cartier and sought reconciliation. At first Cartier rejected his entreaties and called him a rogue, but finally he agreed to a resumption of good relations. There was another feast, and soon the two sides were visiting each other again, "with as much affection as earlier." Then winter set in!

Domagaya and Taignoagny were aware that the winters in France were nothing like the winters in the valley of the great river. The cold that descended shocked the French. The entire river froze over, locking the ships in thick ice. The ships themselves were encased in icy shells, and even the interiors had layers of ice four fingers thick. Snow, more than four feet deep, covered the ground and the frozen river. Then scurvy began to take its toll.

Known today to be caused by a diet lacking in vitamin C, scurvy was a mysterious ailment to sixteenth-century Europeans. When his men began to fall ill, Cartier could do nothing but pray. Soon eight men were dead, and before the winter's end that number increased to twenty-five. The bodies were simply covered with snow because the ground was like iron.

Cartier did not entirely trust Donnacona and did not want to let the Iroquois know how weak the French had become. He made a regular show of coming out of the fort to talk to visiting Iroquois, telling them his men were hard at work in the ships. The two or three men who could still walk would come out to support his bluff, while the sick men in the ships made as much noise as they could. Even though he fooled the Natives, Cartier was sure that most of his men were doomed. Relief, however, came from a most unexpected place.

The Iroquois, too, suffered from scurvy. One victim was Domagaya, whom Cartier saw with a swollen leg, decayed teeth, and gums "rotting and stinking." A little more than a week later, Cartier saw Domagaya "healthy and resolute" and realized there was a cure!

Instead of telling Domagaya that almost all of his men were sick, Cartier said he had one servant who was sick, and that he wanted to know how Domagaya had been cured. The Iroquois told him that a drink brewed from the bark and leaves of a tree they called *annedda* (white cedar) cured the sickness. He even had two women prepare some of the medicine.

At first the sick men were reluctant to even taste the drink, probably fearful that the Iroquois might poison them. Then a few brave souls tried it, and showed almost immediate improvement. Soon the rest of the men clamoured for the brew, calling the white cedar "the tree of life."

At every opportunity Cartier questioned Donnacona through one of his sons, asking him about the country and the people. Two things in particular were of great interest to him. One was the "freshwater sea" that lay far to the west, but which Donnacona had never seen. This sea, the chief said, was so vast no man had ever been to its opposite shore. The other story that intrigued Cartier was that of the kingdom of Saguenay that lay, according to Donnacona, a month's journey to the north. The chief claimed to have been there himself. He said the people there had gold, silver and precious stones. They were white, like the French, and wore woollen clothing. Was Donnacona simply practicing the Iroquoian love of storytelling, and making up a yarn he thought Cartier wanted to hear? He had, after all, told Cartier some pretty far-fetched tales: "He told us also that he had visited another region where the people, possessing no anus, never eat nor digest, but simply make water through the penis. He told us furthermore that he had been … to another country whose inhabitants have only one leg and other marvels too long to relate."

It's possible that Donnacona was relating a legend concerning a long past encounter with whites that had come to him through Native folklore. Wherever this "kingdom of Saguenay" was, nobody ever found it.

At last the spring thaw came and by April 15, 1536, the ice was out of the river. However, trouble was brewing in Stadacona. Donnacona had been away for about a month. When he returned on April 21, he had with him a number of "people who were handsome and powerful" whom the French had not seen before. When Domagaya came to tell Cartier of Donnacona's return, he delivered the message from a distance, and refused to approach the fort. Cartier was suspicious, and sent two of his men who were quite popular with the Iroquois to Stadacona to find out what was going on.

The men were told Donnacona was sick and were not admitted to his home. They then went to see Taignoagny. Though all of the houses were crowded and there were many people there that the Frenchmen did not recognize, Taignoagny would not allow them to speak to anyone. He personally escorted them halfway back to their fort. Along the way he passed on some startling news: Stadacona was in the midst of a political crisis!

A clan led by a man named Agona had challenged Donnacona's leadership and many of the Iroquois were taking Agona's side. Taignoagny told the Frenchmen that Donnacona wanted Cartier to seize Agona and take him to France. If Cartier would rid him of the troublemaker, Donnacona would do anything Cartier asked of him. Taignoagny impressed upon them the urgency of the situation and said Donnacona needed Cartier's answer by the next day.

Cartier carefully examined his options. In his opinion the Iroquois who had caused the most problems were Donnacona and his sons. If he could take *them* away, there would be a new chief in Stadacona—one who might be more manageable. Furthermore, Donnacona would be a magnificent prize to take to the French king.

Cartier sent a message summoning Taignoagny. Two days passed without an answer. In fact, the natives seemed to be avoiding the French, as though out of fear. On the third day Donnacona and his sons went to the riverside, but only Domagaya and Taignoagny would speak to Cartier. Donnacona was leary of treachery.

The young men repeated their request that Cartier take Agona away. Cartier said the king had forbidden him to take men and women to France. He said he could take only two or three boys, so they could learn the language. But to please Donnacona, Cartier lied, he would carry Agona off and leave him on an island off the coast of Newfoundland. This plan satisfied Domagaya and Taignoagny.

On May 3, amidst great ceremony, Cartier erected another tall cross, taking possession of the country for France. The Iroquois were not aware that their land had just become the property of a foreign monarch. All of the people of Stadacona were present at the ceremony, including Donnacona and his sons. At Cartier's signal his men seized the chief and his two sons, as well as two other men known to be important leaders. The rest of the Natives fled "like sheep before a wolf, some across the river, the others into the woods, each to save his own skin."

The captives were taken aboard a ship and placed in "safe custody." All that night the people of Stadacona howled like wolves and demanded the return of their chief. Cartier told Donnacona that he was being taken to see the king of France, who would reward him with many presents, and that in ten or twelve months he would return home. This reassured Donnacona. He was taken on deck so the people could see that he was alive and unharmed. He shouted across the water that he was going to France and would return. He told the women to bring him corn, meat and fish for his voyage. The people rejoiced at this, and presented Cartier with twenty-four strings of wampum.

Cartier sailed on May 6. Because he was short of men, he had to leave the *Petite Hermine* behind. He had a total of ten Native "guests" including Donnacona and his two sons. He also had a small amount of gold, though he left no record of how he came into possession of it. This time, instead of going through the Strait of Belle Isle, Cartier acted on a hunch and sailed through the Cabot Strait, proving at last that Newfoundland was an island. He had fair weather and was in St. Malo by July 16. The ten Iroquois—eight of whom were looking at a strange new world for the first time—would never see their homeland again. By the time Cartier sailed for Canada again, all had died.

Cartier's second expedition had been an enormous success. He had mapped a large part of North America's east coast, brought home samples of gold and furs, and claimed Canada for France. Most importantly, he had discovered the great river that led hundreds of miles into the continent, and he had good reason to believe that river flowed from an inland freshwater sea. Cartier expected another expedition would be arranged as soon as possible.

Unfortunately, Cartier arrived home to find that France and Spain were once again at war. For that and other reasons, a new expedition was not authorized until 1540. This time, there would be an odd twist to the plans.

On October 17 of that year, King Francis gave his permission for a third expedition. He named Cartier "Captain General and master pilot" and gave him instructions to go to Canada and "enter deeper into these lands, to converse with the peoples found there and to live among them if need be." Basically, Cartier was to continue exploring from where he had left off in 1536.

Then, in 1541, there was a complete change of plans. The king authorized the establishment of a colony in Canada. The man in charge was not to be Cartier, but Jean-François de La Rocque, Sieur de Roberval, a courtier who was a personal friend of the king, and something of a scoundrel. Roberval belonged to one of the noblest families in France, but he squandered money and was frequently in debt. He went from one relative to another, seeking loans. He even dabbled in a little piracy. Roberval was also a Protestant. In Roman Catholic France, all that kept Roberval from being killed was his personal relationship with the king.

Everyone in the French court knew of the great fortunes that the Spanish conquistadores were seizing in their part of the Americas. Colonizers, too, were getting rich on crops like sugar. Now that Cartier had claimed new lands for France, Roberval got the idea that he could make a fortune in Canada. He talked the king into supporting a colonizing venture. Roberval was to lead it, with the title of lieutenant general of Canada, a rank that put him above Cartier, who after all was but a commoner. He was to establish a colony by building houses, churches and fortifications. And even though Roberval was a Protestant, he was to spread the Catholic faith among the "savages."

Roberval was given the use of three ships, and was provided with mariners and soldiers. A few aristocrats in search of fortunes and adventure would also join the expedition. Fifty convicts dragged out of prison would provide the manual labour. The colonists would take along cattle, sheep, goats, hogs and horses. These animals would be the first domestic livestock in Canada.

When word of the proposed French colony reached the kings of Portugal and Spain, they protested vigorously, even threatening war. They reminded Francis of the Papal Bull that gave all undiscovered territories to them. Francis replied that the sun gave warmth to him as well as to others, and he would like to see Adam's last will and testament to learn how he had divided up the world.

Cartier was not very pleased to have his voyage of discovery sidetracked by Roberval's colonizing venture. Of course, he could not complain to the king. Francis had provided Cartier with fifteen hundred men and five ships for his expedition: the *Grand Hermine,* the *Emerillon,* the *Georges,* the *Saint-Breiux* and one other vessel.

Cartier was ready to sail by mid-May, but Roberval was still waiting for gunpowder and other necessities. Roberval was still not ready to go when, with the king's permission, Cartier sailed on May 23. It would be a year before Roberval left France.

Cartier's Atlantic crossing was difficult. Storms and contrary winds scattered his fleet. Fresh water ran low, so the animals had to be given cider. All of the vessels made it to Newfoundland, where Cartier took on food and water and waited for Roberval. His patience wore thin, and Cartier set sail for Stadacona. He anchored in the St. Charles River on August 23, five years after he had last left.

Agona was now chief. He asked what had become of Donnacona and the others. Cartier told him that Donnacona had died. This was not a surprise because by the villagers' standards the chief was an old man. This was also good news to Agona because it meant his rival was dead. But Cartier could not reveal that the rest of the people he had taken away were also dead. He said they were all living as great lords in France and did not want to return home. Agona presented Cartier with a headband that was the Iroquois equivalent of a crown.

Cartier knew by now about the Iroquois ruse of showing

friendliness while harbouring hostility. He suspected the Iroquois did not entirely believe what he had told them about the people he had taken away. They were also quite likely concerned about having such a large number of Frenchmen in their country. Cartier also realized that Agona would be no happier about him going on to Hochelaga than Donnacona had been. For those reasons he chose an anchorage upriver from Stadacona, on the western end of Cape Diamond, where the Cap Rouge River met the St. Lawrence. He had some of his cannons taken ashore and set up defensive works.

As the French explored the country around their new base, they were pleased to find an iron mine. Then they found something more: "a kind of slate stone blacke and thicke, wherein are veines of mynerall matter, which shewe like gold and silver." On the riverbank they discovered "certaine leaves of fine gold as thicke as a man's nayle." And there was more. On the high land above the cape the astonished French found "a good store of stones which we esteemed to be Diamants." Treasure at last!

Cartier built two forts to give the French control of the river. He put men to work clearing land and planting vegetables. On September 2, he sent the *Saint-Breiux* and the *Georges* back to France with reports for the king. What was written in those documents is not known, nor is the king's response. But if Cartier reported that he had found gold, silver and diamonds, Francis must have been very excited indeed.

On September 7, Cartier and a group of his people started out for Hochelaga. He wanted to scout the rapids so he could better prepare for an expedition in the spring. En route he stopped at a village called Achelacy, which he had visited on his earlier expedition. The chief there had been very friendly, so Cartier left two French boys with him so they could learn the Iroquois language.

Cartier's journal makes no further mention of Hochelaga, but it does tell of a town called Tutonaguy. There he tried to communicate to the people that he wanted to go to Saguenay. This was difficult, because he had no interpreter. Four Iroquois agreed to guide the French upriver, but it is not certain they understood what Cartier asked. They spent an entire day walking along the riverbank because the rapids were much too powerful for boats. After they passed what would be called the St. Mary rapid, they came to another village at the foot of the rapid that would one day be called Lachine. Here Cartier asked the people how far the rapids continued. They attempted to show him by means of a diagram made from small sticks. From this he judged the distance to be about 18 miles. He decided not to push on any further at that time.

Cartier distributed presents among the people there, and the Natives appeared to be very friendly. However, the French soon learned that the show of hospitality was just that—a show. When they stopped at Achelacy they could not find the chief in whose care they had left the two boys. In fact, this man in whom Cartier had placed such trust had gone to Stadacona to talk to Agona about how to get rid of the white men. Fortunately, the two French boys were unharmed.

Back at the fort, Cartier was told that the Iroquois were no longer coming to barter food for trade goods and that they seemed to have "a wonderful doubt and feare of us." Cartier ordered the forts' defences strengthened. This is where the journal that is the main source of information on this expedition ends.

It seems that Cartier did make an attempt to explore farther up the St. Lawrence, but it is not known how far he got. He would report later that the Iroquois went out of their way to "annoy" him and that he did not have enough men to withstand them. It seems likely that some of his men were killed. Cartier left his encampment early in June 1542. In his hold he had barrels full of what he thought were gold and silver, and a bushel of what he thought were diamonds.

Meanwhile, Roberval had finally sailed with his colonists. On June 7, his three ships arrived at the fishing port of St. John's, Newfoundland. They were still there when Cartier's fleet arrived about a week later.

Because Roberval was officially his commander, Cartier dutifully reported to him all that had happened in Canada. He said he had been obliged to abandon his post there because of the Iroquois' hostility, and he had gold, silver and diamonds to take home to the king. Roberval boasted that he had brought along enough soldiers and arms to deal with the Natives. He ordered Cartier to return to Canada with him.

Cartier agreed, but he had no intention of going back with Roberval. He wasn't about to let the aristocrat take the credit for finding riches, which would certainly happen if they eventually returned to France together. The night after his meeting with Roberval, Cartier's ships quietly slipped out of the harbour and sailed for France.

The Roberval expedition would be marked by tragedy. Trouble began even before they reached Canada. Among the aristocrats sailing with Roberval was a young woman named Marguerite de la Roque, believed to be his niece. While they were in Newfoundland, or shortly after they left, Roberval became aware that Marguerite was romantically involved with a commoner, who had joined the expedition as an ordinary sailor to be near his lady love. To her furious uncle, Marguerite had shamed the family name. The punishment he decided upon was draconian. Roberval had the girl, her lover and her female servant abandoned on an uninhabited island (possibly Fogo Island) off the coast of Newfoundland. There the servant and the young man would die, as well as a baby to whom Marguerite had given birth. In one of the most incredible stories of survival in early Canadian history, Marguerite would endure almost two-and-a-half years of lonely privation before being rescued by fishermen.

Roberval's colonizing venture did not go well at all. He chose the spot west of Stadacona that Cartier had so recently abandoned. Almost no documentary evidence of the colonists' relations with the Iroquois has been found, except that the Natives went to the settlement to trade fish. Perhaps the presence of Roberval's soldiers discouraged them from taking any hostile action. The colonists suffered from cold, hunger and sickness. Evidently Cartier had not told Roberval about the white cedar medicine, because fifty of the people died from scurvy. Roberval was also a harsh commander. Petty offences were punished by flogging. And when there was a threat of mutiny, Roberval had six men hanged. Some of the other mutineers were placed in leg irons and banished to an island. Roberval was forced to return to France in 1543, his colony an utter failure. He was murdered in Paris by anti-Protestant assassins in 1560.

While Roberval was struggling to establish his colony, Cartier arrived in France, reaching St. Malo early in September 1542. The high hopes he had as he sailed into his home port were soon to be shattered. His barrels of gold and silver contained nothing but worthless iron pyrites and his diamonds turned out to be quartz. These rocks gave rise to the catchphrase, "as false as Canadian diamonds." To add to Cartier's troubles, he had committed an act of insubordination against his commanding officer. It is not certain if he was reprimanded for that, but Cartier never again led an expedition of discovery. Certainly the Roberval colony would have had a better chance of success had Cartier given it the benefit of his experience.

Cartier spent his remaining years engaged in business and running his estate at Limoilou. He died in 1557 at sixty-six, an advanced old age in that time. He has gone down in history as the man who discovered and named Canada. A ballad, "Jacques Cartier," was written by Thomas D'Arcy McGee, a Father of Confederation. It begins:

> In the sea-port of St. Malo 'twas a smiling morn in May,
> When the Commodore Jacques Cartier to the westward
> sailed away;
> In the crowded old Cathedral all the town were on their
> knees
> For the safe return of kinsmen from the undiscovered seas;
> And every autumn blast that swept o'er pinnacle and pier
> Filled manly hearts with sorrow, and gentle hearts with
> fear.

Samuel de Champlain

The Father of Canada

After Roberval's failure to set up a colony and the disappointing results of the third Cartier expedition, half a century passed before there was renewed French interest in colonizing the St. Lawrence Valley. France was in the grip of religious turmoil as Roman Catholics launched a vicious campaign of violence against the Huguenots (French Protestants). This did not mean the French had given up on the Americas, however. They attempted to establish colonies in warmer regions that had been claimed by the Portuguese or Spanish, but these settlements were destroyed. The French still went to Newfoundland to fish, and more of them were trading with the natives for furs. The French quickly realized that for a few cheap tools and trinkets they could acquire furs that fetched very high prices back home. As the natives of what is now Atlantic Canada became increasingly aware of the white men's desire for furs, they turned away from their traditional pursuit of getting their living from the sea, and turned instead to the forests to acquire more pelts. Thus, their entire culture underwent a dramatic change.

In 1584, the merchants of Jacques Cartier's hometown of St. Malo sent an expedition up the St. Lawrence specifically to trade for furs. The profits were fantastic. Other European nations, quickly realizing that furs were practically worth their weight in gold, began sending their own ships up the St. Lawrence. Soon there was violence in the valley of the great river, as rival fur traders began to fight over the territory. The French realized that they needed to establish a strong and permanent presence in the valley, or they would risk losing the area to rival traders.

In November 1599, Pierre Chauvin de Tonnetuit obtained an exclusive monopoly on trade in Canada from Henry IV. He sailed the following year with four ships and established a post at Tadoussac, where the Saguenay River flows into the St. Lawrence. Algonquin and Montagnais Natives had already become accustomed to travelling to this spot to meet French traders. Chauvin also brought with him people who would remain as colonists. Unfortunately, while Tadoussac was strategically located for trading, it was a bad choice for settlement. The soil was poor, and the winter was brutal. Of the sixteen colonists Chauvin left there for the winter, only five survived to return to France.

Among those who sailed with Chauvin was Pierre Du Gua de Monts, a man who believed he could succeed where others had failed. In 1603, he was granted a royal license to trade in what was now being called New France, to establish a colony and to spread Christianity to the Natives. One of the men he brought with him was Samuel de Champlain.

Champlain's hometown parish records were destroyed by fire, so very few hard facts are known about his life before 1603. While we do not know what he looked like, historians do know that he was born in Brouage in the province of Saintonge on the Bay of

Biscay, in 1567 or 1570. There has been some speculation that he was the child of a poor fishing family or the bastard son of an aristocrat; however, neither claim has ever been proven. On his marriage contract of 1610, he is identified as the son of "the late Antoine de Champlain, Naval Captain in his lifetime, and of Dame Marguerite Le Roy."

Brouage was famous for its brine, which was used to preserve meat. Ships of all nations went there to pick up cargoes of this pickling solution, so the young Champlain would have been exposed to mariners of many nationalities and would have heard their stories of newly discovered lands. He almost certainly went to sea as a boy. In 1613, he told France's Queen Marie de Médicis that he had been interested in the art of navigation since early childhood.

Based on an autobiographical account Champlain wrote in later years, he began a military career in 1587 when he became a quartermaster in the army of King Henry IV. Then, in 1598, his life changed when he met one of his uncles:

> I went to Blavet [a port town in Brittany], where at that time was a garrison of Spaniards, in which place I found an uncle of mine named Captain Provencal, who was considered to be one of France's first-rate seamen, and who, in that capacity, had been commissioned by the King of Spain as Pilot-General of their sea-forces.

At that time Catholic Spain and France were allies in a conflict with Protestant England and the Netherlands. Champlain's uncle, Guillaume Hellaine ("Captain Provençal" was a nickname that roughly meant "the Southener") took him aboard his warship, the

500-ton *St. Julien,* which was about to transport Spanish soldiers to Cadiz. While in Spain, and probably through his uncle's influence (and if his account is factual), Champlain joined the fleet of Don Francisco Colomo, who was heading for the Caribbean to hunt down English privateers. Historians are uncertain if Champlain actually had command of a ship, but he probably, at least, enjoyed an officer's rank.

Champlain did not see any naval action; no doubt the English privateers cleared out when they got word of the armada that was looking for them. But he did spend the next two years in the Caribbean, visiting such exotic places as Santo Domingo, Puerto Plata, Havana and Panama. He also visited Mexico and considered Mexico City to be one of the most beautiful places he had ever seen. But he was appalled by the "evil treatment" the Natives received at the hands of the Spanish Inquisition. Years later, the cruelty Champlain saw in Mexico may have had some influence on his own attitudes toward the Natives in Canada.

In 1601, Champlain returned to Spain where he made his report to the Crown. Then he went on to France where Henry IV gave him a pension and named him Royal Geographer. At about that time, Hellaine died, making Champlain the sole heir to his considerable estate. In addition to a large sum of money, he inherited a farm near Brouage. This legacy gave Champlain the financial freedom to do whatever he wanted, and what this lover of adventure desired to do was to go fur-trading in Canada, and perhaps find the Northwest Passage.

In 1603, Champlain was with Captain François Pontgrave aboard the small *Bonne Renommée* on a trading mission for Aymar de Chaste, the governor of Dieppe and viceroy of New France. Also on board were two Montagnais Natives who had been taken to France a year earlier and had met the king. Champlain had no official position in his first voyage to Canada. He was travelling strictly as an observer. But he kept a journal that he had published when he returned to France, and that journal is the only known surviving account of the voyage.

According to the journal, Pontgrave and Champlain arrived at Tadoussac on May 26. The French met the Montagnais chief Anadabijou who held a *tabagie* (feast) in their honour. The Montagnais, who had been to France, told the chief that the French king had treated them very well, wished the people of Canada well, and wanted to "people their land." They said that the king would help them make peace with their enemies (the Iroquois), "or else send forces to conquer them."

The Montagnais had already formed an alliance with the neighbouring Algonquin and Etchemin nations. Now Anadabijou welcomed the additional strength the French would bring. He was not interested in peace with the Iroquois. He had recently won a battle against them, and proudly showed the white men the scalps his warriors had taken. Anadabijou said he was pleased to have the king of France as his "great friend," and would welcome the French who came to live in his country.

Over a thousand Montagnais, Algonquins and Etchemins came to Tadoussac to trade furs. Champlain had some of them guide him about 40 miles up the Saguenay River, where they explained to him how they came down to the St. Lawrence from the interior using various rivers and lakes. This helped Champlain to better understand the network of waterways that were the highways of the Canadian wilderness. His guides also told him of a saltwater sea to the north. Champlain did not immediately jump to the conclusion that this must be the Pacific Ocean. Instead, he concluded that "it is some gulf of this sea [Atlantic] whose waters enter from the North into the lands, & in truth it can be nothing else." Without having seen it, Champlain had described Hudson Bay with some degree of accuracy.

On June 18, the French went farther upstream and dropped anchor on June 22 at a place the natives called *quebec,* meaning "the narrows." Champlain's journal reveals that he was generally impressed with the site, but their stop was brief. The place that he described as being "suitable for habitation" was the present location of Trois-Rivières. Blocked by the rapids, Champlain got no farther up the river than Cartier had. But from information given to him by Natives, he was able to construct a remarkably accurate chart of Lake Ontario and Lake Erie, as well as Niagara Falls and the Detroit River. Beyond that, said the Natives, was another lake whose water was not good to drink, and which was so vast, they dared not venture across it. This was an early reference to Lake Huron, but Champlain thought it might be the Pacific Ocean. Champlain also learned of the trade routes (rivers, lakes and portages) by which French trade goods were making their way to the lands of the Algonquins and another nation referred to as "good Iroquois" (the Hurons). Champlain expressed his hope that the other Iroquois "could be brought to friendship."

Champlain and Pontgrave returned to Tadoussac intending to return in a year or two to try and explore past the rapids. In mid-July, they sailed for Gaspé, where they planned to lay in a provision of fish. There they met a Breton trader, Jean Sarcel de Prévert, who had considerable experience sailing the waters off Acadia (Nova Scotia and New Brunswick). He turned Champlain and Pontgrave's heads with stories of all the gold, silver, copper and other mineral wealth that could be found there. Moreover,

Acadia might offer a shorter route to the inland sea than the St. Lawrence, and without all the tribal conflict. When Champlain and Pontgrave finally returned to France in September, it was not with a plan for another expedition to Canada, but to Acadia.

Aymar de Chaste had died, but Pontgrave and Champlain found an eager listener in Pierre Du Gua de Monts, the new lieutenant general of New France. Accepting their accounts of the desirability of Acadia—no doubt full of Prévert's embellishments—he supported their plan for an Acadian colony. The expedition sailed in early March 1604. Among the sixty colonists (all male) was Jean de Biencourt de Poutrincourt et de Saint-Just, who would one day be largely responsible for maintaining a French presence in Acadia. Champlain had no official rank, but his role was to carry out the tasks of a geographer.

They spent some weeks examining the coast of Acadia and the Bay of Fundy, and then, at Champlain's suggestion, chose Île Sainte-Croix (now Dochet Island in the St. Croix River). Although it was only meant to be a temporary habitation until a permanent location could be found, it turned out to be a most unfortunate choice.

While the colonists cleared land and built a little palisaded village, Champlain explored the surrounding country and went as far as 50 miles up the Penobscot River. He was not the first European to see this territory, but he was the first to map it, along with a previously uncharted 150 miles of coastline. When he went back to the Sainte-Croix settlement, he returned to six months of hell.

The island that had looked so inviting in the summer was horrific in the winter. It had no stand of trees, so firewood had to be hauled from across the river. There was no spring from which to draw water, so the colonists had to drink melted snow—a process that required more firewood. The inexperienced Europeans did not know how to build shelters that would give adequate protection from the freezing temperatures and strong winds. To make matters worse, it was an exceptionally cold winter. With a diet of nothing but salted meat, the French were soon suffering from scurvy. They knew that Cartier had made a cure from the *annedda* plant, but they did not know what it was. The local Natives knew nothing of the medicine, and couldn't help them. Before the winter was over, thirty-six colonists were dead, and another twenty were close to it. The survivors were saved by Pontgrave, who had sailed to France in the autumn, and returned in the spring of 1605 with provisions.

The French moved their settlement to a better place they called Port Royal (Annapolis Royal, Nova Scotia). This was still to be but a temporary encampment while de Monts looked for a more favourable location farther south along the coast of what would become New England. This time the French built their homes with an understanding of what winter held for them. They planted gardens, and Champlain even constructed a sluice in which he could stock trout. Most important, they established friendly relations with nearby Micmacs whose chief, Henri Membertou, was said to be so old he had met Cartier.

Champlain searched unsuccessfully for the mines Prévert had spoken of. When winter set in scurvy was again a problem, but it was not as severe as it had been the previous year. Thanks to the Natives, the colonists were able to supplement their salted meat with fresh meat. Two of the six who perished from scurvy that winter were the colonists' Catholic priest and Protestant minister. It was reported that the settlers buried them in the same grave "to see whether they could rest in peace together in death, since they were unable to reach agreement in life."

In the summer of 1606, beset with navigational accidents and a concern that they would see no ships from France, the colonists gave up on Port Royal. The colonists were, in fact, aboard ship and on their way back to France when they encountered a relief vessel heading for the settlement, so they returned to Port Royal. Though it was late in the season, Poutrincourt planted grain, the first to be sown in what is now Canadian soil.

A year earlier the French had explored down the coast to the vicinity of Cape Cod, looking for a place for a permanent settlement. There had been a misunderstanding with the Almouchiquois in the area, and one Frenchman had been killed. The colonists made one more venture south, but this time the Almouchiquois made it clear that they considered the French to be trespassers and would defend their territory. On the morning of October 15, the Natives attacked a French shore party and killed four men.

Angry and bent on revenge, some days later the French lured a group of Natives—who may or may not have been the same ones who had killed their comrades—out into shallow water by waving gifts. As soon as they came within reach, the French shot and strangled them. A few days later there was another fight in which several Natives and Frenchmen were killed.

Generations later, the American historian Francis Parkman would say of European policies toward American Native peoples: "Spanish civilization crushed the Indian; English civilization scorned and neglected him; French civilization embraced and cherished him." In many regards this generalization was true, and Natives usually fared much better in their dealings with the French than they did with the Spanish or English. However the bloody, though brief, encounters between the Frenchmen from Port Royal and the Natives at Cape Cod marked the beginning of a long period of hostility between the colonists of New France and the Natives to the south, particularly the Iroquois.

The winter of 1606–07 was a relatively comfortable one in Port Royal. This time there was sufficient food, milder weather and fewer cases of scurvy. Champlain organized the Order of Good Cheer in which the colonists took turns providing game for a feast. They also put on a play, the first theatrical production in North America.

But in the spring news came from France that de Monts' licence had been revoked. Dutch and English traders, as well as illegal French traders, had been ignoring the licence and scooping up the lion's share of furs. The Port Royal colony was losing money. Everyone appreciated the wonderful work Champlain had done in charting the region, but he wasn't making any money, and he'd found no passage to the Pacific Ocean. The Port Royal colony was closed down—though Poutrincourt would soon return to revive it. Champlain, however, would never return. His destiny lay elsewhere.

Disappointed with the failure of Acadia, which he blamed on "Those who know the least and shout the loudest," Champlain was hardly dismayed. He convinced de Monts that their best hopes lay in the valley of the great river, where the fur trade looked more promising; the area would be easier to defend against rival European nations; the French had strong alliances with the tribes; and the river promised a likely route to the Pacific Ocean. De Monts presented these arguments to the king and, in April 1608, Champlain commanding *Le Dom de Dieu* and Pontgrave skippering *Le Leurier*, sailed for Canada. This time Champlain was the superior officer, with the rank of lieutenant in the country of Canada. He carried with him King Henry IV's commission granting de Monts the monopoly on trade in Canada. Statements on paper, however, did not always reflect reality.

Pontgrave arrived at Tadoussac first. He found the post in the hands of Basque whalers led by a man named Darache, who challenged the French claim to exclusive trading and fishing rights. The whalers had already killed one Frenchman who disagreed with them. Pontgrave, known for being short-tempered and impulsive, did not wait for Champlain to arrive to deal with the situation. Instead, he tried to force the issue right there and then. As a result he was wounded, captured and his ship was seized by the Basques.

When Champlain arrived a few days later, Darache told him he could have Captain Pontgrave and the vessel back on the condition that the French clear out. Darache was making it plain that documents signed in Europe carried weight in the New World only if one had the guns to back them up. With Pontgrave's *Le Leurier* in his control, as well as his own Basque ships, Darache had Champlain outgunned. Champlain must have been furious, because the Basques were in clear violation of the law. But he suggested a compromise to which Darache agreed. He would allow the Basques to continue their activities at Tadoussac for the remainder of the year if they would release Captain Pontgrave and his vessel. They would then allow the courts in France to settle the matter. Superficially, it appeared to be a victory for the Basques. In truth, Champlain had in fact made the very best of a bad situation because he had never actually thought Tadoussac was a very good site for settlement.

On July 3, 1608, Champlain chose an area at the foot of Cape Diamond at the *quebec* of the river for his *habitation.* In the holds of his ships were timbers for pre-fabricated buildings to hasten construction. This new outpost called Quebec was made of three buildings joined by a second-floor gallery and a continuous outside wall that unified them into a single block. A separate building would serve as a storehouse. All this was surrounded by a fifteen-foot-wide moat with a drawbridge, and a stockade of sharpened stakes. This was a small-scale reproduction of a European fortress.

The Habitation was still under construction when the fledgling colony faced its first major crisis. One of the colonists was a locksmith named Jean Duval, a former member of the Port Royal colony. He hatched a treacherous plan to murder Champlain and turn Quebec over to the Basques or the Spanish, whom he believed would pay him well. He was able to draw several other colonists into the plot because there was discontent over the fact that the ordinary settlers would not share in any of the profits from the fur trade.

Unfortunately for Duval, one of his confederates, Antoine Natel, had second thoughts and reported the conspiracy to a pilot named Le Testu. The pilot passed the information on to Champlain, who immediately exonerated Natel. As far as the French colonists were concerned, Champlain *was* the law in Canada and he acted swiftly. He duped the conspirators into coming aboard the ship to join him for a drink, where they were immediately seized and placed under arrest. Champlain assembled a panel of judges, and then held the first recorded trial in North America. Duval was found guilty and hanged, making him the first prisoner in Canada to suffer capital punishment after a legal trial. His head was displayed on a pole as a warning to other would-be traitors or mutineers. Three others who were found guilty were sent back to France to be dealt with by French magistrates. Two more were acquitted.

Champlain had solved one problem, but more trouble awaited. On September 18, a ship set sail for France, leaving twenty-eight men to spend the winter in Quebec. It was to be a winter of disaster. Hunting was poor. The river froze early, cutting short the season for catching eels. Starving Natives went to Quebec seeking food from the fort's dwindling supplies. Seven Frenchmen died from dysentery. Scurvy set in, and neither the French nor the locals knew about the restorative properties of the white cedar. By the time Pontgrave arrived about the end of May 1609 with a shipload of supplies, only eight Frenchmen in Quebec remained alive.

Replenished and reinforced, Champlain decided now was the time to explore westward into the land of the Iroquois. He left Pontgrave in charge of trading at Tadoussac, and Pontgrave's nephew, the Sieur de Marias, in command at Quebec. Then he set out in the company of a few Algonquins and just two Frenchmen.

Champlain met with a party of Natives he had heard of, but had never seen before. They were from the nation the local people called Ouendats, but whom the French called Huron, because the style in which they wore their hair reminded them of the bristly head of a boar (*hure*). The Hurons occupied the area south of Georgian Bay and dominated trade between nations on the Great Lakes. They had been familiar with French trade goods for quite some time, and were anxious to meet the white people who brought them. Linguistically and culturally, the Hurons were much more closely related to the Iroquois than to the Algonquins, but they and the Iroquois were longstanding enemies.

In 1603, the French had agreed to assist their Native allies in their fight against the Iroquois. Now Champlain had to live up to that promise. It is not certain who really wanted the forthcoming battle with the Iroquois. Did the Hurons push for it after

Champlain had demonstrated the firepower of muskets and harquebuses? Did Champlain want it, so he could report to France that he had taken the field against the enemy? Or did Champlain want to put on a show of strength for the Natives? Whatever the reason, Champlain and two other Frenchmen accompanied an Algonquin, Huron and Montagnais war party into the land of the Mohawks, one of the five tribes of the Iroquois confederacy.

The invasion force went up the Richelieu River to "a very large lake," which the French at once named Lake Champlain. They were the first recorded Europeans to see this beautiful body of water that lies between the states of New York and Vermont, but has its headwaters in Canada. At some point about half of the Native force had second thoughts about attacking the fierce Iroquois and turned back. Sixty warriors continued on with the three Frenchmen.

On the evening of July 29, at what is now Crown Point, New York, the allies came upon an Iroquois camp. Champlain was absolutely bewildered at the Native methods of warfare. All element of surprise was lost when the allies shouted insults at the Iroquois, and the Iroquois responded in kind. This continued until morning. Then both sides took time to construct palisades. Next the shamans conducted their rituals. Finally, spokesmen from both sides conferred to decide whether they should fight at all. Meanwhile, the three Frenchmen remained hidden as the allies' secret weapon.

When at last the battle started, it was brief and bloody. The warriors on both sides fought completely naked, armed with bows and arrows, and protected by shields made of wood or hemp. Some two hundred Iroquois came out of their stockade and advanced on the allies. The allies opened their ranks, and

Champlain, wearing armour, strode to the front, armed with a harquebus loaded with four bullets. Champlain fired the gun, which made a noise like a thunderclap, and killed three Iroquois chiefs.

The Iroquois had never seen guns before and, while they were still stunned and confused, Champlain's two French soldiers fired their weapons from the woods, throwing the Iroquois into a panicked flight. The allies pursued them, killing about fifty and taking a dozen prisoners. The victors suffered but a few minor wounds. Though torture was all too frequently practiced by Europeans at that time, Champlain expressed disgust when his Native allies tortured one of the captives to death.

Champlain has been unfairly blamed for starting a war that brought years of hardship and terror to New France, and resulted in the ultimate destruction of the Huron nation. However, the fight at Crown Point was but a skirmish in a tribal conflict that had been going on for many years. Moreover, Iroquois hostility toward the French dated from the time of Cartier. Champlain's involvement did bring new features to the war; most notably firearms and furs. The Iroquois decided after this incident that if the Hurons and their allies were going to get guns from the French, they would get theirs from the Dutch and the English, who were starting colonies of their own. And when the land of the Iroquois began to run out of beaver, the warriors began looking north to the fur-rich Huron country.

Having won a battle and added some new territory to the map of New France, Champlain returned to France in October to report to de Monts and the king. Henry was interested in Champlain's adventures, but he would not renew de Mont's monopoly on trade. For financial support de Monts turned to a cartel of merchants, who were willing to put up the money on the condition that

Quebec be maintained as a centre of the fur trade.

Following setbacks of illness and bad sailing weather, Champlain was finally back in Tadoussac by May 19, 1610. Now that de Monts no longer held a monopoly on the fur trade, the little port was full of ships, which was not good news for the settlement at Quebec. Champlain thought it was in the best interest of the colony if he were to open up new territories for trade, and expand the borders and influence of New France. He wanted the natives to guide him either to the saltwater sea to the north (Hudson Bay), or the freshwater sea to the west (Lake Huron).

The Native allies, however, were more interested in another military expedition against the Iroquois. News of the incredible power of the French guns had spread far and wide, and now the Montagnais, Algonquin and Huron leaders were all anxious to launch a major attack on their old enemy. To entice Champlain, they showed him samples of copper ore that they said came from the Iroquois country. They would not guide him to the saltwater or the freshwater seas, they argued, until he helped them win a crushing victory over the Iroquois.

An advance force of about two hundred Algonquin and Huron warriors started along the Richelieu River toward the Iroquois country. However, the Iroquois had anticipated an invasion and sent their warriors north, where they caught the interlopers by surprise and repelled them. When Champlain arrived with the main force of Algonquin and Montagnais warriors and a few Frenchmen, he found the Iroquois entrenched behind a palisade.

Just getting to this site had been an ordeal for the French. Lugging armour and heavy guns, they trudged through swamps, tormented by clouds of mosquitoes. This time the Iroquois were not frightened off by the sound of guns. They put up a stiff fight, raining arrows into the ranks of their attackers and killing many of Champlain's Native allies. He himself was wounded in the neck and the ear by arrows. Eventually, the French guns prevailed, the walls of the stockade were breached, and those Iroquois who did not flee were slaughtered. Prisoners died slowly and painfully by torture.

After the battle Champlain sent a French youth whom he identified only as "my servant" to live among the Huron and Algonquin people to learn their language and "to learn what was the nature of their country, to see the great lake, observe the rivers, what manner of peoples inhabit them; withal to discover what mines and most rare things may be found among these places & peoples." The French youth Champlain had sent was undoubtedly Étienne Brûlé. The Natives agreed to take Brûlé, on the condition that Champlain take a young Huron named Savignon to France.

When Champlain returned to Quebec the shocking news awaited him that King Henry IV had been assassinated. Queen Marie de Médicis was acting as regent for the nine-year-old Dauphin who would one day be crowned Louis XIII. Champlain would have to go to France to find out where the colony of Quebec stood with the new government in Paris.

He arrived in September 1610 and found prospects bleak. France was in political turmoil and there was no royal funding available for him. His patron de Monts was out of royal favour. Traders who had been to Tadoussac complained that the Natives had learned something of the real value of their furs, and had become sharp businessmen, holding out for the best prices. Champlain himself had little to show in the way of further explorations and new lands claimed for France, and he had found no mines of any kind. His own financial resources were growing thin.

Champlain resolved this last problem in December 1610 when he married Hélène Boullé, who brought with her a substantial dowry. She was only twelve years old at the time of the wedding but, according to the marriage contract, the union could not be consummated until she was fourteen, "unless it is deemed advisable and be decided between them, their relations and friends."

On March 1, 1611, Champlain was once again under sail for Canada, leaving his child-bride in Paris. With him were the reliable old Pontgrave and the Huron youth Savignon. After spending several months in France, Savignon was full of wondrous tales about that strange country, many of which his people would dismiss as lies. They arrived in Quebec on May 11, after the worst Atlantic crossing Champlain had yet experienced.

Champlain wanted to take an expedition up the St. Maurice River to see for himself the saltwater sea (Hudson Bay) the Natives had told him about. The Algonquins, whose lands he would have to pass through, refused to take him. They were middlemen who profited by the traffic of goods and information between the French and the northern tribes, and they saw French exploration of their country as a threat to that commerce. Therefore Champlain had no choice but to look westward.

He travelled up the St. Lawrence as far as the island of Montreal, where he was supposed to rendezvous with the Hurons and some Algonquins. Champlain arrived at the appointed time, but the natives were not there. Meanwhile, Champlain examined the island and declared it a good site for a settlement. He even planted a garden and built an earth wall, to see how it would stand up to the winter.

Portaging through the woods on the riverbank, Savignon guided Champlain and one French companion upstream to the confluence of the Ottawa and St. Lawrence rivers. This was farther than Cartier had gone. But lacking boats for a full expedition, Champlain could proceed no farther that year.

Back at the island of Montreal, the Hurons and Algonquins at last arrived, three weeks late. Étienne Brûlé was with them, "dressed as a savage" and "having most excellently learned their tongue." Champlain had hoped to have no further trouble convincing the natives to assist him in his explorations, but then new problems arose.

French traders, who had swooped into the vacuum created by de Mont's loss of the fur monopoly, squabbled among themselves and left the natives with the impression that the French had no "chief" at Quebec. They had believed Champlain to be the leader, and it confused them that these other Frenchmen claimed to owe Champlain no obedience at all. Champlain would eventually use this situation (unsuccessfully) to try to regain the monopoly for de Monts.

Then another problem arose from an act of compassion by Champlain. A year earlier Champlain had been greatly disturbed by the extreme cruelties his Native allies inflicted upon prisoners who had been condemned to death. At his insistence they had agreed to spare one Iroquois captive from the torture stake, though he was still kept prisoner; most likely as a slave. That prisoner had started the rumour that Champlain was really an ally of the Iroquois, undermining Huron and Algonquin trust in Champlain. Savignon explained to them the actual reason Champlain had wanted the prisoner spared, and assured them he was not an ally of the Iroquois. But the Huron and Algonquin leaders were not convinced.

Champlain knew that above all other things, the Natives

respected and admired courage. To restore their trust in him, Champlain got into a canoe and shot the St. Louis rapids single-handedly. This was a feat no other Frenchman except Brûlé had accomplished. It was especially impressive since Champlain, like most Europeans, could not swim. Champlain's prestige among the natives was restored considerably, if not entirely.

Champlain sailed for France in August 1611, certain that riches were finally within his reach. He had heard more from the natives about the freshwater sea (Lake Huron) and he believed he could reach it with their help, though they insisted the route was difficult. Champlain also took home a cargo of split oak to see how it would do on the French market.

Through no fault of Champlain's, the potentially lucrative fur trade had been mismanaged and the profits were disappointing. It would take more than a shipload of timber to generate further serious investment from France in the Quebec colony. As part of his campaign to generate interest—and funds—Champlain wrote *Les Voyages de Sieur de Champlain,* one of the most important documents from early Canadian history. He also drew a map to illustrate his writings, which served as advertising to help generate interest in his dream of expanding New France. Champlain based his map on his own charts and on information given to him by natives. Though Champlain had never seen Lake Erie or Lake Ontario, his map shows them quite clearly, connected by the Niagara River. However, his map also optimistically suggests these waters lead to the Pacific Ocean.

Champlain sailed for Canada again on March 6, 1613. This time he was the official lieutenant of Henri de Bourbon, Prince de Condé, who had been made viceroy of New France, and who had been granted an exclusive trade monopoly. With such authority behind him, Champlain was now governor of Canada in all but name.

Champlain arrived at Tadoussac in April and stumbled into an unpleasant situation. In spite of the new royal monopoly, illegal French traders were already busy in the St. Lawrence Valley. It would be several years before the scandalous news came out that the Prince de Condé himself was behind this unlawful trading; trying to make more profits from black-market fur-dealing than he could through legitimate commerce. Moreover, during Champlain's absence of a year and a half, many of the French traders had been too high-handed in their dealings with the Natives, and diplomatic relations were strained.

Following a brief visit to Quebec, Champlain went to the foot of the St. Louis rapids to meet the Natives there. He had made up his mind "to go into their country, so as to encourage those remaining there with the good treatment they shall receive," and "with my concern for assisting them in their wars." Champlain especially wanted to find that route to the northern saltwater sea. He had reason to believe not only that it was within reach, but also that the English might already be there. This was due to information he had received from yet another young Frenchman, Nicholas de Vignau, whom he had sent to live with the Natives.

On May 27, 1613, Champlain started up the Ottawa River with four other Frenchmen, including de Vignau, who was acting as a guide. Just above the Long Sault rapids the French met a band of Algonquins who were on their way to join an attack against the Iroquois. They wanted the French to accompany them, but Champlain refused. The Algonquins did not want Champlain to proceed up the Ottawa. They were afraid he would reach the land of the Nipissing tribe, and deprive the Algonguins of their role as middlemen and toll keepers. The Algonquins occupied a commercial crossroads and charged other people a fee for passing through. They told Champlain that upriver there were even worse rapids than the Long Sault. They also warned him that Iroquois war parties often waited in ambush along the river. However, they reluctantly provided the French with a guide when Champlain insisted on pressing forward.

The explorers continued upstream and on June 4 passed the site of the future capital of Canada. Champlain noted the mouth of the Gatineau River, the Rideau Falls and the Chaudière Falls. Two days later they landed on the west bank of the river and became the first Frenchmen on record to set foot in what is now Ontario.

At Allumette Island, near present-day Pembroke, Ontario, Champlain met the Algonquin chief Tessouat. This tough, one-eyed old warrior may have known Champlain as early as 1603, when he'd gone south to make war on the Iroquois. At first Tessouat welcomed the French. But when Champlain expressed his intention of travelling north to Nipissing territory and the saltwater sea, Tessouat became agitated. He told Champlain that the way was extremely difficult, and that the Nippissing were a very unfriendly people.

Champlain expressed surprise at this. He said that his interpreter, de Vignau, who had spent the previous winter among the Algonquins, had been up in that country and had not experienced such difficulties. De Vignau, Champlain said, had even seen the saltwater sea and the wreckage of an English ship.

At this Tessouat became angry. He called de Vignau a liar and said the young Frenchman had never set foot in that country. Other Algonquins howled that de Vignau deserved to be put to death. At that the youth hastily "confessed" that he had lied to Champlain.

The truth of the matter has never been ascertained. Had de Vignau really been lying, or did he say he lied to save his life?

With further exploration barred by the Algonquins, Champlain was back at the St. Louis rapids by June 17. By the end of August he returned to France. Once again seeking support for his endeavours in Canada, Champlain played up his trip on the Ottawa River for all it was worth. He had covered only 175 miles, but presented the Ottawa River as the door to the West. In addition, as part of his campaign of new "ruses, stratagems and inventions," he wrote to Louis XIII on the great value of civilizing the Native peoples by teaching them French and converting them to Christianity so they would become loyal subjects of the king.

With France still in political turmoil, Champlain had a hard fight to get what he wanted, but get it he did. On April 24, 1615, when Champlain sailed from Honfleur aboard the *Saint-Étienne,* he had four Récollet clergymen with him, who were aflame with missionary zeal. Champlain was just as eager to reach the land of the Hurons (Huronia) and look upon the great freshwater sea.

As soon as he reached Quebec, Champlain hurried to the island of Montreal to meet the Hurons and Algonquins at the annual rendezvous. But because Champlain had not been there the previous year, few Natives bothered to make the journey in 1615, and those who did show up were mistrustful. The Iroquois had been raiding their country. They wanted to know where the help was that the French had promised!

Champlain agreed to help his allies fight the Iroquois once more. He would travel with the Huron to their own country and join their expedition against the foe. That would mean travelling through Algonquin country, past the very place where Tessouat had halted him in 1613. But this time, if the Algonquins had any objections, they kept them to themselves.

Champlain proceeded up the Ottawa River with a party of natives and Frenchmen, one of whom was probably Brûlé. He crossed Lake Nipissing and entered a river that flowed to the west (the French River). This stream entered into the body of water the natives called Attigouautan (Lake Huron), and which Champlain named Mer Douce (Freshwater Sea). On August 1, after a three-and-a-half-week canoe journey (with many portages), Champlain was in the land of the Hurons. He didn't know it, but he had scouted out the canoe route that would be the main highway of the fur trade for generations to come. Champlain had, in fact, opened up the West.

Considering the power the Huron nation wielded in the early seventeenth century, their homeland, Huronia, was rather small. Its borders ran from the mouth of the Coldwater River to Lake Couchiching (about 2 miles north of Orillia); and from the mouth of the Nottawasaga River to Lake Simcoe. It measured roughly 40 miles by 20 miles. The principal village was called Cahiague, located near Lake Simcoe in the eastern part of Huronia.

Champlain was anxious to explore further, but he had to first assist the Hurons in war. There was a great council, and messengers brought the welcome news that the Andastes (also called Susquehannas), who lived to the south of the Iroquois, were willing to join the northern tribes in an attack on their mutual enemy. If a two-pronged attack could be properly coordinated, the allied tribes could catch the Iroquois in a pincer and defeat them once and for all. Brûlé volunteered to travel south to hurry the Andastes along.

Champlain found to his frustration that Natives preparing for war could not be "hurried along." They had to dance, feast and wait for reinforcements—many of whom did not show up. The Hurons and Algonquins, who had been so anxious for the French to join them, now took a very long time to mobilize. The European idea of a military campaign was totally alien to them. Not until September 1 was an attack force of about five hundred warriors, accompanied by a handful of Frenchmen, ready to move.

The exact route taken by Champlain and his allies is not known. Taking into account the necessity of avoiding detection by Iroquois scouts, they probably would not have taken well-travelled routes. Some historians have suggested a likely route that begins at the northeastern shore of Lake Simcoe and follows a lengthy portage of about 25 miles to Sturgeon Lake. From Sturgeon Lake they probably paddled through a string of lakes: Pigeon, Buckhorn and Clear Lake, then into the Otonabee River and into Rice Lake. They may have then followed the Trent River to the Bay of Quinte in the eastern end of Lake Ontario. From there, according to Champlain, they made their crossing by way of "five very large islands." Champlain was probably not the first European to see Lake Ontario; in all likelihood Brûlé already had reached it.

On the Iroquois side of the lake (now New York state) the Hurons and Algonquins hid their canoes and proceeded silently toward their destination, a fortified Iroquois town near present-day Syracuse. About 10 miles from their objective they captured a fishing party of eleven Iroquois. Right away the Algonquin chief, Iroquet, began the ritual of torture by cutting off a woman's finger. Champlain angrily told him the French considered such treatment of women cowardly and brutal. The Algonquin reluctantly agreed not to torture the female prisoners, but would make no such promises regarding the men. Meanwhile, the attacking force went off toward the Iroquois town, whooping and shouting their war cries. All element of surprise was lost.

It was October 11, and the Iroquois facing the invading force were probably Onondagas. The stockade around their town was well-constructed, and Champlain expressed admiration for it. There was no sign of Brûlé and the Andastes. Champlain wanted to wait for these allies, but the Hurons and Algonquins were impatient, and attacked immediately. Champlain was utterly exasperated with their lack of discipline. He still had not grasped the fact that Europeans and North American Natives had totally different concepts about war.

The Huron-Algonquin assault was beaten back with many casualties, and the French gunfire proved ineffective against the stockade's stout walls. Champlain had platforms constructed from which his men could fire their weapons down into the fort. But the French were soon driven to seek cover by volleys of arrows and a barrage of rocks. One Frenchman was killed and Champlain himself was struck in the leg by two arrows, one of them lodging painfully in his knee. The attackers then retreated into the trees.

For two days they waited for Brûlé and the Andastes. Native warriors generally had little patience for siege warfare. The Hurons and Algonquins decided they'd had enough and began a full retreat, carrying the wounded Champlain in a basket; an ordeal he called "hell." French prestige among the Hurons and Algonquins suffered considerably from this defeat. The Iroquois, however, now realized that the white men and their guns were not invincible. Many months would pass before Champlain heard Brûlé's explanation of what had happened.

Champlain wanted the Natives to take him to Quebec, but they said they could not spare the canoes. He and the other Frenchmen had no choice but to accompany them to Huronia. With winter setting in, it was a difficult journey, and they did not reach Cahiague until December 24. Since he was compelled to spend the winter with them, Champlain made detailed studies of the Huron way of life. Champlain's in-depth descriptions of Native life, from their everyday recipes for cooking to their manner of courting, would provide Europeans with the first serious study of their ways.

One of the Récollet priests, Father Joseph Le Caron, had already begun his proselytizing mission among the tribes. When he visited Cahiague, he and Champlain took a tour of the surrounding country. They visited the Petuns, who cultivated tobacco and "turkey corn" in their land between the Nottawasaga River and Lake Huron. Then they went southwest to the land of the tribe Champlain called Cheveux Relevés (High Hairs) because of their elaborate hair style. These people called themselves the Andatahouats, but were eventually known as the Ottawas, a name mistakenly given to all of the Algonquin peoples of the Great Lakes. Champlain and Le Caron wanted to go on to meet the Neutral tribes on the shores of Lake Erie, but their Huron guides told them that would be dangerous because the Andatahouats and the Neutrals were at war. Once again, this may only have been a ruse to prevent the French from becoming acquainted with a rival tribe.

During that winter in Huronia Champlain regained much of the respect he had lost following the defeat in battle. He was often called upon to settle disputes, and the sound judgment he exercised impressed his hosts. There was much about the Huron lifestyle that Champlain found alien and even revolting: "Their life is wretched by comparison with ours, but happy for them since they have not tasted a better and believe that none more excellent can be found." However, he also found a great deal to admire. Aside from those instances in which he expressed disgust at the torture of prisoners, Champlain did not make the mistake of being openly judgmental of the natives.

The exploring Champlain did in the early months of 1616 would be his last. On May 22 he set out with the Natives for the St. Lawrence Valley. At the island of Montreal he met Pontgrave, who had given him up for dead. By July 11, Champlain was back in Quebec. His wife, who had spent a few miserable years in Canada, and hated it, remained in France.

The rest of Champlain's career in Canada was taken up with the administration of Quebec and the nurturing of the colony there. He made numerous trips to France to convince people that Canada held great promise for those bold enough to go there and put down roots. In 1628, with England and France at war, a fleet commanded by the privateer Captain David Kirke blockaded the St. Lawrence River, reducing the population of Quebec to starvation. On July 20, 1629, Champlain was forced to surrender the town. To his shock and utter dismay, he learned that Brûlé had gone over to the English and had guided their ships upriver from Tadoussac.

In 1632, Quebec was returned to France, and in 1633 Champlain was back in the community he had founded. He died there on Christmas Day 1635. Champlain was buried in Quebec with all due honours. His gravesite is not known, but it could be said that Canada itself is a monument to Champlain.

Étienne Brûlé

The First Frontiersman

Say the word "frontiersman," and for many people the first names that come to mind are Daniel Boone and Davy Crockett. Thanks to American novels, films and television, historical icons like Boone and Crockett, and even fictional characters like James Fenimore Cooper's Hawkeye have become the most recognized representatives of the "leatherstocking" heroes of wilderness lore. They are the resourceful white adventurers who are as much at home in the forest as any Native. Yet, the predecessor for their kind was not an American; and though he made his mark in Canadian history, he was not Canadian-born. He arrived in Canada as a French boy of uncertain origins. In his relatively short life he would be many things: a pioneer of cultural exchange between two worlds, an interpreter, an explorer, a free spirit who stirred the anger of the Church in early Canada and, in the end, an outlaw damned to a traitor's death.

The time and place of Étienne Brûlé's birth are not certain. There is evidence that he came from a peasant family in Champigny-sur-Marne near Paris, and may have been born in 1592. Brûlé was probably no more than fourteen years old when he sailed to Canada with Champlain in 1608. That year is a calculated guess, because Champlain's writings make no mention of Brûlé until 1618, when Brûlé had already been living among the natives for eight years. Champlain wrote that in 1610 a "youth who had already spent two winters at Quebec" had asked his permission to go and live with the Natives so he could learn their language. Brûlé was the first boy under Champlain's command to be sent to learn the Native way of life.

That a young European would voluntarily go off into the howling wilderness to a totally alien lifestyle tells us a lot about his character. During the two years he had already spent in Canada he would have been exposed to Montagnais and Algonquin people, and he evidently did not consider them "savages." He quite likely had already picked up many dialects from the Natives who traded at Quebec and Tadoussac. It could very well be that he saw in the forest life of the Natives a degree of freedom that Frenchmen, bound by their own cultural restraints even in Quebec, could not enjoy. That Brûlé *requested* the assignment tells us he was a lad who hungered for adventure. He liked the Natives, and they evidently liked him too. The Algonquin chief Iroquet would not likely have agreed to take young Brûlé under his wing if he did not consider the boy a worthy student.

We can only wonder how Brûlé came to be in Canada with Champlain in the first place. Champlain's writings say nothing about it. It could be that the youth heard stories of adventure in the New World, and decided that life behind a plough was not for him. We don't know for certain if Brûlé was present at Champlain's first two battles with the Iroquois. He was most likely with Champlain at the victory in the summer of 1610, because it was the day after the battle Champlain agreed to the exchange that saw his "servant" go away with the natives while the young Huron Savignon was chosen for a journey to France.

Unlike Champlain, Brûlé was not a chronicler. We don't even know if he was literate. He did not write a word about his first year with the natives. If he did write an account of that, or any of his subsequent adventures, he gave the reports to Champlain, who would have incorporated the information into his own journals. We know only that the next time Champlain saw him after he went away in 1610, Brûlé was "dressed like a savage" and "well pleased with the treatment received from the Indians, according to the customs of their country."

While living with the tribe and mastering a new language, Brûlé would have had to learn the basics of wilderness survival: how to hunt, catch fish and find food in the forest. The Algonquins did a little farming, but their land was poorly suited to agriculture. Brûlé would also have had to adapt to the Native diet, which was often unappealing to Europeans. The Natives would have also taught him how to handle a canoe. We know from Champlain's journals that Brûlé was the first Frenchman to meet the dangerous challenge of shooting white water rapids.

For the eastern woodland tribes of Canada, the forest was their universe. It swept, unbroken except by rivers and lakes, halfway across the continent. A squirrel, jumping from treetop to treetop, could have travelled from Nova Scotia to the edge of the western prairies without touching the ground. The forest was spectacular in its beauty, and it provided the Natives with everything they needed to sustain life. But it could also be a place of great danger. An accident on a seldom-used trail could mean death to a careless traveller. It was also the home of bears, wolves and rattlesnakes.

Moreover, the forest was always a potential battleground; foes like the Iroquois could be waiting in ambush anywhere along a path through the bush, or beyond the next bend in the river. Brûlé would have had to learn, and learn well, that in this magnificent but often deadly timberland, one moved with senses on high alert at all times. An unusual mark on the ground, an unfamiliar noise from the forest, a strange scent on the breeze might be all the warning one got that something was amiss.

Among seventeenth-century Europeans the concept of "teenager" did not exist. A person was a child or an adult, with no middle ground. By modern Western standards Brûlé was a teenaged boy when he went to live with the Natives; a boy who suddenly found himself in a society with none of the restrictions or rules he had previously known. That included sexual behaviour. As far as the French were concerned, the natives were lascivious people. Except when the weather was cold, they wore very little clothing, and on festive occasions girls and women danced naked. They had almost no inhibitions about sex. According to one missionary, Brother Gabriel Sagard, the boys "are at liberty to give themselves over to this wickedness as soon as they can, and the young girls to prostitute themselves as soon as they are capable of doing so. Parents are often procurers of their own daughters."

No doubt the Natives would have been bemused, if not downright bewildered, at the cleric's use of words like "wickedness" and "prostitute." To them sexual relations were as natural as the forest around them. Young men and young women slept together for a few nights to help determine if they were suitable for each other as husband and wife. French missionaries and Champlain himself were appalled when Native women offered themselves to them as bed partners. Men in their position, of course, had to turn the offers down.

Young Étienne Brûlé would have felt no such obligation. Given his unique position in the Native community, he would have been seen as quite a novelty to unmarried Native girls. It seems likely that Brûlé had very little religious education. Indeed, he seemed at times to scoff at Christian religious taboos. He once said that at a dangerous river crossing, he made an offering of tobacco to the river god, and that it seemed to work well enough. Brûlé also told the priests that on one occasion, when his life was in danger, he said the *benedicté* (Grace before meals) because it was the only prayer he knew. This would not go over well at all with the missionaries, especially the ultra-conservative Jesuits, whose *Relations* were, for a long time, one of the only sources for information on this period of Canadian history. To the priests, Brûlé was a "wretch" whose "scandalous way of living" was a "great stumbling block to the spread of the gospel" among the Natives. When they wrote their accounts they either condemned Brûlé as a villain "guilty of every vice and crime," or ignored him and credited Champlain with his accomplishments.

Just where Brûlé's wanderings took him in the years 1610 to 1615—during which time Champlain was often in France—no one really knows. He most certainly ascended the Ottawa River before Champlain did, and saw Lake Nipissing, Georgian Bay and Lake Huron. He very likely travelled to Neutral country and saw Lake Erie. He may have been the first European to stand on the shores of Lake Ontario and to see Niagara Falls. Indeed, there is evidence that Brûlé explored four of the five Great Lakes (he probably did not see Lake Michigan), earning the unofficial title, "Columbus of the Great Lakes."

The closest thing we have to actual documentation of a Brûlé expedition of discovery is Champlain's account—as told to him by

Brûlé—of the 1615 journey to enlist the aid of the Andastes against the Iroquois. As explained in the previous chapter, the Hurons and Algonquins were preparing to invade the Iroquois homeland on the southern shore of Lake Ontario. They were accompanied by Champlain and a few French, whose firearms had helped them win battles against their traditional enemies on two earlier occasions. Word came to the Huron village of Cahiague that the Andastes, who lived south of the Iroquois in what is now Pennsylvania, were eager to join in the campaign against a common foe. Twelve of the best and bravest of the Huron warriors were chosen to go to Carantouan, the principal town of the Andastes, and urge them to hurry north. If the allied tribes could coordinate their attacks, they could catch the Iroquois in a vise and destroy them.

Brûlé asked Champlain for permission to go with the twelve braves. Champlain readily granted it, "since [Brûlé] was drawn thereto of his own inclination, and by this means would see their country and could observe the tribes that inhabit it." It was an extremely dangerous mission, because the route lay straight through enemy territory. Whatever other charges might have been made against Étienne Brûlé, no one could call him a coward. However, Brûlé's mission would be a failure and three years would pass before he gave Champlain an explanation.

The exact route Brûlé and the twelve Hurons took is disputed. Some historians think they went ahead of Champlain's main body of men; that is, from Lake Simcoe down through the Kawartha lakes to the Trent River and then through the Bay of Quinte into eastern Lake Ontario. Others think it more probable Brûlé crossed Lake Simcoe, went up the Holland River as far as possible, portaged to the Humber River and followed that stream to its mouth on Lake Ontario, thus making Brûlé the first European to visit the future site of Toronto. They would then have crossed the western end of Lake Ontario at Hamilton Bay and stealthily slipped into Iroquois country.

En route to Carantouan, Brûlé and the Hurons surprised an Iroquois hunting party. There was a fight in which four of the hunters were killed. The other two were taken as prisoners to the Andastes village and tortured to death. The Andastes had a feast in honour of their guests, performing their war dances and singing their war songs. They did everything except respond to Brûlé's requests for haste. Like Champlain, Brûlé was learning that Natives made war in their own good time, and no amount of argument could hurry them into it.

The Andastes were still dancing and singing when Champlain attacked a major Iroquois settlement with a force of Algonquins and Hurons. The attack failed, Champlain was wounded, and the invaders had to retreat back across Lake Ontario, wondering all the while what had become of their Andaste allies. Two days after the northern allies gave up the fight, Brûlé arrived with the Andastes. From the walls of their fort, the Iroquois shouted taunts at their enemies. They boasted that they had driven off the interlopers, killing many of them, and they waved bloody scalps to prove it. The Andastes withdrew immediately and returned to their town.

The twelve Hurons who had travelled south with Brûlé now probably returned to Huronia, while Brûlé remained in the Andastes' country. Whether he did so at Champlain's instructions is not known. Brûlé then became the first European to set foot in what is now Pennsylvania. He spent that autumn and winter exploring the countryside. He travelled down a river—probably the Susquehanna—all the way to the sea; most likely Chesapeake

Bay. Brûlé was not the first European at Chesapeake Bay; the Englishman, Captain John Smith, had been there before him. But Brûlé was the first to reach it from the interior. He would later report meeting many tribes who were well-disposed toward the French because they had been badly treated by the Dutch.

Brûlé's descriptions, as reported by Champlain, provide an accurate geographic picture of the Susquehanna River and Chesapeake Bay. Yet some historians dispute Brûlé's claims, saying he only passed on information given to him by the Andastes; that, in fact, he never even left the Andastes' village. Those scholars believe Brûlé lied because he had to tell Champlain *something* to redeem himself after failing to bring the Andastes to the battlefield on time; though the Natives' tardiness was clearly not his fault.

In the spring of 1616, Brûlé decided to return to Huronia, which meant another trip through Iroquois country. Six Andaste warriors went with him as an escort through the land of the Senecas, one of the tribes in the Iroquois confederacy. Somewhere along the trail they were attacked by an Iroquois war party. The Andastes scattered and fled, leaving Brûlé to his own devices. Brûlé managed to escape, but found himself alone in unfamiliar and hostile territory. Soon he became lost. After a few hungry days he decided to give himself up to the Iroquois, "through the trust he had in God," as he shamelessly told Champlain later, but, in truth, trusting more in the fact that he spoke the Iroquois language. It is at this point, according to some historians, that Brûlé's story becomes somewhat incredible.

Brûlé claimed he saw three Seneca fishermen returning to their village with the day's catch. When he called out to them, they were about to drop their fish and run, but Brûlé spoke again, reassuring them that he meant no harm. He put down his weapons and convinced them to do the same. Then he smoked a pipe with them, and told them a tale of woe about how he came to be lost in their woods. The three men then took Brûlé to their village.

At the village, a crowd gathered around Brûlé, wanting to know who he was and where he came from. Was he not a Frenchman, one of the "men of iron" who made war on the Iroquois? Brûlé said that he came from a people who were better than the French, and who were friends of the Iroquois.

The Senecas didn't believe him. They tied him to a tree and some began to tear his beard out while others burned him with firebrands. A chief tried to speak in his favour, but to no avail. Then, according to Brûlé, a "miracle" occurred. Around his neck Brûlé wore an Agnus Dei medal, and when one of the torturers reached out to take it, Brûlé warned, "If you touch that, the God of the French will strike you dead!"

The warrior ignored the threat and grabbed at the medal. Just then the sky darkened and a thunderclap shook the heavens as though a god had indeed been grievously offended. Terrified, the superstitious natives fled for cover. The chief who had tried to protect Brûlé undid his bonds, took him into his longhouse and cared for his wounds.

Now that his life was no longer in danger, Brûlé called the tribal leaders to a council. He told them that the French were "next of kin to the angels or good spirits of Paradise," and that the Dutch, who were then at Albany, were "the bad manitous or spirits." The Senecas honoured Brûlé with a feast, and when he expressed a desire to return to Huronia, they sent an escort to guide him at least part of the way. When he left, he promised the Iroquois that he would speak on their behalf to make peace between them and the French.

Brûlé arrived safely in Huronia in the summer of 1616, but took his time getting back to Champlain; two more years, in fact! Was he recuperating from injuries for part of that time? Historians have speculated that his tortures might have gone beyond those described in his story; that he may have had his fingernails torn out and been forced to run the gauntlet. He certainly would have had to show Champlain scars to verify his tale.

Modern historians take Brûlé's story with a rather large grain of salt. "Miracles" don't generally stand up very well to scrutiny. They believe Brûlé was captured and was initially subjected to pretty rough treatment; after all, the French were allies of the Hurons and Algonquins, the Iroquois' mortal enemies. But then someone—possibly the sympathetic chief of Brûlé's story—realized that Brûlé could be an important emissary for the Iroquois. The Iroquois wanted to get in on the fur trade with the French. Who better to carry a message of peace than a Frenchman they had captured and then spared?

So why the story about the Agnus Dei medal and the thunderclap from God? Brûlé knew that his Huron friends would not be very pleased if he admitted the Iroquois had released him on his promise to be a peacemaker. But he had to explain how he had been able to walk out of the Seneca camp alive. He knew that the Hurons, Champlain and especially the devout missionaries would be all too willing to believe in a tale of divine intervention, even when the beneficiary was a sinner like Brûlé. Brother Gabriel Sagard, who probably heard the story first hand from Brûlé, wrote in his *Histoire du Canada:* "The poor man was very much frightened. He did not know to which saint he could give himself; for to hope for mercy he knew very well he could not, and so he had recourse to God and to patience, and submitted himself to the

Divine wishes more because he was obliged to than otherwise, for he was not devout, judging by what he told us."

When Champlain finally met Brûlé again, at Trois-Rivières in the spring of 1618, he was still angry over Brûlé's failure to bring the Andastes warriors to the Iroquois village. After hearing Brûlé's amazing story, Champlain wrote: "He is more to be pitied than blamed for not reporting to me before, because of the misfortunes which he experienced on his journeys."

Over the next decade Brûlé was active as an agent in the fur trade. It was his job to make sure that the largest volume of furs possible went to Quebec and not to the Dutch in Albany. Brûlé seems to have handled this assignment well, and for that he was well-paid. Money never seems to have been of great importance to him, but his annual salary of one hundred pistoles a year (a pistole being roughly the equivalent of an English pound) was ten times the annual wages of a common labourer. Ironically, Brûlé was also essential to the work of the missionary priests because they needed him as a guide and language instructor. It has even been suggested that Brûlé assisted Brother Sagard in compiling a dictionary of the Huron language.

But relations between Brûlé and the priests were never good. To the clerics, and even Champlain, men like Brûlé who had "gone native" were debauched. They had turned their backs on Christian civilization to live the inferior lifestyle of degenerate heathens. The self-righteous were quite vocal in their disapproval of, and even contempt for, such men. There were, in fact, times when Brûlé and other interpreters stood together and refused to give the missionaries instructions in Native dialects. Small wonder that Father Jean de Brébeuf, a future martyr and now honoured as a saint, despised Brûlé.

For years the French had been hearing stories from the Natives about a big island (Manitoulin) in Georgian Bay. Beyond that, said the Natives, was a channel that led to a vast body of fresh water, even larger than Mer Douce. Champlain wanted to learn more about this new lake and asked Brûlé to investigate. Brûlé probably did some exploring among the thousands of islands in Georgian Bay, but it was not until sometime between 1621 and 1623 that he took his canoe through the North Channel that separates Manitoulin Island from the mainland, and then up the St. Mary's River to the rapids at Sault Ste. Marie. From there, accompanied by another Frenchman named Grenolle, and perhaps a few Huron guides, Brûlé went on to Lake Superior, thus becoming the first European known to have seen and explored that great inland sea. He evidently travelled from one end of the lake to the other, finding no connection to Hudson Bay or the Pacific. He did take back to Champlain a big copper ingot that might have come from Île Royale, where there are large copper deposits. This would be Brûlé's last known important expedition of discovery. After a few more years during which nothing was heard of him, Brûlé's career and life entered a phase that was both dark and final.

As a member of the Huron nation, Brûlé belonged to the Attignawantan, or Bear Clan. For some twenty-three years, when he wasn't exploring, on the warpath, or guiding priests to and from Quebec, Brûlé lived in the Huron village of Toanche, near present day Penetanguishene on Georgian Bay. In that time he was a brother hunter and a fellow warrior to the Huron men, a lover of Huron women and most likely father to several children. He had been living, what was to him, an ideal life, disturbed only by the Récollet priests and then the even more meddlesome (but politically powerful) Jesuits. In fact, it would appear that the Jesuits had the authority to order any Frenchman in Canada—including woodsmen like Brûlé—back to France.

In 1627 war broke out between England and France. Captain David Kirke (whom the French called a pirate) had a commission from King Charles I to capture "Canida." In the summer of 1629, Champlain sent Étienne Brûlé and another interpreter down from Quebec to guide the relief ships he had been expecting from France, unaware that Kirke had already captured the ships. When Brûlé and company reached Tadoussac, they found the English holding the post. There was absolutely no hope of any French help reaching Quebec. Brûlé agreed to guide the English ships upriver. On July 19, Champlain surrendered. When he boarded the English vessel, he was shocked to see Brûlé on board, and not as a prisoner. Brûlé said the English had forced him into their service, but Champlain did not believe it. He denounced Brûlé as a traitor and prophesied he would end his life as a renegade, "abhorred by both God and man."

Champlain was taken to England, where he argued his case that Quebec had been illegally seized. Brûlé returned to his home in Huronia. The English held Quebec until 1633, when it was finally restored to the French. During that time the English took a fortune in furs out of the St. Lawrence Valley, and no doubt Brûlé worked just as hard directing the fur fleets into Kirke's warehouses as he had done for Champlain. The English were, after all, the new masters on the great river.

Why Brûlé betrayed Champlain has never been satisfactorily explained. We have only Champlain's version of events, and that is quite understandably biased. Was Brûlé truly a turncoat who sold out to the English? Did he, knowing that the occupants of Quebec were on the verge of starvation, see no alternative but to do the bidding of the English? Had he, like so many others in

Quebec, grown weary of the autocratic, condescending attitudes of the Jesuits; so weary, in fact, that he was willing to dabble in a little treason if it meant getting them out of the country? For surely, the Protestant English would not permit the Catholic missionaries to carry on their proselytizing among the Natives!

Just as mysterious is Étienne Brûlé's death. All we know for certain is that shortly after Champlain returned to Quebec on May 22, 1633, Brûlé was dead; murdered by his brethren of the Bear Clan. But why?

The most accepted version is that the Hurons killed Brûlé because he had betrayed Champlain. In fact, according to this story, they tortured him to death, and then cooked and ate him. But if the Hurons felt Brûlé deserved to die for betraying Champlain, why would they tolerate his presence amongst them for so long before finally putting him to death? Only one original account, written by Brother Sagard many years after Brûlé's death, says anything about him being tortured and eaten, and those gruesome features may have been figments of the priest's imagination. Brébeuf, in discussing Brûlé's death only a year after it happened, says nothing of torture or cannibalism.

It is possible that Brûlé was killed because he committed some sexual indiscretion. Or could it be that in order to get back into Champlain's good books, he risked Huron anger by acting on his old promise to the Seneca to arrange peace negotiations between the Iroquois and the French? The French would have been delighted to see Iroquois fur canoes coming to them instead of going to Albany, but such an arrangement would have been perceived as disastrous by the Hurons. If Brûlé was, in fact, plotting such a scheme, many former friends would have seen him as a threat to be removed.

Shortly after Champlain returned to Quebec, he had an Algonquin executed for the murder of a Frenchman. The Algonquins then passed word on to the Hurons that Champlain might take revenge on them for murdering Brûlé. But if the Hurons feared retribution, Champlain soon reassured them there would be none. Brûlé, he told them, was no longer a Frenchman, but a traitor and an outlaw. They had done no wrong in killing him.

Nonetheless, the Hurons expressed regret over killing Brûlé. Some of them told Brébeuf they were afraid the Algonquins or even members of their own tribe would seek vengeance. Other Huron chiefs treated the head of the Bear Clan as a pariah after Brûlé's murder.

Not long after Brûlé's death a smallpox epidemic swept through Huronia, killing thousands. The people of Toanche, feeling that the ground upon which Brûlé had been killed was now cursed, abandoned their village and built a new one nearby. A story spread throughout the land that a ghostly, pale woman, Brûlé's sister, wandered the forests, breathing pestilence upon the people who had slain her brother.

Every twelve years the Hurons held a major ceremony called the Feast of the Dead in which the remains of all who had died since the previous Feast were gathered from temporary graves for re-burial in a mass grave pit. Three years after Brûlé's death the time came for a Feast of the Dead, and Brûlé's bones became the centre of a major controversy. The Hurons told Brébeuf that they wanted to include Brûlé's bones, perhaps in the hope of making atonement for his death. But the Jesuit would not allow it. Brûlé had been baptized a Christian, and even though he had not been a devout one, Brébeuf could not allow his remains to be buried with those of unbaptized heathens. He suggested a compromise, whereby he would have Brûlé's remains buried in a Christian grave, next to the pit into which the Native remains would be cast.

That seemed to be satisfactory to the Hurons. But then a dispute arose as to which village should have Brûlé's bones. The Bear Clan of Toanche said the bones should go in their grave pit, since Brûlé had lived with them, and they had the greatest need to make peace with his ghost. Other villages argued that Toanche did not deserve such recognition, because they had killed Brûlé. In the end Brûlé's bones remained in the unmarked grave in which the adventurer had been buried. And Father Brébeuf was relieved that he did not have to honour that "infamous wretch" with a Christian burial after all. The location of Brûlé's grave remains unknown.

Whatever his personal flaws—and they might not have been as enormous as his contemporaries made them out to be—Étienne Brûlé stands out as a great man in early Canadian history. In addition to being an explorer without whom Champlain's accomplishments would have been greatly diminished, Brûlé was the first European to fully immerse himself in the wilderness and the native way of life. He was the first of a unique breed of woodsmen who, long before Daniel Boone and Davy Crockett, would spread out from the St. Lawrence Valley in search of furs, adventure and a life of freedom. They would penetrate the forests of central Canada to the prairies and even to the Rocky Mountains. In what is now the United States, they would push westward beyond the Mississippi long before the Lewis and Clark Expedition was even dreamed of. Most of them would not leave their names for historical record, but as a breed of men they would become known as the legendary coureurs de bois.

Henry Hudson

Arctic Mutiny

When Henry Hudson sailed his ship, *Discovery,* down the Thames River on April 17, 1610, little did he know that his quest for a Northwest Passage would end in what has become the most infamous mutiny in Canadian history. (Perhaps only the mutiny on the ill-fated *Bounty* is better known.) Indeed, Hudson was confident that he would be in the Far East by the following February.

Hudson had good reason to be optimistic. In three short years the middle-aged sea captain had emerged from obscurity to become one of the leading explorers of his day. In 1607 and 1608 he led two expeditions to find a northeast route to China by rounding the northern tip of Norway. Though he failed in his primary objective, he still registered some noteworthy accomplishments: He set a record by sailing farther north than any other European before him; he discovered the Spitsbergen whaling grounds for England; he observed that in the high Arctic, the sun stayed above the horizon for twenty-four hours a day during the height of summer.

In 1609, sailing the Dutch East India Company ship *Half Moon,* Hudson explored what is now called the Hudson River inland as far as present-day Albany, New York, blazing the way for a Dutch colony in America. It wasn't long before France and England took notice of his work and began clamouring for his services. In the end, it was King James I who convinced Hudson that he ought to be working for his own country. In fact, he strongly suggested it might be treasonous for Hudson to be working for a foreign power.

A group of prominent London men—among them Sir Dudley Digges, Sir Thomas Smith and Sir John Wolstenholme, with Henry the Prince of Wales as their titular head—wanted Hudson to penetrate the Furious Overfall. This treacherous stretch of water in the Canadian Arctic, now called Hudson Strait, was a bottleneck of icebergs, fog and devilish currents that no European ship had yet conquered. Several English captains had tried, but their ships had either been turned back or had vanished without a trace. The men in London were certain it was a key to the Northwest Passage, and they believed Hudson was the man to conquer it. Though we know almost nothing of Hudson's early life, there is evidence that he may have sailed with the explorer John Davis and possibly saw the Furious Overfall for himself as a youth.

In spite of all his qualifications as an explorer and experience as a mariner, Hudson should have had some misgivings about the trip. The 55-ton bark *Discovery* was barely adequate for a long, rugged Arctic voyage. Her twenty-two-man crew, which included Hudson's teenage son Jack, had more than its share of malcontents and troublemakers; a puzzling situation since, with the Prince of Wales as one of his sponsors, Hudson should have had the pick of the very best seamen.

The first mate was Robert Juet, a vile-tempered, elderly seaman who had shipped with Hudson on two earlier voyages. Juet had developed a hatred for Hudson that the captain was not fully aware of until it was too late. Juet should have been a strong right arm for Hudson, but at critical moments he became a taunting adversary, undermining the commander's authority. Robert Bylot, the second mate, was an able-enough seaman, but was a man of weak character. Quartermaster John King was bad-tempered and had an abrasive personality. The ship's bos'un (boatswain), Francis Clemens (or Clement), was a competent and reliable man, as were the ship's carpenter Philip Staffe, the cooper, Sylvanus Bond, and seamen Michael Perse and Arnold Lodlo. Another seaman, Adrian Motter, signed aboard with letters of recommendation, which later turned out to be forgeries.

Edward Wilson, the ship's doctor, was a twenty-two-year-old gentleman who was going to sea for the first time. The ship's cook Bennett Matthews was moody and unpredictable, as was the ship's boy, Nicholas Syms. Seaman William Wilson was foul-mouthed, intemperate, quarrelsome and a braggart.

Abacuck Prickett, a former haberdasher, was aboard as a lackey for his master, Sir Dudley Digges, the man who put up most of the money for the voyage. Prickett considered himself a pious man and liked to quote scripture. While he openly ingratiated himself to those in authority, secretly he was a schemer. Thomas Woodhouse, a mathematics student at Oxford, was also aboard at Digges' insistence. He, too, was going to sea for the first time.

Young Jack Hudson, who had sailed with his father before, was aboard as a common seaman. He was an able lad who was always willing to pitch in and shoulder his share of the work. He ate with the crew, and not at his father's table, but nonetheless was never fully accepted by the other sailors as one of them.

The other crewmen were Syracke Fanning, Adam Moore, John Thomas, Michael Butt and ship's gunner John Williams. Nothing is known of them except that they did not survive the voyage. A man named Coleburn signed aboard the *Discovery,* but Hudson dismissed him just before setting sail because he thought he might be a troublemaker.

Then there was Henry Greene, a young wastrel Hudson secretly took aboard at Gravesend. The relationship between this youth and Hudson is still mystifying. Greene was the black sheep son of a prosperous farmer in Kent. He was handsome, with "the broad shoulders of a river bargeman, and even greater strength," according to Juet's account, but he was thoroughly dishonest. All but disowned by his family, he also "had lost the goodwill of all his friends," according to one observer, because of his acid tongue, his scandalous behaviour and his tendency to be argumentative. He was known to revel with the lowest riffraff in London, and was often seen in the company of pimps, prostitutes, pickpockets and counterfeiters.

Greene went to Hudson looking for a place on the *Discovery.* Inexplicably, Hudson took a liking to this young libertine and agreed to take Greene aboard. He also promised Greene that upon their triumphant return he would introduce him to his friend the Prince of Wales and have him accepted into the Royal Guard. Weeks before *Discovery's* departure, Greene moved into Hudson's comfortable house in one of London's better middle-class districts. This did not at all please Katherine Hudson, who quickly developed an intense dislike for her husband's new friend. Greene's family hoped the great explorer would be a good influence on the young rogue, and they happily gave Hudson five pounds to help outfit Greene for the sea. Officially, he was not even a member of the crew. He went aboard as a passenger and the captain's guest. Henry Hudson and Henry Greene would not be friends for long.

Perhaps the greatest liability aboard the *Discovery* was Hudson himself. He was a brilliant navigator and a man of unquestionable courage, but he was also capricious in dealing with men under his command. While other sea captains controlled their superstitious, unruly sailors through steady enforcement of strict rules and harsh discipline, Hudson was inconsistent. At times he asserted his authority, while at others he meekly gave in to demands made by insubordinate officers. His three major voyages before 1610 had all been marred by shipboard rebellions, in which Hudson, in order to avoid a mutiny, capitulated to his crew. On his trip up the Hudson River in the *Half Moon,* the captain had failed to restrain his men from debauching and murdering Natives. For all his great accomplishments as an explorer, Henry Hudson was a poor leader, and this failing would ultimately prove to be his undoing.

Still, as he put the coast of England behind him, the captain anticipated a successful voyage. He was certain that if he could navigate his way through the Furious Overfall, the rest of the way would be clear sailing right to the Orient. "There, I know, lies the sure sea path to the Indies," he wrote in a letter to his friend the great geographer Richard Hakluyt, "and he who finds it will be remembered for all time, even as Drake will not be forgot. I pray with all my heart. Be it by northern path or western, I would that my name be carved on the tablets of the sea." Hudson's name would indeed be remembered, but not for the reason for which he prayed.

Trouble began early aboard the *Discovery.* The ship was

barely under way when William Wilson began picking quarrels with other crewmen. Hudson offended the rank and file when he showed favouritism toward the arrogant and pretentious Henry Greene. When Greene realized that Prickett was a devout Christian, he went out of his way to insult the man's religious beliefs. Then, during a stopover in Iceland, Greene deliberately picked a fight with Edward Wilson. Greene was an experienced street brawler and gave the young physician a savage beating. First mate Juet could have stopped the fight, but didn't. When Hudson arrived on the scene, to the disgust of all, he took Greene's side and reprimanded Dr. Wilson. When Hudson realized he had angered most of his men, he did a complete turnaround and charged Greene with causing the fight. He then infuriated the young troublemaker by cutting off his ale ration for a week. Juet, reprimanded for not using his authority to quell the disturbance, went into a sulk.

A few days later, when Juet was drunk, he spread the rumour that Greene was Hudson's spy below deck and that when they returned to England, "he will crack the credit of anyone who won't bow down to him." Soon there were whispers of mutiny, and Juet advised the men to keep their swords and muskets handy.

Several days passed before Hudson heard the rumours. The enraged captain threatened to sail back to Iceland and put Juet ashore, where he'd be forced to return to England with a fishing fleet. Hudson cooled down and reconsidered when he realized a return to Iceland would cost him precious time. Furthermore, Hudson needed a first mate, and he did not think any of his other officers were qualified enough for the job. In the end, Hudson decided to push on, "hoping of amendment" with Juet.

On June 25 the *Discovery* reached the entrance of the Furious

Overfall. Fog gripped the *Discovery* and the proximity to the North Magnetic Pole rendered the ship's compass useless. The crew probably paled at the sight of the crashing ice and swirling tides.

For weeks the ice pans thundered down the strait, blocking the *Discovery*'s path and forcing her south into Ungava Bay. Trying to battle through that gauntlet of jagged ice in a small, wooden-hulled ship was like sailing through a minefield. One mistake and the ship would go down with all hands.

The men were terrified and the rumblings of mutiny began again. It was reported later that Clemens said that if he had one hundred pounds, "hee would give four score and ten to be at home." But Staffe, who was made of sterner stuff and was absolutely loyal to the captain, responded that if he had one hundred pounds, "hee would not give ten upon such condition, but would think it to be as good money as hee ever had, and to bring it as well home."

There was no time for arguments. The men had to fight the sea and ice. At one point Hudson was actually on the verge of *asking* the crew if they wanted to continue or go home. But the matter was never put to a vote. The struggle at hand was simply to stay afloat and survive.

Hudson drew on every ounce of his considerable skill as a navigator. He pushed his less-than-ideal crew to their best efforts as he stubbornly held to a western course. After a grueling six-week battle up a 450-mile hell's alley of sea and ice, Hudson guided the *Discovery* between Cape Wolstenholme and Digges Island, and out into open water. For a glorious moment Hudson was a miracle worker. He had beaten the Furious Overfall! For this singular accomplishment he would enter history as one of the great Arctic explorers. But for Hudson at the time, the mission was only half completed. He still had to reach Cathay.

On August 3, in the last surviving entry in Hudson's journal, he wrote, "Then I observed and found the ship at noon in 61 degrees, 20 minutes, and a sea to the westward." The "sea" Hudson looked upon was the giant bay that would be named for him. Hudson sincerely believed he had reached the Pacific Ocean and would soon be coasting along Oriental shores.

Hudson sent men ashore at Digges Island to climb to the highest point for a better view of the world around them. The party found some Inuit food caches and spotted wild game. When they returned to the ship they reported their findings to Hudson and suggested they stay a few days to rest and replenish their supplies. Hudson refused. China and Japan were within reach, he said, and he was anxious to get under way.

For the next few weeks Hudson sailed down the eastern shore of the bay, sure that he would soon be in warmer waters. The *Discovery* entered what is now called James Bay, when the coastline suddenly turned north again. Hudson refused to accept the evidence in front of him: He had reached a dead end. He sailed back and forth along the coasts of what are now Ontario and Quebec, probing for an opening that would allow him to continue south. Juet, for all his personal flaws, was an experienced mariner. He knew that the waters and landforms around him matched nothing on the captain's charts. The mood of the crew darkened again. Juet did not help matters when he whispered to the crew that they were lost. Talk of mutiny was soon in the air again.

Tales of a coming insurrection reached Hudson's ears, and this time he took action. He interrogated members of the crew and was astonished at how far Juet's plot against him had gone. One sailor after another reported that Juet had spoken of "manslaughter" and had made numerous bloody threats. The first mate had even told the men to keep weapons ready for the moment when he took over the ship.

Before the assembled crew, Hudson stripped Juet of his rank and demoted him to common seaman. While this certainly would have been humiliating for Juet, every man on board knew the former first mate was getting off lightly. Many other ship's master would have hung Juet from a yardarm and would have been justified in the eyes of any court for doing so. On a ship at sea the captain was the law and there was no crime worse than mutiny. To even suggest it could put a man's head in the noose.

Clemens was also demoted, on suspicion of being Juet's chief confederate. If the former bos'un had not been in Juet's camp previously, he was now. Hudson promoted second mate Bylot to first, and seamen Wilson and King to a shared rank of bos'un. Seaman Motter was made bos'un's mate. Then Hudson announced that the men he considered guilty of conspiracy to commit mutiny would forfeit a portion of their pay, and that money would be divided among the loyal crewmen. This divided the crew even more. Amazingly, Hudson later apologized to Juet and Clemens and promised them all would be well if they behaved themselves. A good ship's master never apologized to insubordinate underlings he had been obliged to discipline, and respect for Hudson slipped lower.

Hudson continued his futile search for a southern exit from James Bay. But bad decisions soon became compounded by bad luck. The *Discovery*'s anchor was fouled and had to be cut loose: a considerable disadvantage to a vessel probing a strange coastline. Then a party Hudson sent ashore on an exploratory mission found human footprints in the mud. They reported this to Hudson, adding that they feared the country was populated by savages who might be cannibals. Hudson laughed at the men, and scorned them in the presence of the other crewmen. Next the *Discovery* ran aground in shallow water and was stuck for twelve hours before the tide raised her off the bottom. Meanwhile, the temperature was plummeting and ice began forming in the bay. The demoralized sailors soon realized they were going to be trapped for the winter.

Sometime in early November Hudson had the *Discovery* beached and ordered the men to prepare a winter camp. They would be the first Europeans to spend a winter in the Canadian Arctic. Henry Hudson had no idea how long and harsh a winter on James Bay could be, and he and his men were not prepared for it. As the ice locked them in, the captain's erratic behaviour swept away whatever confidence the men might still have had in him. Some historians have speculated that Hudson became mentally deranged.

It soon became clear that food would have to be rationed. The *Discovery* could have, in fact, carried far more provisions than she actually did, but on leaving England Hudson had not wanted to overload his ship. He wanted her light and fast, so as to make good time in the race to the Orient. Now the men longed for the game on Digges Island that the captain had not allowed them to hunt.

Philip Staffe wanted to build a cabin immediately, before the weather became too cold for working outdoors. Hudson refused permission, saying they could live in the beached ship. A week later it was obvious that the cramped, difficult-to-heat quarters of the *Discovery* were inadequate. Instead of discussing the situation with Staffe directly, Hudson sent Bylot to Staffe with orders to get out and build a hut.

With the exception of young Jack Hudson, Philip Staffe was

the most loyal man in Hudson's crew. But by this time even the stalwart carpenter had ragged nerves and a short temper. When Bylot delivered Hudson's order, Staffe refused. It was so cold that boards were iron-hard, and nails froze to a man's fingers. Bylot went back to Hudson with Staffe's reply that "hee neither could nor would goe in hand with such work."

Hudson, who had been lenient with men for greater acts of insubordination, flew into a rage. He dragged Staffe out of his cabin, cursed him, struck him and threatened to hang him. Afterwards, Staffe built a small hut on shore. Survivors later testified, however, that it wasn't of much use. Greene went out of his way to be companionable to Staffe, as a way of stirring up greater ill feeling toward Hudson.

Meanwhile, the *Discovery*'s crew suffered their first fatality. John Williams, the ship's gunner, died either from scurvy or exposure. The men hacked a grave in the frozen ground and buried him. It was customary when a seaman died for any personal effects that might be useful to others to be put up for auction, and the proceeds given to the dead man's family when the ship returned home. Hudson did that with Williams' few possessions. But he held back the one thing Williams owned that was most coveted: a long, grey, warm woollen coat. Instead of giving everyone a fair chance to bid on the coat, Hudson made a gift of it to Greene, increasing the crew's resentment toward both of them.

To supplement the food supply, Hudson allowed the men to hunt for partridge and other wild fowl, but never alone, as a safety precaution. To show his contempt for Hudson, Greene went on a hunting trip with the disgraced Staffe as his partner. If this was meant to provoke Hudson, it was successful. When the hunters returned to the camp, Hudson peevishly took back the warm coat he'd given Greene and sold it to Bylot.

Greene exploded with fury and fired a barrage of abuse at Hudson. Hudson shouted back, calling Greene an ingrate, a rascal and a thief. He warned Greene that if he did not show the respect that a captain was due, he would forfeit any wages he had coming to him when they returned to England. Hudson then apologized to Staffe, who gladly shook the captain's hand.

It was a hard, bitter winter for the Englishmen on James Bay. In addition to suffering from scurvy and frostbite, they drank the brackish water from the bay and became sick to their stomachs. Prickett also suffered from an inflammation of the joints and could not walk without the aid of a pair of homemade crutches. After a while, the wild birds they had been hunting disappeared. While huge flocks of migrating waterfowl descended on the bay, the men were not good enough hunters to catch them, and the guns they had—primitive blunderbusses—were not equal to the task. They tried fishing as well, but with very limited success. The men were reduced to supplementing their dwindling supplies with frogs and boiled moss.

Hudson tried to keep the men's spirits up, but both nature and Robert Juet conspired against him. During the long hours of darkness the men could hear the howling of wolves; an unnerving sound to Englishmen who had never seen a wolf, but had heard tales of the animal's ferocity. Then Juet filled their superstitious heads with stories of devils and ghosts lurking in the darkness all around them. Afterwards, some of the sailors refused to go hunting in the bush, or to even venture out of sight of the ship in broad daylight. They also began to whisper that the expedition had been cursed from the outset. There were ugly mutterings, too, that Hudson had been hoarding food in his cabin.

On one occasion a Native hunter came across the camp. He was just as astonished to see the Englishmen as they were to see him. The man was familiar with the idea of trade and indicated through signs that he was willing to do some bartering. He went away and returned the next day with a sleigh on which he had some animal skins and a small amount of venison. He offered a deerskin and the meat in exchange for a steel hatchet. Hudson insisted, however, that the hatchet was worth two deerskins. The Native reluctantly agreed, but after the exchange was made, he went away and never returned. Juet grumbled that the man might have returned with a sleigh load of meat if Hudson had not driven such a hard bargain.

Eventually, a spell of mild weather blew in and the ice went out of the bay. Hudson sent several men out in the ship's boat to try their luck with fishing nets. The men could hardly believe it when the fishing party came back with a catch of almost five hundred fish. Some of the fish were trout, while many other species were completely foreign to them.

The men prepared to have a feast but soon discovered that they had almost no appetite due to the many weeks they had been on short rations. Hudson assumed that with the mild weather, spring was just around the corner and they would soon be able to set sail again. So instead of salting down the fish they had not been able to eat, the men left it on deck, where it spoiled and had to be thrown away. Further fishing expeditions met with very little success.

Greene and Wilson plotted to steal the ship's boat and go off on their own to find fish. Greene even wrote a note he intended to leave for Hudson, mocking the captain by telling him about all the delicious fish he and Wilson would soon be eating. Their plan was a feather-brained scheme at best since afterwards the two deserters would have no way of returning home. Whatever their plans were, Greene and Wilson did not get the chance to put them into action.

On the very morning the pair planned to abscond with the ship's boat, Hudson arose early and saw a column of smoke in the clear blue sky to the west. There were Natives nearby, and that meant food. Hudson immediately ordered trade goods—hatchets, knives, blankets and beads—loaded into the ship's boat, along with a few days' rations. Taking John King and two other men with him, Hudson set out to find the Natives, promising the others he would return with food and warm hides. He left first mate Bylot in charge of the camp, with orders to continue the strict rationing program.

Hudson's party was gone for a week. They never did get to barter with the Natives because they fled every time the Englishmen approached. They even started a forest fire to keep the strangers at bay while they packed up their camp and disappeared into the bush.

Meanwhile, back at the *Discovery,* Bylot was being pressured by the others to give them access to the food supplies. They said they were tired of living on short rations and were willing to take their chances with the captain. After all, they reminded him, the captain had promised to bring back more food. Bylot gave in to their demands, and gorged himself with the rest of them.

When a frustrated Hudson returned empty-handed, he was furious to find the supplies so depleted. He immediately demoted Bylot to the rank of common seaman, and elevated King to first mate. King had no qualifications for that position, and now Bylot was ripe for recruitment by the mutineers.

Hudson now kept the key to the provisions storage room on his person, and would not allow anyone to accompany him when he went in there. Soon no one but Hudson had any idea how much food was left. Rumours surfaced again that the captain was hoarding food and sharing extra rations with only a select few.

On June 11, Hudson sent men out for one more try at fishing. They returned with about eighty small fish, which were all consumed at one sitting.

By now enough ice had gone out of the bay for the crew to refloat the *Discovery.* June 12, 1611, was significant for two reasons. First, Hudson went into the storage room and brought out all of the remaining food—some bread and cheese—much of which was mouldy. He divided it equally among the men, telling them that each man was now responsible for his own rationing. Each crewman was given a pound of bread and seven pounds of cheese. When that was gone, a tearful Hudson warned, there would be no more. The second major event was the captain's order to set sail. They were finally leaving the godforsaken corner of nowhere that had held them for seven and a half months.

William Wilson gorged himself and, in a matter of hours, his food was gone. He spent the next three days in his hammock with agonizing stomach cramps. Henry Greene ate up his ration of bread and cheese in two days. Then he joined Robert Juet in gossip mongering about the hidden stash of food in the captain's cabin. One night after he had recovered from his stomach cramps, Wilson allegedly caught Staffe stealthily eating a piece of pickled beef, a food item that had supposedly run out many weeks ago. The surprised Staffe confessed that the captain gave it to him because, "it is necessary that some should be kept up."

Then Hudson inflamed the men by accusing *them* of hoarding food and had their seabags searched. For a common sailor there was no privacy aboard ship, but a sailor's seabag was inviolate. What he kept in it was his business and no one else's. Hudson's search turned up thirty small biscuits and nothing more. The act of searching their seabags had turned almost every man against the captain. Now they were all thinking mutiny. It would take just one more irrational act on Hudson's part to push them over the edge.

As the *Discovery* began her voyage up James Bay, the men believed they were heading for England. They knew they'd be lucky to make it home at all since they were practically out of food. On June 23, they sailed out of the confines of James Bay and into the vast expanse Hudson had mistaken for the Pacific Ocean. He now believed that in the previous autumn he should not have sailed south, but west. He gave orders to set a westward course.

The men couldn't believe their ears. *West!* Had the captain gone totally mad? The men begged Hudson to reconsider. They had no food! How could he possibly expect them to continue the search for the Northwest Passage? Hudson told them they would find food and would not change his orders. The fear-stricken men turned the *Discovery* to a western course. Throughout that day, and out of the view of Hudson and any of the crew thought to be loyal to him, men gathered in small groups and plotted.

That night after most of the half-starved, bone weary sailors had crawled into their hammocks in the foc'sle (forecastle), Greene, Juet and Wilson quietly entered Abacuck Prickett's quarters. They told him they were going to seize the ship. They planned to put Hudson, his son, any sailors who were loyal to him, and any men who were too sick to function into the ship's boat and cast them adrift "to fend for themselves."

According to his own journal and later testimony, Prickett begged them to reconsider. "Do not commit so foul a thing in the sight of God and man as that would be," he pleaded. Greene said he would rather hang for mutiny than starve to death. He and the other mutineers argued that the castaways would be able to forage for food ashore. They could then make their own way to Newfoundland and the English fishing fleet. Nobody would be murdered. But Prickett knew that casting people adrift in that frigid, hostile place was tantamount to murder, no matter how one tried to justify it.

The conspirators told Prickett he could join them, or be put in the boat with the victims. They said they hoped he would remain with them because they needed an educated man to doctor Hudson's log, and to plead their case when they finally reached England. They were sure they would be exonerated of any wrong doing, if the court heard the facts from a gentleman like Prickett.

Prickett decided upon a rather convenient compromise. He said he would not interfere with the mutiny, meaning he would not try to warn Hudson. This meant Prickett would not be forced to join the castaways, but he would not participate in the mutiny, either. This way he did not run the risk of being hanged back in England. Prickett negotiated the best deal for himself in a very difficult situation. Then, hypocritically, he made the lead mutineers swear an oath: "I swear truth to my God, my Prince and my country. I shall do nothing but to the glory of God and the good of the action in hand, and harme to no man."

The three ringleaders left. Moments later John Thomas, Michael Perse, Adrian Motter and Bennett Matthews came and took Prickett's oath. That, at least, was Prickett's version. His journal did not say whether Robert Bylot, who was also in on the plot, took the oath.

The mutineers struck early on the morning of June 24 (possibly when the *Discovery* was near the Cape Hope Islands or Pebble Island). Bylot lured John King to the hold, and then locked him in.

King began pounding and shouting. The noise aroused Hudson, who appeared at the doorway of his cabin dressed in his sleeping gown, but armed with a cutlass. He had no opportunity to use it because Thomas and Matthews quickly jumped on him and pulled him down. Wilson then came up from behind and got a rope around Hudson. Soon the captain was trussed and dumped into the ship's boat.

The noise also brought Edward Wilson to the door of his cabin. When the young doctor asked what was going on, Hudson shouted that he had been bound. Two mutineers told the doctor that "if he were well he should keep himself so." Deeming discretion the better part of valour, Dr. Wilson went back into his cabin and closed the door. Bylot deliberately kept out of the assault on Hudson, so he could not be accused of laying a hand on the captain. He would argue later that he did not know mutiny was afoot. He thought the others only wanted to put the captain aside while they searched for food, and that later they would release Hudson from his bonds.

Into the boat with Hudson went young Jack, who struggled uselessly against the strength of grown men. If any of the mutineers had any pangs of conscience about sending a boy to his doom, the others would no doubt have reminded them of what the boy's testimony could do to them back in England. Sylvanus Bond was hauled to the ship's boat because he'd been crippled by frostbite; Syracke Fanning, Adam Moore and Thomas Woodhouse were ill, and so they, too, were taken to the boat. Woodhouse pleaded all the way, promising the mutineers his family would reward them if they took him back to England, but his pleas fell on deaf ears.

Juet went to get King, who was still locked in the hold. When

Juet opened the door, he was startled to see King brandishing a cutlass. The conspirators had forgotten that weapons were stored in the hold. King flew at Juet and knocked the sword from his hand. Juet beat a hasty retreat as King pursued him, ready to cleave him in two. Luckily for Juet, several of the other mutineers came to his aid. King put up a fight, but three men overpowered him and forced him into the boat.

Then the mutineers pulled a double-cross. Two of their own company, Michael Butt and Arnold Lodlo, were ordered into the boat, while Bond was allowed to return to the *Discovery*. No explanation was given for the treachery shown to Lodlo and Butt. Perhaps someone held a grudge over something that had happened during the winter or maybe they were considered untrustworthy. As for Bond, two of the mutineers spoke on his behalf out of friendship, and Greene reluctantly agreed to allow him back on board.

That left only Philip Staffe. The carpenter had been asleep on deck when the ruckus began and awoke to find three armed mutineers standing over him. Staffe was a big, powerful man, and the conspirators had been afraid he might do them some serious harm if given a chance to fight. As it was, all Staffe could do was watch helplessly as the drama unfolded before his eyes.

When all of the men the mutineers considered expendable had been tossed into the ship's boat, the ringleaders told Staffe he could remain with them on the *Discovery*. A good carpenter, after all, was a valued member of any ship's company. Staffe replied without hesitation. "I will not stay in this ship unless you force me to stay," he said loudly so all could hear. "Give me my tools, and may your souls be damned for all Eternity. For the love of God and master I will go down into the boat rather than accept of likelier hopes with such villains."

The ringleaders tried to argue Staffe into staying. He suddenly grabbed Matthews and, in spite of the guns and swords pointed at him, he clenched a big fist and held it to the frightened sailor's face, threatening to pound him to a pulp if his request was not met immediately.

Awed by this show of loyalty and courage, several of the mutineers hurried below and returned with Staffe's tool chest. The carpenter flung Matthews aside like a rag doll and took his precious chest. Then he climbed down into the boat and took his place beside Hudson.

The mutineers gave the castaways an iron cooking pot, a tiny bag of flour, a blunderbuss, a small amount of powder and shot, and some clothing and blankets. Prickett, who had remained in his quarters throughout the mutiny, opened a porthole and looked out at the boat and its nine occupants. Hudson saw him and called out, warning Prickett not to trust the villainous Juet. Prickett answered that Greene, not Juet, had led the mutiny. To that, Hudson made no reply.

For a short distance the *Discovery* towed the little boat and its doomed passengers. Then the line was cut. The castaways were left to the Arctic elements.

The mutineers turned the *Discovery* east, then began to ransack Hudson's cabin. Prickett claimed in his journal that they found two hundred biscuits, a cask of beer and several jars of brandywine. Using Hudson's key, they opened the food storage locker and found barrels of flour and pork, two casks of butter, half a bushel of dried peas, and small amounts of oatmeal, barley and pickled beef. It was more than they had expected, but not nearly enough to last them the long voyage home. The mutineers also went through the property of the men they had cast adrift, and began quarrelling over shoes, shirts and other loot. Then they saw to their horror that the ship's boat was following them! Hudson and Staffe had raised the boat's small sail, and with Hudson at the helm, the little craft was nimbly skirting around the ice floes to keep up with the ship. The mutineers quickly put the *Discovery* under full sail and fled, to quote Prickett, "as from an enemy." The boatload of castaways fell behind until it was but a dot on the horizon. Then it disappeared altogether. As far as is known, Henry Hudson and his fellow castaways were never seen again.

Henry Greene may have been the leader of the mutiny, but he was no seaman. The mutineers elected Robert Bylot captain, having little trust in Robert Juet. They did, however, restore Juet to his old rank of first mate. Greene, William Wilson and John Thomas were soon drunk on the liquor from Hudson's cabin. Greene, ever the bully, and dressed in Hudson's boots, velvet suit and silk-lined cape, swaggered around and demanded to be called "captain." When Prickett pleaded (or so he claimed later) with the mutineers to go back and pick up the other men, Greene told him that he had wanted to throw him into the boat with the others, and that it was only because they would need an educated man like Prickett to defend them when they got back home that he had been allowed to stay. Wilson drunkenly declared that they didn't have to go back to England at all. He was all for turning pirate, and anyone who didn't like the idea should be thrown overboard.

These were all just words on the wind, however. Their first major concern was food. The *Discovery* put in at a small island where the men tried unsuccessfully to fish. They shot two ducks, and gathered some weeds and herbs that they boiled into an unpalatable soup. They remained for two days, during which they nervously watched the horizon for any sign of the abandoned men.

Meanwhile, all was not harmonious on the *Discovery.* Prickett had the task of reading Hudson's journal and destroying any entries that might be damaging to the mutineers. Greene dictated that Juet should have no access whatsoever to Hudson's log. This, combined with the fact that *he* had not been elected captain, made Juet even more churlish. He quarreled constantly with Bylot, boasting that he was the more experienced seaman. Greene also resented Bylot, and was all for throwing him overboard, but that would have left Juet, whom Greene despised, as the only man capable of getting the ship back through the Furious Overfall and onto the Atlantic Ocean. Juet and Greene, both of them frequently drunk, questioned Bylot's navigational decisions and told the rest of the men Bylot had gotten them lost. But Bylot held his course and finally brought the *Discovery* to the entrance of the Furious Overfall.

On July 26, as Bylot attempted to navigate his way through the channel, the *Discovery* ran onto a rock and was stranded for an entire night. The men became hysterical, and Wilson and Greene got into a vicious fight. The others had to break it up before one or both were killed. Then, just before daybreak, the tide suddenly roared through the channel and lifted the ship free.

Since the mutineers had used the *Discovery*'s only boat to set the others adrift, they had to construct a small craft to use for landing. They had lost the skilled Staffe and his tools, so the vessel they made was crude. The same morning that the tide freed them from the rock, the mutineers made a landing on an island where they managed to catch thirty birds. Two days later they were approaching Digges Island where they hoped to find nesting gulls, when they suddenly encountered a fleet of canoes bearing at least sixty Natives.

At first both groups were startled. Then the Natives pointed toward the island, indicating that they would like to meet the white strangers on shore. Greene was immediately suspicious. He told Prickett—whose life he considered expendable—to go out and meet the "savages."

Prickett went over the side and stepped into a canoe. The Englishmen lowered their boat—full of armed men including Greene and Wilson—and a Native climbed into the odd-looking craft. Having exchanged hostages as a guarantee of peaceful intentions, both groups went ashore.

The Natives took the strangers to their camp, a semi-circle of tents just beyond the beach of a small cove. They showed the Englishmen how they captured birds with a long stick fitted with a rawhide noose. Not one to be outdone by primitive heathens, Wilson blasted the birds with his blunderbuss and killed eight of them. The startled Natives were certainly impressed with this demonstration of a firearm.

The Natives and the Englishmen gathered up a large number of birds and then went back to the camp. The hosts entertained the guests with a dance and gave them gifts of walrus tusks and furs. Greene saw that the women were roasting great quantities of venison over open fires. Communicating through signs, he told the people that he would return the next day with goods to exchange for food. They seemed to agree with the arrangement. Then the English returned to their ship.

The next morning Greene, Wilson, Thomas, Perse and Motter went ashore. They took Prickett along to serve as a hostage if necessary, but they did not really anticipate trouble. Greene had a package of mirrors, beads and other trade trinkets.

When they arrived at the cove Prickett, still hobbled by pain in his legs, stayed in the boat. Greene, Thomas and Wilson went to meet the natives, who were waiting to greet them. Perse and Motter clambered onto some rocks to gather sorrel (an edible plant).

Prickett watched as Greene showed the natives his trade goods. Prickett was surprised to see that the natives had brought no meat to trade. He could hear Greene impatiently trying to make the people understand that he wanted to barter for food.

Then Prickett was distracted by a Native who was wading toward the boat. Something about the man alarmed Prickett, and he gestured for the man to go back. The Native kept coming, so Prickett waved in a clear sign that he wanted the man to go. The Native finally began to withdraw, but at that very moment Prickett realized that a second Native with a knife was climbing into the boat behind him.

He struck just as Prickett caught sight of him. Prickett's right arm deflected the blow. Then the two men grappled in a life-or-death struggle in the rocking boat. Prickett was gashed in the right thigh and had the little finger of his left hand almost cut off. Somehow, Prickett's right hand found the knife in his belt. The former haberdasher, who had probably never wielded a blade in anger in his life, pulled his knife and slashed his assailant's throat.

Meanwhile, the Natives on shore suddenly attacked the other Englishmen. The assault was so unexpected the English didn't have a chance to use their guns. Wilson and Thomas were struck down and disembowelled. They died "cursing and swearing in a most fearful manner." Greene and Perse were both wounded, but managed to tear free from the clutches of the attackers and make a run for the boat. Motter had wandered high into the rocks as he gathered sorrel. When he saw what was happening on the beach, he dove into the icy sea and swam for the boat. So far, no one on the *Discovery* was aware of the battle on the island. High rocks blocked the view of the cove.

Prickett was desperately trying to turn the boat away from the shore, but this was almost impossible for one man to do, especially an injured one. Motter reached the boat at the same time as Greene and Perse, who were pursued by Native warriors. Perse split open one man's head with a hatchet and Greene killed two more with a pike. Perse got into the boat, and then hauled in the half-drowned Motter. He left Greene to deal with the Natives who were trying to climb into the boat, while he helped Prickett turn the craft around. As soon as the bow was pointed seaward, Motter and Perse seized the oars and frantically rowed for deep water. Greene and Prickett fought off the Natives who still clung to the stern. It seemed as though they had made good their escape, but the nightmare wasn't over.

Native bowmen stood on the beach and unleashed a volley of arrows, while other warriors launched canoes to pursue the Englishmen. Greene tried to fire his pistol, but the powder was damp. He knocked the useless charge out of the pan and was about to pour in fresh powder when an arrow pierced his stomach. Then a second arrow thudded into his chest. Greene collapsed over the stern, but Prickett kept him from falling out of the boat. In trying to keep Greene in the boat, Prickett had turned his back to the shore. A moment later an arrow struck him in the back. The wound was not fatal, but Prickett was in extreme pain. Then Perse was hit. He continued to row, but after a few minutes he fainted.

By now the boat had passed through the entrance of the cove and was within sight of the *Discovery*. Motter was the only man who had not been hurt, though he was numb from his plunge in the frigid water. Two Native canoes were rapidly closing in, and Motter could not row the boat by himself. He stood up, shouted to the *Discovery* and waved his oar.

This finally got the attention of Bylot, who realized at once that something was wrong. When he saw the Native canoes racing toward the little boat full of bloodied crewmen, Bylot ordered one of the *Discovery*'s cannons to be fired. The shot didn't hit anyone, but the roar of the gun frightened the Natives into breaking off their pursuit and they quickly returned to the safety of the cove.

When the *Discovery* picked up the men in the boat, Greene was dead. His body was dumped into the sea without ceremony. Perse died two days later. The *Discovery* was down to nine men. Two of those, Prickett and Edward Wilson, were not even sailors. Prickett was wounded and Bond was half-crippled. Their situation looked grim at best.

Bylot knew they had no chance of reaching England alive unless they found food, so he sailed to the north side of Digges Island and took the *Discovery* as close to shore as he dared. He loaded both the ship's cannons and put Prickett in charge of one and Nicholas Syms on the other. Then he sent the other six men ashore while he stood lookout on the *Discovery,* scanning the shoreline and forest with Henry Hudson's telescope.

The men of the shore party were armed with blunderbusses, pistols and cutlasses. As soon as they landed the Natives appeared, poised to attack. Syms fired his big gun and placed a shot right in the Natives' midst, killing several of them. The rest vanished into the trees and did not return. Under the protection of the *Discovery*'s guns the men spent the next few days hunting birds. They salted down hundreds of them for the journey home, but even that would not be enough.

The voyage was one of the most horrific in the annals of navigation, and only Robert Bylot's seamanship brought the *Discovery* through. Even though Bylot strictly rationed the food, the men were eventually reduced to eating birds' bones cooked in the grease from candles made from animal tallow. Soon the men became too weak to work the ship properly. A man had to sit in a chair to take his turn at the helm. If a rope broke or a sail tore, no one had the strength to climb into the rigging to fix it. Prickett wrote in his diary that the sails became "brown skeletons of leaves." Bylot, scarcely able to stay on his own two feet, staggered around with a crude leather whip that he used to beat the others into doing the jobs that had to be done. Juet went raving mad then one day simply dropped dead. The others pushed his corpse overboard.

Finally, on September 6, they sighted the coast of Ireland. A Cornish fishing captain hailed what must have looked to him like a ghost ship and towed the *Discovery* into the tiny port of Berehaven. The *Discovery* and her eight survivors finally reached London on October 20.

According to the English law, mutiny was punishable by hanging. A court of inquiry held on October 24, and presided over by the *Discovery*'s owners, was of the opinion that all eight survivors should go to the gallows. But only the High Court of Admiralty could pass the death sentence on convicted mutineers, and that body did not even question any of the men until a year later. This was largely due to the actions of Abacuck Prickett, who presented the right people with Hudson's somewhat edited journal, as well as his maps and charts.

The maps accurately showed the eastern and southern coastlines of Hudson Bay, but not the western coastline. Prickett, with

Bylot in agreement, expressed Hudson's belief that they had reached the Pacific Ocean, and that the way to the Orient was open. The Furious Overfall, they said, was indeed the Northwest Passage. Henry Hudson was now a national hero. Ironically, the men who had sent him to almost certain death were too valuable to hang. They were the only Europeans who had sailed that deadly stretch of water.

In 1612, two ships, the *Discovery* and the *Resolution,* were sent to follow up on Hudson's explorations. Bylot was the *Resolution*'s second mate, Prickett was the boatswain's mate and Edward Wilson was the ship's doctor. Soon Bylot was captain of the *Discovery,* and made two more voyages to Hudson's Bay. The explorers soon learned that the great body of water was in fact a bay, but its value to the growing, extremely lucrative fur trade was incalculable.

The Admiralty did not begin a serious investigation into the Hudson mutiny until 1617, and the mutineers were not brought to trial in the High Court until 1618. Nicholas Syms had been a minor at the time, and so was excused of any responsibility. Bylot now had the reputation of an experienced Arctic explorer, and so was not prosecuted. Sylvanus Bond and Adrian Motter had died. That left Francis Clemens, Abacuck Prickett, Edward Wilson and Bennett Matthews in the prisoner's box. Fortunately for them, time had obscured much of the evidence against them. Also, Prickett had done a thorough job of placing most of the blame on men who were already dead: Henry Greene, Robert Juet, William Wilson and John Thomas. Some people might have thought that Prickett's journal was largely a work of fiction, created to save his own neck and throw a bad light on Hudson, making the captain the author of his own demise. No doubt some passages in it *were* slanted in that direction; some of those dealing with Hudson's hoarding of food being particularly suspect. But unknown to anyone else, Thomas Woodhouse had also kept a journal in which he recorded events right up to the eve of the mutiny. That document was found in a desk in his quarters, and much of what he had written supported Prickett's descriptions of events. The four accused mutineers were acquitted.

What became of Henry Hudson and his fellow castaways? That is one of the great mysteries of the sea and of Canadian history. They might have drowned, starved to death, died of exposure or been killed by Natives. There have been many tales and legends. An English merchant captain named William Connor was in Hudson Bay in 1629. Back in England he claimed that he and his men went ashore for water at a location in the southeast corner of the bay and found a cabin built with planks of wood that had been hewn with carpenter's tools. In the cabin was a rusted iron cooking pot. He and his men searched the area, he said, but found no other European artifacts and no human remains. Some of Connor's crew vouched for the story, but others said it was the fabrication of a man who hoped to somehow profit from it. Connor could not satisfactorily explain why he had not brought back the cooking pot as evidence.

Other visitors to the bay took home stories of wild, blue-eyed, shaggy haired white men who wore animal skins and lived in the woods, but who fled at the approach of English sailors. There was even a story about an Englishman who, on a hunting expedition, killed a deer with a single musket shot, only to find that the animal had been previously wounded by a shot from a blunderbuss. He did not take home any of the lead shot as evidence.

Prince Rupert, a cousin of England's King Charles II, and a

founder of the Hudson's Bay Company, was intrigued by the Hudson mystery. In 1674 he sent Captain Edwin Edwards into the bay to hunt for clues to Hudson's fate. Edwards and his crew spent a year retracing Hudson's route and visiting all of the places at which the castaways might have landed. They found nothing.

At about the time Hudson was set adrift, far to the south in Quebec, Samuel de Champlain sent a young man named Nicolas de Vignau into the wilderness to live with the Algonquins. A year later de Vignau returned to Quebec with so many far-fetched tales that Champlain dismissed him as "the world's greatest liar." But one of the stories Champlain disregarded as a lie may, in retrospect, have been true.

The natives told de Vignau that some Englishmen had been cast out of their ship in the great saltwater sea to the north. The tribe that lived on the shore of that sea had killed all of the castaways except a young boy whom they adopted. Considering the fact that the *Discovery* did not get back to England until October 1612, and there was no other possible way de Vignau could have known anything about the Hudson mutiny, this could be the one legitimate clue to the end of the tragedy. De Vignau's story might even have support in another report that came out of the bay in 1725.

That year a Hudson's Bay Company agent named Miller wrote to headquarters in London about a Cree with "surprisingly pale skin." This man had come to a company post to trade furs and said that one of his ancestors was an Englishman. He claimed that his ancestor had been one of a few Englishmen who were living in the forest. All of his companions died, and he was taken in by the Cree. He took a Cree wife, and had children.

It could be that the man who told Miller this story was the

product of some other English-Native union, for by 1725 the English were well-established in Hudson Bay country. He might have heard of the Hudson legend, and then told Miller a tale he thought the white man would like to hear. On the other hand, he could have been telling the truth. His English ancestor could have been Henry Hudson, one of his men, or the boy from de Vignau's story—young Jack Hudson.

Regardless of his personal shortcomings and the mystery surrounding the end of his life, Henry Hudson deserves his place as one of Canada's great explorers. His conquest of the Furious Overfall eliminated a major hurdle to further Arctic exploration. His name on the body of water that is the second largest bay in the world is a fitting memorial.

The Quest for Furs

European explorers came to Canada looking for gold, silver, precious stones and a Northwest Passage through this most inconvenient North American continent. At first they found very little in the way of precious metals or gems; and the Passage, while it always seemed tantalizingly within reach, would elude discovery until the twentieth century. What the Europeans did find was a commodity that, in the long run, turned out to be much more valuable than the gold and silver the Spanish were pillaging from ancient empires in Central and South America. The French and the English found furs; in particular, beaver. Other furs were valuable, of course. Fox, wolf, otter, mink, marten, ermine and seal skins all fetched good prices in Europe. But for centuries in the fur trade, beaver was king. It was upon this animal's pelt that the Canadian nation was founded.

At about the time European explorers were probing the eastern coastlines of North America, beaver hats became the fashion rage all over Europe. There were a variety of styles for both men and women, and no person who had any sort of respectable social standing would appear in public without one. If possible, a person would own several hats to go with a variety of social occasions. Of course, only the very wealthy could afford this kind of vanity.

The valuable part of a beaver's pelt was the layer of soft underfur closest to the skin. This was removed and made into felt, from which the hats were manufactured. It took the fur from many beaver pelts to make one hat. Beaver, therefore, had to be available in great numbers.

The Natives the Europeans met along the coastal areas had relatively few beaver pelts to trade because the local geography lacked the extensive network of rivers, lakes and wetlands necessary for a large beaver population. However, as the Europeans made their way into the hinterland and the vast St. Lawrence drainage system, they encountered tribes with access to beaver by the tens of thousands. But this was not wealth one could simply go and take at gunpoint (as the Spanish had done with the Aztecs and Incas). A system of trade had to be developed.

Native trappers went into the woods to harvest the pelts, and then took them to posts where they bartered for European trade goods: initially steel tools, iron pots and kettles, coloured beads and cheap trinkets like mirrors and combs. Eventually the white men's trade items would include guns, powder, ammunition and alcohol.

Native skills such as the fashioning of tools and weapons from stone and copper were lost as the people became more dependent upon European goods. As this dependency increased, Natives had to trap even more beaver. Father Chrestien Le Clercq wrote that a Native said to him, "In truth, my brother, the Beaver does everything to perfection. He makes for us kettles, axes, swords, knives, and gives us drink and food without the trouble of cultivating the ground."

The Natives' reliance on the beaver led to violent rivalries as local hunting grounds became trapped out. Hunters who had exterminated the beaver in their own territories began to force their way into neighbouring lands.

The whites, meanwhile, looked farther afield for new sources of pelts. They set up posts that would be accessible to distant tribes, bypassing those tribes who had been acting as middlemen. To do this, they had to send men out to explore new ground and new water routes, often in dangerous circumstances. There were not only rival tribes at work here, but also rival whites. The French and the English battled tooth and nail over the fur trade. They spread the conflict from the St. Lawrence River valley all the way to the Arctic. And even after the French and English wars were long over, rival commercial entities like the Hudson's Bay Company and the North West Company continued the struggle, carrying it ever farther west and north, until just one emerged victorious. Some men, working for one country or another, or one company or another, became Canada's greatest explorers.

Radisson and Groseilliers

Canadian Caesars

Generations of Canadian schoolchildren have known this pair of remarkable fur traders and explorers as "Mr. Radishes and Mr. Gooseberries." Unfortunately, the catchy nicknames that might serve as memory aids during a history exam tend to diminish the importance of these men. They were unquestionably the most formidable and ambitious of the coureurs de bois, the woodsmen of New France whose origins went back to the legendary Étienne Brûlé. The coureurs de bois (runners of the woods) were boys and men who turned their backs on the farm life of the *habitant* to live in the woods with the Natives. They took Native wives (much frowned upon by the Church), and they made their living by hunting and trapping. Technically they were outlaws. They broke the law when they fled the settlements in favour of the woods. They broke the law when they hunted more than a league from their official place of residence. They broke the law when they traded in furs, because only a few privileged individuals were licensed to engage in commerce with the natives. Coureurs ran the risk of being fined, flogged or even hanged if captured. But while officials from France may have looked down their aristocratic noses at these rugged frontiersmen, it was the illegal coureurs who kept the fur trade alive; the industry that led directly to the formation of Canada as a country.

If the coureurs were outlaws, then Radisson and Groseilliers were the bandit kings. Together, they took scheming and intrigue in the fur trade to a whole new level, playing one side against the other when it suited them, and shifting allegiances as easily as the wind changes direction. Indeed, there were times when they were barely a step ahead of the hangman. But despite all their subterfuge and chicanery, Radisson and Groseilliers were adventurers whose work helped to open up the heart of the continent, and they did it in spite of the meddling of corrupt officials.

Groseilliers was the elder of the two by about twenty-three years. He was born Médard Chouart in 1618, in Charly-sur-Marne in the French province of Brie. His parents owned a farm that was called Les Groseilliers because of the gooseberry bushes that grew there. Later, when Chouart had a farm of his own near Trois-Rivières, he proudly named it after the family farm in France, and called himself Sieur Des Groseilliers.

Groseilliers probably arrived in Canada about 1641, either as a labourer or a soldier. By 1646 he was working with the Jesuits in Huronia, and it was most likely there that he heard about the "great sea that is beyond that of the Hurons," referring to either Lake Michigan or Lake Superior. (Étienne Brûlé had already been to Lake Superior, but information on that Great Lake was still scant in the mid-seventeenth century). Groseilliers was married to a woman named Hélène Martin, who was the daughter of Abraham Martin, for whom the Plains of Abraham were named. Through this marriage Groseilliers became acquainted with the La

Tours, an influential fur-trading family in Acadia who also had connections in Newfoundland and New England. Hélène died in the early 1650s, and Groseilliers married a widow named Marguerite, whose younger half-brother was Pierre-Esprit Radisson.

Radisson's date of birth is not certain, though there is evidence that he was born in 1636, in or near Avignon. Being from Provence, which held itself culturally and linguistically apart from France, could explain why Radisson would not necessarily have a strong sense of French loyalty. It is not known when he arrived in Canada. His sister Marguerite was certainly in Quebec in 1646, but whether Pierre-Esprit came to Canada with her or at a later date cannot be determined. Whenever Radisson first set foot on Canadian soil, he would have just been a boy. Given the taste for adventure he exhibited as an adult, the young Radisson must have been thrilled at the prospect of living in the wilds of Canada.

Radisson arrived during an extremely difficult period for the French settlers. The once powerful Huron nation, weakened by smallpox epidemics, was now reeling before the onslaught of the Iroquois. The Algonquins and Montagnais were also withdrawing deeper into bush country to escape Iroquois wrath. The isolated French settlements in the St. Lawrence Valley were extremely vulnerable, and Iroquois war parties raided almost with impunity. One victim was Claude Étienne, Marguerite's first husband.

One day, possibly in 1651, Radisson and some French companions were duck hunting near Trois-Rivières when they were ambushed by a band of Iroquois. Radisson's friends were killed and scalped, but he was taken prisoner. He would later claim that the Iroquois spared his life because they admired the courage he had shown in putting up a fight, but more likely he owed his good luck to his age. Radisson was only fourteen or fifteen at the time, and the Iroquois often adopted young captives to replace people who had died.

The warriors who had seized Radisson were Mohawks, and from the beginning they treated him like an adopted member of the tribe. They stripped him, painted him, and tied his hair in a Mohawk style. A man whom Radisson had wounded in the fight took the boy under his wing, teaching him how to paddle a canoe and throw a spear. When Radisson could not eat the putrid meat the Mohawks carried along the trail, they went out of their way to find food more suitable to his stomach. Nonetheless, the young Radisson must have despaired as he was carried farther and farther away from his family in Trois-Rivières. No doubt he had heard chilling stories of Iroquois torture.

When the war party reached their home village near Lake Champlain, Radisson was immediately adopted by a family who had lost a son in battle. Radisson's adoptive father was a renowned warrior who had nineteen scars on his thigh, the tally of enemies he had slain in combat. His new mother was a Huron captive who not only doted on him, but also encouraged him to "make meself more familiar with her two daughters, which weare tolerable among such people."

Radisson adapted remarkably well to Mohawk life. He learned their language, and just as importantly, he gained a sharp insight into Native psychology—something that would be to his advantage in later years. Radisson was soon accompanying the men and boys on hunting expeditions and even raids on other Native villages. Just as Étienne Brûlé had once learned the lore of the forest from the Hurons and Algonquins, Pierre-Esprit Radisson learned the same lessons from the Iroquois.

He still longed for his family hearth in Trois-Rivières, however. A little over a year after his capture, he and an Algonquin captive went hunting with three Mohawks. They camped for the night, and when the Mohawks fell asleep, Radisson and the Algonquin killed them. Then the Algonquin took the dead men's heads for trophies. The pair made a dash for Trois-Rivières, which was a little more than a day's journey away. They were within sight of the town's walls when they were intercepted by Mohawk pursuers. The enraged Mohawks killed the Algonquin on the spot. Radisson's life was spared, but he would soon have reason to believe his slain Native companion was the lucky one.

As far as the Mohawks were concerned, Radisson was an ungrateful wretch who deserved the most agonizing death they could devise for him. He and several other French, Algonquin and Huron captives were dragged back to the Mohawk village. There Radisson was forced to watch in horror as his fellow prisoners were put to excruciating tortures. Radisson would later describe how the men's testicles were cut off, and then tossed around by the hooting, jeering women.

When Radisson's turn came he was stripped naked and forced to run the gauntlet. But that was just for softening up. His torturers burned the soles of his feet with red-hot irons, and pierced one foot with a heated sword. Then they tore off his fingernails, and seared his fingertips with burning coals. The Mohawk children also participated, chewing on Radisson's mangled fingers. Luckily, Radisson's adoptive family came to his rescue. Satisfied that the youth had learned his lesson, the tormentors handed him over to his Iroquois "parents." The old man and woman dressed his wounds and, in recognition of the courage he had shown during his ordeal, they gave him the name Orimha, which had been their deceased son's name. Roughly translated, it meant "lead" or "stone."

Radisson spent another year among the Mohawks, during which time he worked to regain their trust. Sometime in 1653 he was allowed to accompany a trading party to the Dutch post of Fort Orange, near Albany. Even though the French and the Dutch were rivals, it was considered un-Christian to leave a white prisoner in the hands of "savages." The governor of the post offered to ransom Radisson. Probably fearful of how the Mohawks would react if he showed any signs of eagerness at this prospect, Radisson declined the offer, saying he preferred to remain with his Iroquois family. He returned with them to the village by Lake Champlain. However, now that Radisson knew the way to the Dutch colony, at the first opportunity he fled the Mohawk village and made his way back.

The Mohawks trailed Radisson to Fort Orange and demanded that he be given back to them. The Dutch kept him hidden and denied that he was there. Unwilling to damage the good trading relationship they had with the Dutch, the Mohawks went home without him. The Dutch smuggled Radisson to New Amsterdam (New York), where he was put on a ship sailing to Holland. There, in 1654, he got passage on a French fishing vessel that took him to Gaspé. Radisson arrived back in Trois-Rivières shortly after Groseilliers and an unidentified Frenchman set off on an expedition to the west. Radisson would later claim to have been with his brother-in-law on this journey, but documentary evidence proves he was not.

By the time Radisson returned, Canada was on the verge of bankruptcy. Numerous Iroquois raids had interrupted trade and the fur warehouses in Quebec were empty. It appeared that Quebec would have to be abandoned. Neither the French government nor French financiers were going to waste money on a colony that did not turn a profit.

Then, in 1653, a group of Huron and Ottawa Natives made their way to Trois-Rivières, using a roundabout route that kept them away from the marauding Iroquois. They told the French that their people were hiding in a territory well beyond Huronia, which by this time was an almost deserted no man's land. They said they had accumulated great quantities of beaver pelts and other furs, and expected to bring them to Trois-Rivières the following summer, when they could travel in sufficient numbers to discourage Iroquois attacks.

In 1654, the French managed to strike a truce with the Iroquois and late in the summer a fleet of fur-laden canoes arrived from the west. The people told of a "great river" that emptied into a "great sea." When they made the return journey, Groseilliers and his unnamed companion went with them.

Precisely where Groseilliers went is not known, but it seems likely he travelled up the Ottawa River to Lake Nipissing, down the French River to Georgian Bay, and across Lake Huron past an eerily silent Huronia. So far he was covering ground already known to the French through the explorations of Brûlé and Champlain. From this point, following Groseilliers becomes a little more difficult. He possibly went through Lake St. Clair and *le detroit,* the strait connecting Lake Erie and Lake Huron. He might then have crossed the lower Michigan Peninsula to Lake Michigan, and followed the shoreline north to the Straits of Mackinac. He may also have visited Green Bay, and there heard from the Natives about the beaver-rich country north of Lake Superior.

All through these months of travel Groseilliers was gathering information on unexplored lands and on the peoples who lived there. He was also harvesting a fortune in furs. By the time Groseilliers and his partner arrived back in Trois-Rivières in 1656, each had furs valued at fourteen to fifteen thousand livres, which was more than enough for the Groseilliers family to live on comfortably.

Meanwhile, Radisson was off on yet another sojourn among the Iroquois. The Jesuits had decided to take advantage of the truce to establish a mission near the site of present-day Syracuse, New York, in the Onondaga country, and the Iroquois apparently were receptive to the idea. Fifty-three Frenchmen—priests, labourers and soldiers—built a stockaded post called Sainte-Marie-de-Gannentaa. Their interpreter was described in the *Relations* as "a young Frenchman who had been adopted by a renowned Iroquois, and had learned their language." That could only have been Radisson.

Though the Onondagas initially welcomed the mission, after a while they began to resent the presence of the foreigners. The French soon felt that they were prisoners inside the walls of their fort. They needed a means of getting out of Iroquois territory without being massacred. So Radisson came up with a plan.

He told the Onondaga headmen that he had had a dream in which he'd been instructed to prepare a great feast for his Iroquois friends, and that all the food at the feast must be eaten or there would be grave consequences. The Natives were strong believers in the power of dreams, so they accepted the invitation to the French feast.

The French kettles brimmed with corn, pork, poultry, wild game and fish. Most likely the food was laced with laudanum from the mission's medicine chest. As the Natives gorged themselves, a Frenchman played a guitar and encouraged them to dance and sing. After an evening of overeating and dancing, the stuffed, exhausted and drugged Natives dropped off to sleep. The French already had their possessions packed and ready to go, and they piled into their boats and headed for home. The priests had to prevent some of the men from cutting the throats of the sleeping Natives.

Back in Trois-Rivières, Radisson began making plans for an expedition with Groseilliers, to whom he would always refer in his journals as his "brother." By August 1659, they were ready to head for Lake Superior to explore the country to the south and west of the great lake. The governor at Montreal, the Marquis d'Argenson, refused to give them permission to go unless they took along two of his men and gave him 50 per cent of the profits from whatever furs they acquired. The Jesuits also wanted a priest to accompany them as a missionary to the natives. Groseilliers, never noted for his tact, said the governor's demands were unreasonable, and that he wasn't going to be burdened with inexperienced men. "Discoverers before governors" was his policy. D'Argenson angrily denied the pair permission to leave. Groseilliers, who had the rank of captain, simply bluffed his way past the town guard. That he willingly took along Radisson, who had barely started to shave, indicates that he considered his young brother-in-law quite capable of looking after himself in the wild.

Radisson and Groseilliers joined a party of Algonquins going up the Ottawa River. By this time, the truce with the Iroquois had ended and the group encountered a stockade at one of the portages. Facing French guns and Algonquin arrows, the Iroquois fled, leaving behind eleven dead. The Algonquins also took four Iroquois captives, whom they promptly burned at the stake.

The adventurers followed what had become the traditional route along the French River and through Georgian Bay to the St. Mary's River and Lake Superior. At Chequamegon Bay on the Wisconsin shore they set up their post, a small stockade surrounded by a clever alarm system of strings and bells. As a precaution against murder and robbery, they convinced visiting Natives that their possessions were guarded by a devil. To this new trading post came the Cree and a people who as yet had not experienced any first-hand encounters with Europeans: the Sioux. These tribes were at war with each other, and both were anxious to obtain guns. The Natives came not only to trade their furs, but also to offer their services as labourers in hopes of receiving "a brasse ring, or an awle or an needle." As Radisson noted, "We were Cesars, being nobody to contradict us."

Radisson and Groseilliers were taken on a journey to a village of Ottawas and Hurons who had been displaced by the Iroquois wars, where they were treated like demi-gods. They witnessed the Feast of the Dead—a rare honour—and they won the Natives over with gifts of hatchets, needles, combs and mirrors. The winter, however, was an extremely hard one. The Natives and their French guests were reduced to eating dogs and crows. On one occasion when he was crossing water, Radisson broke through the ice and almost froze to death.

Radisson and Groseillers continued their explorations after the winter. They travelled to parts of Wisconsin and Minnesota, and may have even crossed Lake Superior to explore some of the Cree country on the north shore. Radisson claimed they travelled all the way to James Bay, but given the time restrictions that would have been impossible.

On their journey, Radisson and Groseilliers heard about the

vast and virtually untouched beaver country that lay between Lake Superior and Hudson Bay. They also learned of the great "Stinking Lake" (Lake Winnipeg), a place no Frenchman had even heard about up to that time. Quite likely the Frenchmen also learned of the Grand Portage, the beginning of the best canoe route between Lake Superior and the West.

In the summer of 1660, Radisson and Groseilliers headed back to Trois-Rivières, having made the longest and most successful canoe journey of any Europeans in North America. They had a fortune in furs, and they led a fleet of Native canoes loaded with pelts for the empty warehouses of Quebec. As they descended the Ottawa River they came upon the site at the Long Sault where Adam Dollard and his tiny band of Frenchmen had made their heroic stand against an overwhelming Iroquois force, and had been massacred only days earlier. It was also about here that Groseilliers' canoe overturned and he lost all his diaries, leaving only Radisson's accounts of their adventures for posterity.

Radisson and Groseilliers' return should have been a triumph. For the second time Groseilliers had saved the colony from bankruptcy. Moreover, he and Radisson had brought back a wealth of information about new territories. They deserved to be welcomed as heroes. Instead, d'Argenson had Groseilliers arrested for leaving the colony without permission. Furthermore, because they had been trading without a licence, d'Argenson had most of their furs seized. The governor said the proceeds from the confiscated pelts would be spent on fortifications. Radisson bitterly complained that d'Argenson kept a large portion of the money for himself, "that he might yet better maintain his coach and horses at Paris." To add insult to injury, the governor also slapped both men with fines.

A furious Groseilliers sailed to France, hoping to obtain

redress as well as backing for an expedition to Hudson Bay. He failed on both counts. Nobody would overturn the ruling of Governor d'Argenson. There was interest in Hudson Bay, but for reasons that are not clear, the Jesuits opposed Groseilliers' plans. Groseilliers returned to Canada and picked up Radisson under the pretence that they were making another journey up the Ottawa River. Instead they went to St. Peter's on Cape Breton Island. There they met Nicolas Denis, a French fur trader who had worked for the English and was connected with the La Tours, whom Groseilliers also knew through his first wife.

The two coureurs de bois had decided that if they could not get fair treatment from the French, they would sell their considerable talents to the English, and lose no sleep over it. In fact, they would awaken in the English an interest in the fur trade, Hudson Bay and eventually Canada that would result in years of conflict, the seizure of the Dutch colony of New Netherland, and finally the capture of Canada. In the long run, d'Argenson's greed had serious consequences indeed.

Radisson and Groseilliers sailed from Cape Breton with letters of introduction to influential men in New England. Already gaining a reputation as sharp "Yankee traders," the New England men saw profit in an expedition to Hudson Bay. In 1663 a ship with Radisson on board sailed out of Boston, bound for the great bay. But the captain found the bad sailing conditions in Davis Strait unnerving, and he turned back. A second vessel on the same mission was shipwrecked on Sable Island. Disappointed, New England sponsors brought a lawsuit against Radisson and Groseilliers to recover their losses, though the Frenchmen were not responsible for the venture's failure.

Rescue for the adventurers came in the form of Sir George

Cartwright, who arrived from England with a team of commissioners representing the newly restored King Charles II. The commissioners were in New England to win support for the monarch, and were very interested when they learned of the Frenchmen's plans for Hudson Bay. They persuaded Radisson and Groseilliers to go to London and present their ideas at the Court of King Charles. Now the New England financiers tried to convince the pair to lead another expedition for them, even offering the use of any ship they wanted. Radisson wrote later, "wee answered them that a scalded cat fears ye water though it be cold."

On August 1, 1665, Radisson and Groseilliers sailed from Boston on the *Charles,* commanded by Captain Benjamin Gillam, who would play a part in their story a few years later. The voyage to London was interrupted when a Dutch privateer captured the *Charles.* The privateers looted the vessel, threw the ship's papers overboard, and then dropped the passengers and crew off in Spain. Radisson and Groseilliers quickly made their way to London, their expenses all covered by the English Crown.

The Frenchmen arrived in England during the Great Plague, when Londoners were dying by the thousands. They would also witness the Great Fire of 1666 that swept away most of the old city. Meanwhile, Cartwright took them to Oxford, where King Charles' Court had fled to escape the epidemic. There they were taken under the wing of Sir George Carteret, a man who had made a fortune in privateering and was now a member of the King's Privy Council and possibly the richest man in England.

Carteret was excited by the prospect of an expedition to the frozen Northwest. He still believed Hudson Bay was key to a sea route to China and arranged for Radisson and Groseilliers to have an audience with the king. Charles commanded them to write an account "of the Manners Languages and Scituacon of the severall parts of that Country [Canada]."

And so Radisson began writing his journal. If he embellished certain parts it was because he had to make the most favourable impression he possibly could on the English king and his advisers. The journal was subsequently lost for two hundred years, before a translated copy turned up in the papers of Samuel Pepys (a contemporary of Radisson) in 1885. It is now in the Bodleian Library in Oxford. Radisson's original French manuscript has never been found.

Epidemics and conflagrations aside, Radisson and Groseilliers arrived in England at an opportune time. The English were emerging from years of repression under the religious dictatorship of Oliver Cromwell and the Puritans, and Englishmen with money were looking for ventures in which to invest. Provided with a generous expense account by the king, the two Frenchmen were welcomed into the best London homes and country estates. Among those who entertained them was Sir Peter Colleton, head of a cartel of aristocrats and merchants willing to invest in a voyage to Hudson Bay. This group included Sir John Kirke, who had helped his brother David capture Quebec from Champlain and whose daughter would one day marry Radisson. There was also John Fenn, admiralty paymaster, who wasn't above borrowing government funds for private investment, and Sir Robert Vyner, the biggest banker in London. Most important of all the backers, at least as far as prestige was concerned, was King Charles' flamboyant cousin, Prince Rupert, a genuine Renaissance man with strong interests in art, science, the military and financial profit. For two years these men worked with Radisson and Groseilliers in planning their grand venture.

There were setbacks, largely due to conflict between the English and the Dutch. Then, when the Dutch and the French got wind of what Radisson and Groseilliers were up to, they both tried to lure the pair out of England. The truly international makeup of the intrigue became apparent when a French spy known as La Tourette was arrested in London while attempting to recruit Radisson and Groseilliers for the Dutch. The two denied having any intentions of going to France or the Netherlands, but the English watched them closely, suspecting they were renegades who would gladly sell out to the highest bidder.

The expedition finally sailed on June 3, 1668. Radisson's vessel, the *Eaglet,* was disabled in a violent Atlantic storm and had to turn back for England. But Groseilliers' ship, the small ketch *Nonsuch,* with Zach Gillam as skipper, sailed into Hudson Bay and down into James Bay. There, at the mouth of the Rupert River, Groseilliers had the sailors build a house surrounded by a log wall and called it Fort Charles. He spent a long cold winter trading with the James Bay Cree, and did very well. When Groseilliers returned to England in October 1669 he had more than 1,300 pounds' worth of beaver pelts that had been purchased with a few pounds' worth of tools, beads and trinkets. (On later expeditions Natives sometimes refused to deal with Groseilliers because he drove too hard a bargain.)

The men of the English cartel were thrilled to see such promising returns on so tiny an investment. They immediately began making plans for another voyage. Meanwhile, they drafted a charter, which received the Royal Seal on May 2, 1670. It gave the "Governors and Adventurers trading into Hudson's baye" absolute control over all lands whose rivers drained into that bay. The territory included large parts of what is now Ontario and Quebec, all of Manitoba, most of Saskatchewan, half of Alberta, and a considerable part of Nunavut, as well as bits of Labrador, the Northwest Territories, North Dakota and Minnesota; in all more than 1,486,000 square miles. At the time no one knew just how large Rupert's Land, as the new company called their domain, really was. But the Hudson's Bay Company charter was so well-constructed that political and commercial rivals tried unsuccessfully for more than two hundred years to find a loophole. In return for this magnificent monopoly over so vast a region, the Hudson's Bay Company was obliged to present the Crown with an annual payment of the skins of two elk and two black beavers.

The first official governor was Prince Rupert, who held the position until his death in 1682, though he never actually set foot in Rupert's Land. The first colonial governor appointed to run things in the bay was Charles Bayley, a peculiar man who had been a childhood friend of Charles II. Bayley was a fanatical Quaker who had gone so far as to try to convert the Pope to his brand of Protestantism. His obnoxious proselytizing had caused him to be jailed in Italy, France and finally England, where he was imprisoned in the Tower of London. He was released from the Tower to serve in the bay, possibly as a convenient means of getting him out of England. Radisson and Groseilliers did not trust him; nor did he trust them. But Bayley actually served the company well for a number of years.

For the next few years, Radisson and Groseilliers worked energetically for the company they had done so much to found. They made trips to the bay, traded with the natives and helped expand Fort Charles. They explored inland from the shores of the bay, and recommended that trading posts be established in the interior along the most well-travelled canoe routes. But the gentlemen adventurers who never set foot outside London dismissed these recommendations. They were content to let the Natives come to the post on the bay.

Radisson and Groseilliers had, in fact, become quite unhappy in their service with the English. They felt that once the trade had been established, they were "look'd upon as useless persons that deserved neither reward nor encouragement." Each of them was paid the comfortable salary of one hundred pounds a year, but that was hardly the fortune they'd expected to make. Nor did it compare with the huge dividends the businessmen in London were making.

The French government had been alarmed at what it considered English aggression in Hudson Bay right from the start. As far as the French were concerned, the claims made by Cartier included all of the land from the St. Lawrence Valley to the shores of Hudson and James bays. Henry Hudson, they said, had wintered on ground that was already French. Charles II politely disagreed.

The English presence in the bay was seriously disrupting the French fur trade. Natives who might have sent their furs through middlemen to Quebec were taking them directly to the English, and getting a better deal for them. Moreover, the furs coming out of Hudson Bay were of a superior quality to those coming from the St. Lawrence Valley. That was because the animals in the colder climate grew more luxuriant pelts. The French decided that if they could not, for the moment, expel the English from Hudson Bay, they had to get Radisson and Groseilliers back into the French camp. The coureurs were secretly approached by agents of the French king. If they would return to France, Louis XIV would pardon them for their error in going over to the English, they would be paid a substantial sum just for returning home, and they would be usefully and profitably employed in the service of France. In 1675, Radisson and Groseilliers quietly left London and crossed the English Channel to France.

The promises of profitable employment were empty. No one in Paris would finance an expedition into the bay. The French government sent Radisson and Groseilliers to Canada to consult with the governor, Louis de Buade de Frontenac. But the governor did not trust them, and was more interested in the ideas of René-Robert Cavelier, Sieur de La Salle, who wanted to explore beyond the Great Lakes for a water route to China. Groseilliers returned to his home at Trois-Rivières and the family he had not seen in years. Radisson went back to France in search of any employment he could find. He spent some time at sea as a privateer, fighting the Dutch. But even after putting his life on the line in the service of his country, Radisson was not trusted in France. Part of the reason was that his wife (whose first name is not known), the daughter of Sir John Kirke of the Hudson's Bay Company, was still in England. Her father had forbidden her to leave the country.

Radisson went to England under the pretence of making arrangements to take his spouse to France. Kirke was still adamant that his daughter, even though she was a married woman, could not leave England. While he was in England Radisson put out some cautious feelers to see how receptive the Company might be to welcoming him back. The signs were not favourable. Radisson did learn, however, that the Company was planning to establish a post at the mouth of the Nelson River. This was a location he and Groseilliers had always thought a prime spot for a trading post, but previous attempts to establish one there had failed. Moreover, the French and English governments were currently trying to settle their disputes over Hudson Bay diplomatically, and for the English to open a new post before negotiations were even concluded seemed a bit presumptive.

By this time, Radisson was in cahoots with Charles Aubert de La Chesnaye, an ambitious Canadian merchant, who was also quite possibly a fur smuggler. La Chesnaye had the ear of Charles Colbert, an important man in the court of Louis XIV. Colbert obtained a fur-trading charter for La Chesnaye's new Compagnie du Nord, which was to be the French equivalent of the Hudson's Bay Company. However, the French had to maintain secrecy about this company because France was, for the time being, at peace with England and Louis did not want to provoke a war. When Radisson and La Chesnaye went to Canada in 1682 the situation was so confused that the Buade would not grant them a licence to trade in furs. The best they could obtain was a permit to fish off Anticosti Island, which they had no intention of doing. But the permit did give Radisson and Groseilliers an excuse for leaving Quebec in two small fishing vessels, the *St. Pierre* and the *Ste. Anne.* One of their crewmen was Groseilliers' son, Jean-Baptiste Chouart. Their real destination was the mouth of the Hayes River, a few miles south of the Nelson.

There were actually three expeditions heading for the bay that summer of 1682. The first to arrive—about August 18—was a party of New Englanders in the *Bachelor's Delight,* captained by Benjamin Gillam, son of old Zach Gillam. Though they had a "charter" from the governor of Massachusetts, these men were in fact poachers, with no legal right to be trading there. They set up a post on an island in the Nelson River, a few miles upstream from the mouth.

Next to arrive were the French. They sailed a short distance up the Hayes River, and were only a few miles overland from the

New Englanders. While Groseilliers set up a trading post, Radisson and young Chouart took an eight-day exploratory trip upstream until they reached a Cree encampment. Radisson concluded a "treaty" with the Natives that gave the French exclusive trading rights in that region, and he requested the Natives spread the word to others, asking them to bring their furs to the French post on the Hayes.

Radisson was on his way back to the French post when he heard the sound of a cannon shot come from a place where there should have been no cannon. (The New Englanders had fired a salute for a member of their party who had died.) Radisson investigated, and was both surprised and angered to see the New Englanders trespassing on what he now considered French territory—and which he formerly would have considered Hudson's Bay Company territory. Radisson now began the most brazen game of deception in his career.

Radisson took a few French and native companions, and paid the New Englanders a visit. He told Ben Gillam that his Massachusetts licence was worthless because he had already claimed this territory for the king of France. He said the French were constructing a big post nearby, and had sent fifty marines to enforce French authority. He promised the New Englanders he could provide them with protection from the natives, but they must remain at their post and conduct no illicit trade. Ben Gillam, who had but a dozen men with him, had no choice but to accept Radisson's terms.

The coureur and his companions left the New England camp and were headed down the Nelson, when they saw a ship enter the mouth of the river. This was the Hudson's Bay Company vessel *Prince Rupert,* commanded by Zach Gillam. On board was John

Bridgar, sent to establish a new post at Port Nelson and be its governor.

Radisson could not let the Englishmen go upstream and discover the New Englanders, because if the two joined forces they would outnumber the French. He had his men build a large, smoky fire that he knew would get the attention of the skipper on the *Prince Rupert.* Zach Gillam saw the smoke and dropped anchor. The following morning he and Bridgar went ashore to investigate.

Radisson was waiting on the riverbank, his companions covering him from the trees with their muskets. To the astonishment of the Company men, Radisson said he had claimed the territory for France a year earlier, and that a French army of three hundred soldiers had built a fort just a few miles away. The Englishmen argued the matter, but Radisson's bluff worked. The *Prince Rupert* advanced no farther upriver. It was too late in the season for the ship to turn back for England, so the crew went ashore to build a shelter for the winter. Radisson spied from the woods for a few days to be sure the English did not wander too far.

Then the Company men had a bad stroke of luck, but one that would be beneficial to Radisson. The *Prince Rupert,* running in newly formed ice, cut through her planking at the water line and sank. One of those lost with the ship was Captain Gillam. John Bridgar and his company of fewer than twenty men were now completely at Radisson's mercy, as most of their provisions were gone.

For months Radisson kept the two English parties ignorant of each other. Neither knew just where the French "fort" was, because Radisson had given them false information. When men from the Hudson's Bay Company camp caught sight of men from the New England camp, they took them for a French patrol and kept their distance. From time to time Radisson visited the Company men with gifts of food—the only thing that kept them alive. Meanwhile, Groseilliers was filling the storehouse of the French post with top-quality furs.

In the spring the two French ships, *St. Pierre* and *Ste. Anne,* were badly damaged by ice. The French used timber salvaged from one to patch up the other, but the result was a leaky contraption that could hardly be depended upon to carry them back to France. Radisson had a better idea. Taking along a group of armed men, he descended upon the New England camp, took Ben Gillam's men prisoner and seized the *Bachelor's Delight.* This was technically an act of piracy for which Radisson and Groseilliers had no authority whatsoever.

Soon Bridgar learned that he and his men were also Radisson's prisoners. He complained vigorously when he realized how he had been hoodwinked, but to no avail. Radisson and Groseilliers confiscated all of the trade goods from both parties. Then Radisson burned down their posts. The Englishmen and New Englanders were loaded onto the patchwork French ship and sent to the Hudson's Bay Company post at the bottom of James Bay. Radisson and Groseilliers sailed away in the *Bachelor's Delight* with more than two thousand beaver pelts in the hold.

Radisson had allegedly plotted with La Chesnaye to meet a ship aptly named the *Black Eagle* at Perce Rock off the Gaspé Peninsula, which was then a notorious rendezvous for smugglers. The *Black Eagle* was to take the cargo of furs to Spain or the Netherlands, and sell them illegally for top prices. But French authorities uncovered the conspiracy, and the *Black Eagle* did not show up. The two coureurs had to sail on to Quebec. There the new governor, Joseph-Antoine Le Febvre de La Barre, seized the furs and took for himself the quarter share of the profits that should have gone to Radisson and Groseilliers. Once again the greed of a short-sighted bureaucrat would be costly to New France.

Radisson and Groseilliers sailed to France one more time to seek justice, and once again they were denied. Their patron, Colbert, who might have spoken for them, was dead. Louis XIV was more concerned with soothing English anger than he was with the complaints of a pair of backwoodsmen. Disgusted, Groseilliers, went back to his farm in Canada. He was sixty-five and tired of making fortunes for other men. He is believed to have died peacefully at Trois-Rivières in 1696, though Radisson wrote that the old explorer died "in the Baye."

Radisson, meanwhile, was again feeling out the possibilities of returning to the Hudson's Bay Company. Lord Richard Graham Preston, the English ambassador to France, got word of this and sent his aide, a Captain Godey, to meet Radisson at his lodging in Paris. Godey provided a rare physical description of the famous explorer, describing him as:

> ...apparelled more like a savage than a Christian. His black hair, just touched with grey, hung in a wild profusion about his bare neck and shoulders. He showed a swart complexion, seamed and pitted by frost and exposure in a rigorous climate. A huge scar, wrought by the tomahawk of a drunken Indian, disfigured his left cheek. His whole costume was surmounted by a wide collar of marten's skin; his feet were adorned by moccasins. In his leather belt was sheathed a long knife.

Godey also found that Radisson was thoroughly disillusioned with the French and was anxious to go back to England. Radisson himself wrote: "I yielded to these solicitations and am determined to go back to England forever, and so strongly bind myself to his Majesty's service … that no other cause could ever detach me from it." Radisson snuck out of Paris, possibly with the help of Frenchmen in the English embassy, and crossed the channel again. Radisson was declared an outlaw with a price on his head by French officials who wanted him to be thrown into the Bastille.

In London, Radisson was welcomed back into the hierarchy of the Hudson's Bay Company with the title of Superintendent and Chief Director of Trade at Port Nelson. He was given a silver tankard and two hundred pounds in Company stock, plus an annual salary of one hundred pounds. Still, some of the leading shareholders regarded Radisson with suspicion. After all, his shifty ways had just cost the Company two thousand pelts and a shipload of trade goods. Radisson won their trust when he told them his nephew Jean-Baptiste Chouart was still sitting at Port Nelson with furs he had been accumulating ever since his father and uncle had sailed for Perce Rock. The young man would be anxiously awaiting a French ship.

The ship that sailed into the Nelson River in the summer of 1684 was not French, but the Hudson's Bay Company vessel *Happy Return*. Radisson was on board, anxious to win his nephew over to the Company. Radisson found the post deserted, and learned from local Natives that young Chouart had retreated inland upon sighting the English ship. He was also told that all had not been quiet in his absence. The English traders down in James Bay had paid a Cree warrior to assassinate Jean-Baptiste. Chouart had overcome the would-be-killer in hand-to-hand combat, thus winning the admiration of the Natives. He would certainly be a valuable man to have in the Company fold.

Radisson found the French camp a few miles upriver. Of course, young Chouart was confused to see his uncle with the hated English, but Radisson soon convinced him to turn over the twenty thousand beaver furs he had acquired. Jean-Baptiste and the Frenchmen with him accepted employment with the Hudson's Bay Company, but they would not renounce their French citizenship or take an oath of loyalty to the English Crown. At about the same time that Radisson was loading Chouart's pelts into the *Happy Return,* yet another governor in Quebec, Jacques-René de Brisay, Marquis de Denonville, issued a warrant for Radisson's arrest. There would be a reward of fifty pistoles for anyone who could bring the outlaw to Quebec where he could be hanged.

French privateers actually prowled Arctic waters, hoping to seize a ship on which Radisson might be travelling so they could collect the bounty. One man who fell into their hands was Bridgar, on his way to take command of a post in James Bay. When Bridgar angrily demanded to know why his ship had been seized when England and France were not at war, the French captain told him he was looking for Radisson. At the sound of that name Bridgar flew into a rage. He called Radisson a traitor and a thief, and swore he would kill him if he ever set eyes on him again.

For the next two years Radisson looked after Company business at Port Nelson. He supervised trade and sent younger men to explore the interior. One of them was Henry Kelsey. Radisson also founded York Factory at the mouth of the Nelson River. In the end, Radisson became was a victim of the infighting that was a constant pastime of Company employees in the bay. Governors and officers of various trading posts wrote to London, accusing Radisson of illegal trading and other abuses. Always regarded with a degree of suspicion, Radisson was sent to England in 1687 as a prisoner on an HBC ship.

Radisson was acquitted of the charges against him, but he never returned to Hudson Bay. The company that largely owed its existence to him gradually pushed him aside. The pension he had been promised was whittled away to almost nothing. But Radisson showed some of his old tenacity when he battled in the courts for five years to get it back. Still, he was reduced to begging the Company for a job as a warehouseman in London; a request that was refused. Radisson spent his final years in poverty.

In June or July 1710, Radisson died. In his will he bequeathed to his widow (his third wife) and his children the eighteen hundred pounds he believed the company still owed him. His family saw none of it. All the company would release from its rich coffers was six pounds to cover Radisson's burial expenses, which they took care to designate that as "charity."

Radisson and Groseilliers opened large parts of present-day Canada and the United States to trade and further exploration. They were co-founders of one of the greatest and most enduring commercial enterprises in the history of the world; a company that is still in operation in the twenty-first century. Yet both men died in obscurity and today lie in unmarked graves. The greatest of all the coureurs de bois certainly deserved better.

Henry Kelsey

First to the Prairies

But for the accidental discovery of his journal in 1926, more than two centuries after his death, explorer Henry Kelsey might have remained to this day Canada's "forgotten man." His lifelong employer, the Hudson's Bay Company, saw fit for various reasons not to publicize the story of his accomplishments as a pathfinder. Certain historians dismissed his great journey from the shores of Hudson Bay into the Canadian interior as the unimportant wanderings of an impetuous boy who had run away from his post. The word "boy" would, in fact, cloud history's perception of Kelsey. In 1688 he was referred to in a Hudson's Bay Company document as "the boy Henry Kelsey," leaving the impression that he was at that time still in his teens. Historians have since deduced that by the time the "boy" statement was written, Kelsey was actually twenty-one years old.

Though almost nothing is known of Kelsey's early years, there is circumstantial evidence that he was born in East Greenwich, England, in 1667, the eldest son of a mariner named John Kelsey. He received at least a basic education and, given his love of writing in rhyme, may have been slightly better schooled than the average lad from his social class.

We know for certain that Kelsey was indentured to the Hudson's Bay Company on March 15, 1684, for a term of four years. It has been speculated that this was Kelsey's second term of indenture with the Company. However, it seems more likely that he was indentured elsewhere in 1677, and that his indenture was taken over by the Company at a later date, perhaps 1683, and then renewed in 1684. There is little doubt he made his first trip to Hudson Bay in May of 1684, when he sailed in the *Lucy* under Captain John Outlaw, who was accompanying Pierre-Esprit Radisson's ship the *Happy Return.*

Kelsey was assigned to the post on the Nelson River, but was later relocated to the new post of York Fort (renamed York Factory) on the Hayes River. A few weeks after Kelsey's arrival, the post was unsuccessfully attacked by the French. There is no record of what action—if any—Kelsey saw in this engagement. As a mere apprentice he would not have been considered worthy of mention even if he did participate in the fight. He wrote nothing of the episode himself.

As an indentured employee, Kelsey would have worked long hours for little money. He would have had to learn all the tasks necessary to the operation of a trading post: cooking, carpentry, hunting, fishing, and, of course, keeping accounts. Later he would be taught the finer points of the fur trade: how to assess the value of pelts, how to deal with the natives, and just as importantly, how to deal with the Company administrators in London. From his accomplishments as an adult, it is clear that Kelsey also learned to be a sailor. For his work with the Company, Kelsey received room and board, and the promise of eight pounds and two suits of clothes at the end of his apprenticeship. If he did exceptionally well, and if his masters were feeling generous, he might also receive gratuities.

Life at a trading post on Hudson Bay was far from comfortable. For a youth from England, there was hardly a more isolated place than the bleak shores of the frigid bay. Between Hudson Bay and the ocean lay deadly, ice-choked waters that were open for only a few weeks during the summer. For the rest of the year, the post was cut off from the outside world.

The men were discouraged from taking families with them, which meant wives and children remained at home. Relationships with native women were also frowned upon; as far as the Company directors in London were concerned, the men working in the bay were expected to live celibate lives. Daily life was lonely and also quite regulated, as demonstrated by this list of Company rules:

> All persons to attend prayers.
>
> To live lovingly with one another not to swear or quarrel but to live peaceable without drunkenness or profaneness.
>
> No man to meddle with, trade or affront any of Indians, nor to concern themselves with women … Men going contrary to be punished before Indians.
>
> No man to go abroad or to hunt without obtaining leave.
>
> No person to embezzle powder or shot entrusted to them to hunt with or to keep defence of factory.

> Not to carry fire about warehouse, nor smoke tobacco on any of the flankers but to be always careful. To have but one lamp that the watch lamp burning for public.
>
> No man to go off duty until he sees the next one up, not to suffer drinking.
>
> To live lovingly and do things with cheerfulness.
>
> People who go hunting trapping for fox, marten, wolf or any skin — company lays claim to one-half as they find victuals, drink and wages — other half to do with as they please. All such skins to be registered and account set home as those skins were not traded.

Winters on the bay were cold and monotonous. The wooden buildings were not insulated, and even though fires were kept roaring in the brick fireplaces, ice formed on the insides of the walls, so dampness was always a problem. Spring thaw was accompanied by floods. Summers were short but hot, and plagued by hordes of black flies and mosquitoes. For much of the period that Kelsey lived on the bay, there was also the danger of attack from the French. The English posts on Hudson and James bays were seriously undermining the French fur trade, which was now based in Montreal. Since the Hudson's Bay Company's charter, granted by King Charles II of England, meant nothing to the French, they took it upon themselves to grab some of the rich trade by force of arms.

The world of a Hudson's Bay Company employee was a narrow one. On his doorstep was the great bay. Behind him was the unknown wilderness; a frightening haunt of fierce beasts and savage

Indians. The Natives were well-behaved when they came to the posts to trade, but the men had heard enough stories to know that they should fear them. Tales of cannibalism and other unholy practices regularly drifted in to the white men manning the posts. The Cree who traded at the posts encouraged such fears among the Englishmen because they didn't want the white men travelling into the interior and meeting the more distant tribes. The Cree knew this would undermine their position as middlemen in the trade and reduce their profits. The governors of the Company didn't encourage inland exploration either. They wanted their traders where they could keep an eye on them, so they wouldn't be tempted to engage in any independent business transactions. It was for this reason that they thought it better to have the Natives trade at the posts on the bay. The leading men of the Company even concluded that it would not be in their best financial interests if one of their men should stumble across the Northwest Passage, as such a discovery, they felt, would threaten their precious monopoly. One of the conditions of the Hudson's Bay Company charter, however, stated that the gentlemen adventurers had to engage in exploration.

By 1690, the Company's men found a reason to send an explorer beyond the fringes of the bay; all of their posts, except York, had fallen into French hands, thanks to the exploits of the Chevalier Pierre de Troyes and Pierre le Moyne d'Iberville, whose daring raids all but drove the English out of Hudson Bay. While the English held York and hoped to regain their other posts through negotiation or war, they decided on an expedition into the hinterland. Their purpose was to contact distant tribes and convince them to trade at York rather than with the French. The man in the field was also to be a peacemaker, as the rival tribes were constantly at war, often over the benefits of the fur trade. The Company was concerned about this because tribal warfare hurt business. So even as the French and English slugged it out in the bay, the Company wanted the natives to spend less time warring and more time harvesting beaver pelts. The man chosen for this mission was Henry Kelsey.

Most of the Englishmen who worked in the Hudson's Bay Company posts held the typical European attitude that the Natives were an inferior race. Kelsey, on the other hand, liked the Natives. He learned their language and their customs. A report on him sent to London early in his apprenticeship described Kelsey as "a very active lad Delighting much in Indians Compa., being never better pleased than when hee is Travelling amongst them." Indeed, Kelsey had already been entrusted with assignments that would have been beyond the abilities of the average apprentice from England.

In 1688, the governor at York gave three Natives a package of letters to take to the post at the mouth of the Severn River, about 250 miles away. Though they had been paid to do this errand, the natives soon returned with the letters undelivered. Kelsey then made the journey himself accompanied by one Native boy, in the dead of winter. He handed the letters to the head man at Severn, and then returned to York with the replies. The round-trip took him a month. This was an impressive accomplishment for the young man.

So impressive that in the summer of 1689 Kelsey was chosen as a member of a small party sent to establish a post on the Churchill River. The Company thought the Natives north of the Churchill might be encouraged to trade white whale oil. Kelsey sailed north in the *Hopewell* with Captain James Young. Men were put ashore at the mouth of the Churchill River to begin construction on the post, while young and Kelsey continued north in the ship, looking for Natives. Due to ice conditions they covered only 90 miles in ten days, so Kelsey volunteered to go ashore and search for Natives with a Native boy who claimed to know the territory.

The trek across the Arctic tundra was brutal. The ground was hilly and stony, and river crossings were dangerous. Kelsey wrote in his journal on July 25: "To day put from ye shore it being dread-full to behold ye falls we had to pass Considering we had nothing to tye our Raft but small Logline & were forced to shoot 3 Desperate Falls ye Raft struck upon two of ym (them) but gott safely over."

The searchers found debris where Natives had camped, but they found no Natives. To make matters worse, Kelsey's "guide" did not know the land as well as he had claimed, and he displayed considerable fear of the local people. After hiking about 140 miles, Kelsey gave up in disgust. He and the boy walked back 140 miles to the place where Young had put them ashore, then an additional 90 miles to Fort Churchill. The mission had been a failure, but it helped to condition Kelsey for the greater journey to come. The post on the Churchill was in operation for barely a year before it accidentally burned down and the site was abandoned.

On June 12, 1690, Kelsey set out from York Fort on the journey for which he is best known. He had orders from Governor George Geyer "to call, encourage, and invite, the remoter Indians to a Trade with us." He carried with him samples of the trade goods the natives would find at York if they took their furs there. Kelsey was also looking for signs of mineral deposits and plants that could have medicinal value. The fact that Kelsey travelled with Assiniboine natives who knew the route well and had been over it many times does not diminish his achievement. For an Englishman to travel hundreds of miles into the wilderness, over some of the most difficult terrain in the world, in the company of people from an alien culture, was quite remarkable.

As Kelsey travelled through the wild country, he wrote about the waterfalls, rapids and many portages that made the going slow. It has been estimated that he travelled almost 600 miles on that first leg of his journey, crossing five lakes and making thirty-three portages. He described the birch and poplar forests he passed through, along with many wild cherry trees. While it is difficult to precisely follow his route on a map, he probably went up the Hayes and Fox rivers to Moose Lake. On July 10, he was at a location he called Deering's Point, after Sir Edward Deering, deputy governor of the Hudson's Bay Company. No one is positive just where Deering's Point was located, but the most accepted idea is a bend in the Saskatchewan River about 12 miles below The Pas, on the border of Assiniboine country. Kelsey took possession of Deering's Point and all the surrounding territory for the Hudson's Bay Company. It is worth noting that in so doing, Kelsey was ascribing to the Company sovereignty similar to that which earlier explorers had recognized only in the crowned heads of Europe.

Kelsey had a penchant for writing parts of his journal in verse. The following passage from his diary describes the countryside, and offers insight into the military situation of the people who lived there:

> This plain affords nothing but Beast and grass
> And over it in three days time we past,
> getting unto the woods on the other side
> It being about forty sixe miles wide
> This wood is poplo (poplar) ridges with small ponds of
> water

> there is beavour in abundance but no Otter,
> with plains and ridges in the Country throughout;
> Their Enemies many whom they cannot rout,
> But now of late they hunt their Enemies
> And with our English guns do make them flie

Kelsey spent the rest of that year in the vicinity of Deering's Point. In the spring of 1691 he gave a party of Natives heading to York a letter for Geyer. Kelsey said in his report that "the Indians are continually at war within land, but have promised to get what Beaver they can against next year, others not before the next Summer come twelve-months when they promise to come down." The combatants in this case were the Cree (whom Kelsey called "Home Indians" because they were already frequent visitors to Hudson's Bay Company posts) and the Gros Ventres. The Cree had acquired guns from the English, but the Gros Ventres were still armed only with bows and arrows. Kelsey managed to get a grudging promise out of the Cree to stop waging war, but the peace was short-lived. With their superior arms the Cree were soon raiding Gros Ventre country again, settling old grudges.

Natives passing back through Deering's Point in July brought Kelsey a reply from Geyer. The governor renewed Kelsey's commission to explore, sent him some supplies and trade goods, and instructed him once again to try to mediate peace amongst the tribes. On July 15, 1691, Kelsey set out on the second leg of his journey.

We know that Kelsey was the first European to see the Canadian Prairies, although as with the first part of his expedition, no one is sure exactly where he went. After he left Deering's Point, he seems to have travelled more than 40 miles by canoe, using side streams to avoid the strong current of the main river, before entering the Saskatchewan River at a place that would one day be the site of Cumberland House. He then went about 20 miles downstream before turning inland. He cached some supplies and equipment, and then may have followed the valley of the Carrot River south. After travelling about another 150 miles, Kelsey sighted bison. He was not the first European to see these magnificent animals, which were misnamed buffalo. The Spanish and French had seen them on the American Plains to the south. But Kelsey was the first white man to see them on the Canadian Prairies, and possibly even the first European to witness a Native buffalo hunt. He was also the first European to record the sighting of a grizzly bear, an animal the Natives regarded as a god.

Kelsey travelled more than 500 miles, hoping to establish contact with the people he called the "Naywatamee Poets." Where this term came from is a mystery. It might have originated with the expression *pwat*, which was another name for the Sioux. Kelsey most likely reached the Touchwood Hills, near present-day Saskatoon, where he met people called the Atsinas who told him about a range of high mountains, far to the west. These of course were the Rockies, which no European had heard of up to that time. The news of a great mountain range forced the whites to seriously reconsider the possible routes that a Northwest Passage might take, realizing it might be at higher latitudes than they had previously anticipated.

Kelsey found that other tribes generally lived in fear of the Cree, who jealously guarded their position as middlemen between the Hudson's Bay Company posts and the more distant Natives. Moreover, when the other tribes sent deputations seeking English protection from the Cree, the Cree tried to convince Kelsey to join them in making war on the others. Following his orders, Kelsey wrote in his journal that he advised the natives:

> Telling ym [them] yt [it]must Imploy their time in Catching of beaver for yt [it] will be better liked on then their killing their Enemies when they come to ye factory neither was I sent there for to kill any Indians but to make peace with as many as I could but in all my arguments prevailed nothing with ym [them] for they told me wt [what] signified a peace with those Indians considering they knew not ye use of Canoes and were resolved to go to wars so I seeing it in vain I held my peace.

The Cree had a point in arguing that their rivals, who had not mastered the use of the canoe, would not be able to travel to Hudson Bay anyway. But Kelsey persisted in trying to convince the native leaders to forget old grievances. He wrote of an encounter with one chief:

> So then I made a speech to him and told him that he should not mind what had passed formerly as concerning the nayhaythaways killing Six tents of his Countrymen and for the future we English will seek for to prevent it going any farther, for if so be they did so any more the Governor says he will not trade with them if they did not cease from killing his friends. And when I had done I presented him with a present: coat and sash, Cup and one of my guns, with knives, awls, and tobacco with small quantities of powder and shott and part of all such things as the Governor had sent me. So he seemed to be very well

> pleased and told me he had forgott what had past although they had kill'd most of his kindred and relations.

But though the chief said he had "forgott what was past," before long there was bloodshed amongst the tribes again, and Kelsey's peace mission came to naught. The "Naywatamee" (who may have been Sioux) agreed to meet him the following year at Deering's Point, but fear of the Cree prevented them from keeping that rendezvous. It was very unlikely that one young Englishman, hundreds of miles from his trading post, could have had much influence over tribes whose hostilities were probably many generations old.

It is not known if Kelsey spent the winter of 1691–92 south of the Saskatchewan River or if he went back to Deering's Point. He added nothing to his journal after September 12, 1691. He returned to York Fort in the summer of 1692, and Geyer was pleased to report that he brought in a "Fleet of Good Indians." In addition to his journal and his rambling poems, Kelsey wrote an account of Native customs, and is believed to have compiled a dictionary of Native words, most likely Cree.

Kelsey never travelled into the interior again, and it would be almost fifty years before the Hudson's Bay Company sent anyone else inland. His journal was not published in his lifetime, and was eventually lost and forgotten. When it turned up in the twentieth century, it was, strangely enough, found among Major Arthur F. Dobbs' possessions, a descendant of Arthur Dobbs who had been a sharp critic of the Hudson's Bay Company. Henry Kelsey was the heart and soul of the Company in the bay for almost forty years. Between 1684 and 1722 there were only three years (1704, 1705 and 1713) in which he was absent from Hudson Bay.

Kelsey was at York on October 4, 1694, when it was surrendered to d'Iberville. He was one of the men sent out to discuss terms with the French commander. Kelsey was not held responsible for what the Company considered the shameful capitulation. Nonetheless, his pay was docked—as were the payments to all other Company employees in the post—from the moment of the surrender.

It seems that the French, being short of supplies, turned most of the English—including Kelsey—out into the woods to fend for themselves over the winter. Only three or four of the senior English administrators were allowed to remain in the post. Many of the English died of scurvy. No record exists that tells how the others survived, but it would be fair to assume that those who made it through alive owed their lives to Kelsey's experience as a woodsman and his rapport with the Natives. The following year, Kelsey and his men were shipped to France as prisoners, and eventually made their way back to England in late 1695 or early 1696. Kelsey returned to Canada with the English squadron that re-took York later that year. There is no record of what part, if any, he took in the action.

History repeated itself in September 1697 when d'Iberville captured York again. Once more Kelsey was sent out to negotiate, and was again held blameless for the loss. D'Iberville had already beaten English ships in Hudson Bay, and York could not hold out against his force of nine hundred men. Once again Kelsey was sent to France as a prisoner, and was then repatriated to England. This time the French would hold York until 1714.

In 1698, Kelsey was sent to Albany, the only post the Hudson's Bay Company still held in the bay. For three years he served as a trader and as master of the Company frigate *Knight,* a 50-ton vessel that ran between Albany and a new post the Company established at the mouth of the East Main River on James Bay. In 1703, he returned to England, apparently dissatisfied with his pay of fifty pounds a year, and possibly in poor health. The Company evidently missed his services, because a year later he was hired back at one hundred pounds a year.

Kelsey was sent back to Albany as chief trader. He also handled much of the East Main trade. The Company instructed Kelsey "to Educate the men in Literature but Especially in the Language that in time wee may send them to Travell if wee see it Convenient." This odd wording has been interpreted to mean that Kelsey was expected to teach his men to read, and to teach them the language of the natives.

Under the terms of the Treaty of Utrecht in 1713, France was obliged to return York to the Hudson's Bay Company. Kelsey was present when the English re-occupied the post in September 1714, and was given the task of rebuilding. According to Kelsey, the French had allowed it to become "all rotten and ready to fall" and it was "not scarce defensible against the natives if they have a mind to assault us."

Kelsey worked under Governor John Knight, but in 1717 when Knight was sent to establish a new post at Churchill, Kelsey was made governor of York. A year later Knight was summoned to England and Kelsey was made governor of all the Company posts on the bay, including Churchill. Then, for reasons that remain unclear, Knight made complaints against Kelsey in London. Documentation concerning the charges has been lost, but it seems Knight accused Kelsey of private trading and of being too soft on the natives. Whatever Knight's accusations were, we know that Kelsey, after so many years of service to the Company, became deeply resentful. In a letter written in February 1720 he said, "It is a great Dolor to be represented so Odiously to our Masters and tuched in ye most Sensable part yt [it] is a mans reputation wch is more Valuable yn [then] Life itselfe." The Company dropped the affair, and Kelsey remained in command until 1722. For his part, Knight, at the age of eighty, sailed off in 1719 to look for Arctic gold and to find the Northwest Passage. Neither he nor his two ships were ever seen by white men again. Henry Kelsey found evidence in 1721 that both ships had been wrecked. A year later a captain named John Scroggs would claim to have found more wreckage, as well as evidence that the men had been "killed by the Eskimos." This account would be challenged later.

In 1722, after Kelsey had completed four years as governor in the bay, London sent him a letter that stated: "Wee think it Convenient to Call you home." Kelsey returned to England, but later tried to secure a position as captain on a vessel that would take him back to Hudson Bay. He was still waiting for the appointment when he died in 1724, at his home in East Greenwich. He was buried on November 2. Though he owned property in London, Kelsey did not have much money to leave to his wife and three children. In 1730 his widow, Elizabeth, had to petition the Hudson's Bay Company for ten guineas for the cost of apprenticing her son. Four years later she had to ask for an additional four guineas to buy the boy clothing. As was the case with Pierre-Esprit Radisson, the Company to which Henry Kelsey had given most of his adult life was found wanting when it came to recognizing the debt it owed to a great man.

Samuel Hearne

Trek to the Arctic

The thought of an Englishman "going native" would have been not only unacceptable to the British-born explorers and traders who came to what is now Canada, it would also have been repugnant, too shockingly immoral to even consider. To the English (and most other "civilized" Europeans) the North American Natives were an inferior race. Their ways were perceived by the whites as barbarous and degenerate. They were heathens who had to be converted to Christianity and "taught" the ways of civilized people—even if they never would be the equals of whites. To have suggested to an Englishman that *he* learn Native ways would have brought, at the very least, snorts of indignation. The English regarded the French Canadian coureurs du bois with contempt, because they were white men who debased themselves by living like Natives and sometimes among Natives. Even among the Hudson's Bay Company men who dealt with Natives on almost a daily basis, this condescending attitude was prevalent.

Yet, the Natives in what is now northern Canada survived in a hostile climate and on a harsh land. They did so without the houses the English had to build, and without the supply ships that came from England. They lived in the wilderness without the tons of equipment that would be required by even a small party of Englishmen. They ate food that no Englishman would consider eating, and they dressed in a manner the English considered "savage." No Englishman (Henry Kelsey excepted) would live the way the Natives lived, until Samuel Hearne went on his unique journey of discovery.

Samuel Hearne was born in London in 1745 to Samuel and Diana Hearne. His father was the managing engineer of the London Bridge Water Works. The elder Hearne was an ambitious, capable and imaginative man. He was also something of a nonconformist, taking issue with some of the doctrines of the Church of England. In these traits, the son would take after the father.

Samuel Hearne Sr. died in January 1750. Diana now had to raise her son and daughter, Sarah, without her husband's income. They'd been living in a comfortable company house, which they were obliged to vacate. Diana took her children to her hometown of Beaminster in Dorset, where they could afford to live relatively well.

Young Hearne attended the Tucker Free School, where he was often in trouble for misbehaving. He enjoyed learning, but rebelled against the monotony of sitting in a classroom for hours on end, completing dull exercises and drills. He was actually very bright and inquisitive. According to one eighteenth-century chronicler, "He was particularly fond of drawing, and though he never had the least instruction in the art, copied with great delicacy and correctness even from nature."

Hearne's boyhood hero was Daniel Defoe's fictional character Robinson Crusoe. He expressed an early desire to go to sea, and obstinately rejected suggestions that he pursue a career in business. Late in 1756, his mother secured a position for him as a servant to Captain Samuel Hood, a renowned naval officer who had distinguished himself in battle.

As a "Young Gentleman" in the captain's service, Hearne was in fact serving an apprenticeship. His pay from the Royal Navy went to the captain, who in turn instructed the boy in all aspects of being an officer and a gentleman. Hearne's mother had to provide him with an allowance of thirty pounds a year so he would always be properly dressed and groomed, and to pay for his food and education.

Hearne served under Captain Hood on several vessels. As an officer-in-training he did not have to do menial chores like the boys who served on the lower deck. In fact, in the act of relaying the captain's commands, young Hearne would be giving orders to grown men. He and the other Young Gentlemen in Hood's service spent a few hours each day with a schoolmaster who gave instruction in both nautical and academic subjects. Hearne was fortunate to be in the service of an enlightened commander like Hood. Like all Royal Navy officers, Hood believed in strict discipline. But in an age when far more naval sailors died from disease and bad food than from wounds received in battle, Hood believed in running a clean ship. Even so, mariners lived on a monotonous diet of soup, salted beef, cheese and hardtack biscuits, washed down with beer. The hardtack biscuits were usually full of weevils, the cheese was rock hard and the beer frequently sour.

At age fifteen, Hearne advanced to the rating of ordinary seaman and moved into the midshipmen's mess. This was a crowded room where an assortment of Young Gentlemen and other members of the crew ate, slept and socialized when they were off duty.

Here, boys like Hearne were often bullied by older youths, and neither the captain nor other officers interfered. It was up to the Young Gentlemen to look after themselves. Hearne, who was brighter than the average midshipman, could often talk his way out of an unpleasant situation. As he became older and more muscular, Hearn developed a social conscience and stood up for younger boys who were being victimized. While he was still very young he heard of the execution by firing squad of the British admiral John Byng. Admiral Byng had lost an important battle with the French and had been charged and convicted of neglect of duty. The trial was a great sensation all over England. Mobs cried for Byng's head, saying he had shamed the nation. Others begged clemency for Byng, including the great French writer and philosopher Voltaire. Letters Voltaire wrote in Byng's support appeared in publications all over Britain and won over many sympathizers. Nonetheless, the sentence was carried out. Hearne was greatly affected by the cold-blooded execution, which to him was a shameful act. The incident drew Hearne to Voltaire's writings.

Hearne had been in the navy only four months when he experienced his first sea battle. His ship, the fifty-gun *Antelope,* took on a French warship off the north coast of France. Standing on the quarterdeck, the twelve-year-old saw men smashed to pieces by iron balls as the deck ran with blood. While the cannons roared, he threw up over the side. He was told he'd get used to it, but Hearne never did learn to stomach carnage. Captain Hood won the battle, and a week later he captured two French privateers. The money made from the sale of such ships was divided proportionately among the officers and crew. Even the smallest share, such as the sum a boy like Hearne would receive, could be considerable. Hearne sent the money to his mother.

Over the next four years, Hearne saw further action, and visited exotic ports in Italy, Greece, Turkey and North Africa. Captain Hood saw great officer potential in Hearne, and put him in command of a gun crew. But Hearne knew he did not fit well in the brutal world of the Royal Navy. He hated the regularity of the beatings and floggings. He witnessed two hangings, and was disgusted. Like Voltaire, Hearne questioned the morality of war. When the war with France ended in 1763, Hearne left the Royal Navy.

What Hearne did for the next three years is not known. He almost certainly worked on merchant vessels, quite likely rising to the position of first mate or even captain. Early in 1766, Samuel Hearne joined the Hudson's Bay Company as first mate on a whaling sloop operating out of Prince of Wales Fort on Hudson Bay. If he proved satisfactory, he would be promoted to captain when there was an opening. Hearne left England for the bay on the supply ship *Prince Rupert* at the end of May.

Hearne arrived at Prince of Wales too late in the summer for a trading or whaling voyage to the north, so he sailed in the HBC sloop *Churchill* to York Fort to help stow the vessel away for the winter. Then he returned to Prince of Wales. Hearne did not share his fellow employees' enthusiasm for drinking and gambling in their spare time. He explored the country in the vicinity of the post, and met the Natives who came to trade. He also began to learn the Cree language.

In the summer of 1767 Hearne prepared to sail north with the *Success* and the *Churchill.* Before he left, he chiselled his name into a large flat stone near Prince of Wales. The inscription on what is now called Hearne's Rock can still be seen today: "Sl Hearne, July ye 1, 1767." It is no crude carving, but an aesthetically attractive inscription.

This expedition combined trade with whaling. The Inuit who lived in the northern barrens wanted the white man's trade goods, but were afraid to cross the territory of the Dene, Cree and other Native peoples who lived to the south of them. These other nations despised the Inuit and killed them on sight. It was they who gave the northern people the name "Eskimos," which means "eaters of raw meat." The Company sent ships north to trade with the Inuit in their own territory. During Hearne's first trip north two Inuit boys came aboard the ship. He took the opportunity to learn some basic Inuktitut, while teaching the boys some English.

The Hudson's Bay Company hoped to develop trade in whale oil. They soon abandoned the endeavour as uneconomical. However, while on this voyage the men of the *Success* and the *Churchill* found further evidence of the demise of the Knight expedition that had disappeared in 1719, and whose members Scroggs concluded had been killed by Inuit. Hearne would disagree with Scroggs on this issue.

Hearne and a few men went ashore at Marble Island, where Knight's two vessels had been wrecked. Besides some guns, cables, anchors and other items, they found the remains of a house and "the bottoms of the ship and sloop, which lie sunk in about five fathoms of water, toward the head of the harbour." They also found graves. Captain Joseph Stevens of the *Success* wrote in his log: "on their digging up part of a soft raising ground they found ye skulls & bones of different human bodies."

Captain Magnus Johnston of the *Churchill* wrote: "They had found a great number of graves, one of which Mr. Hearne caused the people to dig up in order to see if they find any thing remarkable—but could not—only the bones of a stout man who without doubt is one of the unhappy sufferers."

The Inuit had always denied killing Knight's men. The Englishmen had been no threat to them. On two later trips to Marble Island, Hearne would find additional artifacts from the doomed expedition. By that time he was fairly fluent in Inuktitut, and he later claimed he interviewed two elderly Inuit men who had seen Knight's men and who gave him their version of what had happened.

Writing about the event years later in London, Hearne said that forty or fifty of the shipwrecked men built a house on the barren, windswept island. They died from hunger, sickness and the cold. Only a few were still barely alive when some Inuit found them. The Inuit gave the men seal meat and whale blubber, which they devoured raw. The weakened Englishmen could not digest such food, and soon they, too, died. The Inuit had no blood on their hands.

Hearne's version was accepted as fact for generations. Then historians learned that Hearne had made up the story about the elderly Inuit witnesses. Why would he do such a thing?

From the evidence he saw first hand on Marble Island, Hearne probably deduced that the Inuit had nothing to do with the deaths. But he had nothing that would prove his conclusion beyond the shadow of a doubt. By the time he wrote about the incident he had lived among Native peoples and probably knew their ways better than any other Englishman alive. He was also very aware of his own people's prejudices about "savages." He knew that much of what Europeans believed about North American natives was the fanciful nonsense of bigotry. So he probably tried to offset it with a yarn. Historians still don't know just what happened to Knight and his men, but there was never any real evidence against the Inuit.

During his early years in Hudson Bay, Hearne met three men who would have a great influence on him. The first was Andrew Graham. This jack-of-all-trades employee of the Hudson's Bay Company was, among other things, a dedicated student of natural science. He was one of the first naturalists to collect specimens of North American fauna, and even discovered five new species. He became a mentor to Hearne, and encouraged the young man to gather and record all the information he could about wildlife.

The second was William Wales. A noted mathematician and astronomer, Wales went to Prince of Wales Fort in 1768 to make specific astronomical observations. He was the first professional scientist to set foot on the shores of Hudson Bay. Lodged in a freezing stone hut, he was probably pleasantly surprised to find that young Samuel Hearne wanted to learn all the great man could teach him about the science of astronomy.

Then there was Moses Norton, one of the most controversial figures in the history of the Hudson's Bay Company. He was the governor of Prince of Wales Fort, and the son of former governor Richard Norton. There is still disagreement as to whether he was English-born, or the child of one of his father's Cree wives. Moses Norton was schooled in England and served on Hudson's Bay Company ships before taking over as chief at Prince of Wales. Depending upon which account one reads, he was either a sinister character or a very misunderstood man. He was allegedly a tyrant to those who had to work for him. He strictly upheld the Company policy of not allowing employees to have sexual relations with Native women, yet he himself regularly took Native girls to his bed. It was rumoured that he poisoned Natives who forbade him the use of their daughters. Yet, the governors in London clearly placed their trust and confidence in Norton, or he would not have held such a high position. Norton and Hearne quickly developed a mutual dislike. On Hearne's part, the dislike would grow into hatred.

Beaver pelts were the mainstay of the trade, but the Company governors in London wanted to diversify. There had to be other commodities besides furs from which the gentlemen adventurers could make money! Their investment in whale oil hadn't been as profitable as they had expected. But they had heard reports of copper in the wastelands beyond the great bay. Copper in fact, was one of the resources James Knight had been looking for when he vanished.

Natives had been bringing pieces of copper into Hudson's Bay Company posts for many years, but they were vague about the source. In 1765, Norton sent two Natives named Matonabbee and Idotliazee to find the mine. Three years later the pair returned with some copper samples and a map. They said they had found the copper "far to the northward where the sun don't set." The map, of course, was a fake. But Norton was enthused enough that on a trip to London, he convinced the governors to let him send a white man north to find the copper mine. At the same time the Company would be fulfilling its obligation to search for the Northwest Passage. The gentlemen adventurers agreed, and Norton recommended Hearne for the job.

Hearne had spent most of his young life at sea, but they felt he was qualified to lead an overland expedition because he liked the Natives and spoke their language. He also knew astronomy and could take the readings necessary to make an accurate map. Furthermore, he was a first-rate hunter, who was tough and determined, and wouldn't run back to the post at the first sign of hardship. Hearne had made overland hikes before, and while so doing had become expert in travelling on snowshoes. Moreover, he had been pestering Norton for the captaincy of a ship. A good long trek across the tundra would get him out of the governor's hair.

The task given to Hearne was three-fold: find the copper mine, find the Northwest Passage, speak to natives who previously had no contact with the white men and convince them to bring their furs to the trading posts. Hearne was surprised to be given the assignment, and he wasn't entirely unprepared. He had been working in the bay for three years, and he had read the accounts of Henry Kelsey and two other Company men who had travelled with the natives. He had a very good idea of what he was getting himself into, and he did not hesitate to accept the assignment.

Hearne knew that he would not "lead," but rather travel with natives. He would rely on them as guides, and he would live off the land because it would simply be too difficult to take along all the food he would need. He wrote in his journal: "I took only the shirt and clothes I had on, one spare coat, a pair of drawers, and so much cloth as would make me two or three pair of Indian stockings, which together with a blanket for bedding, composed the whole of my stock of clothing."

Hearne also took his gun, a large supply of powder and ammunition, his astronomical equipment, parchment for making maps, a knife and other tools, and a supply of trade goods. Norton provided Hearne with two Company men as labourers; a sailor named William Isbester and a landsman named Thomas Merriman. He also hired two local Cree men to help carry Hearne's equipment. When a band of Dene led by a chief named Chawchinahaw arrived at Prince of Wales to trade, Norton arranged for Hearne's party to travel with them.

Norton told Hearne that Chawchinahaw would take him as far as "Athapuscow Lake," which was a point of confusion at the time. The white men did not realize that there were not one, but two huge lakes far to the west: Lake Athabasca and Great Slave Lake. Norton also told Hearne that Matonabbee would meet him there. Hearne would write later that he wondered how he was supposed to rendezvous with Matonabbee, when Matonabbee had no way of knowing anything about the expedition.

Norton also made it clear that Hearne was not to take along any women. His orders stated: "It is sincerely recommended to you and your companions to treat the Natives with civility, so as not to give them any room for complaint or disgust, as they have strict orders not to give you the least offence."

Hearne was not travelling south, as Kelsey had done, he was going northwest into one of the most inhospitable regions on Earth. It was and still is a land of extremes: long, dark winter months of sub-zero cold intensified by gale force winds; a few brief weeks of summer with intense heat, twenty-four-hour sunlight and clouds of voracious mosquitoes and black flies. If the other men in Prince of Wales Fort had been fully aware of what Hearne was willingly walking into, they might well have thought him mad.

Hearne's party set out on November 6, 1769, to the roar of a salute from the post's big guns. Two days out of Prince of Wales, one of the Natives quietly deserted in the night. This man had been assigned the task of pulling a sixty-pound sledge full of equipment. Hearne took over that job himself. But trouble was only beginning.

Isbester and Merriman quickly consumed much of the food they had brought from the post. Game was scarce, and what the

Native hunters did bring in, they were reluctant to share with Hearne's "common men." They showed respect for Hearne, but they treated the other two white men with contempt.

Then Chawchinahaw wanted to return to Prince of Wales. Hearne reminded the chief that he had given Norton his word to take the Englishmen to Athabasca, and had accepted payment. Chawchinahaw had been taking the whites through the very worst country he knew of, and likely thought the foolish Englishmen would be glad to go back. He hadn't counted on someone as resolute as Samuel Hearne.

The Dene chief had no intention of keeping his promise to Norton. He only wanted to go into his winter camp without these bothersome white men. But he didn't know how to get rid of them without causing a problem for himself and his people.

Late one November night several of Chawchinahaw's men slipped out of camp, taking with them much of Hearne's property, including trade goods, tools and ammunition. When Hearne confronted Chawchinahaw in the morning, the chief denied any knowledge of the theft. He said that it would now be impossible for the white men to continue on to Athabasca. Taking his people in another direction, he told Hearne the way back to Prince of Wales, then abandoned him. Hearne wrote that the Dene made "the woods ring with their laughter, and left us to consider our unhappy situation, near two hundred miles from Prince of Wales Fort, all heavily laden, and our strength and spirits greatly reduced by hunger and fatigue."

On December 11, Hearne's party arrived back at Prince of Wales: "to my own great mortification, and to the no small surprise of the Governor, who had placed great confidence in the abilities and conduct of Chawchinahaw."

Hearne wanted to go out again as soon as possible. He had learned some valuable lessons. Out in the wilds he could not "order" the natives to go where he wanted to go. He would have to travel where they went, at their pace. He also learned that women were essential to any expedition, because they did the work the men would not do. Women pulled the sledges, gathered firewood, pitched tents, did the cooking, dressed skins and repaired clothing. Moreover, Hearne decided, he would be better off if he took no other white men along, as they were more of a liability than an advantage. Unfortunately, he could not convince Norton of all these points.

Norton found a promising guide in a Dene named Conne-e-quese, who said he had been to the "metal river" where the copper was found. Norton hired him, two other Dene and two Cree, but he was insistent that no women join the expedition. He also wanted Hearne to take two Englishmen with him (Isbester was willing to go, but Merriman had had enough), but Hearne flatly refused, saying the Natives' low regard for these men was such that he feared for their lives.

Hearne set out on his second attempt on February 23, 1770. They followed the Seal River westward, and bad weather made for slow going. Conne-e-quese said they should settle into a camp until mid-May when the weather improved. Hearne agreed, and used the time to fill his journal with observations of Native customs. In April, a large number of Dene who had been travelling the barrens arrived at their camp. Hearne's party was low on food, and the new arrivals had a good supply of dried meat. However, they would share it only with Hearne's Dene companions, and not with Hearne or the two Cree. Fortunately, migratory birds began to return and soon there was food for all. Once again, however,

Hearne would have cause to regret Norton's choice for a guide.

Conne-e-quese did not know where the "metal river" was. He took Hearne out of the taiga and onto the barrens without advising him that he would have to bring along poles for his tent, because there were no trees where they were going. When it rained, as it did frequently, the explorer had no shelter. Moreover, whenever it rained there was no possibility of a fire, so meat had to be eaten raw. The Natives were quite accustomed to raw meat, but Hearne had to overcome his revulsion and force himself to eat it. He had a particularly difficult time with raw muskox meat, which he found to be coarse, tough and stinking. In time he would learn to eat caribou stomachs, beaver wombs and animal fetuses. However, he would draw the line at lice and flies.

Hearne noted that it was a matter of feast or famine with the Natives. When there was plenty of food they gorged themselves, rarely putting anything aside for another day. When food was scarce, they lived on berries, burnt bones and scraps of leather.

As Hearne wandered across the barrens, more and more Natives joined the band until by the end of July there were about six hundred of them. He noted in his journal that they made constant demands on him for tobacco, medicine, ammunition and cloth, "as if indeed I had brought the Company's warehouse with me."

On August 12 disaster struck. Hearne's quadrant was accidentally broken. Without it, even if he found the copper mine or the Northwest Passage, he would be unable to determine the location. He was 600 miles from Prince of Wales Fort, and he would have to go back. When word spread among the Dene that the Englishman and his Cree companions were leaving, a group of men robbed them of almost everything they had.

On August 19 Hearne started south with the two Cree, Conne-e-quese and a few Dene who had furs to trade. He had some skins that he wanted the women in the group to make into clothes for him, but their husbands would not permit it. As the weather began to turn cold, Hearne knew he was in a perilous situation. Snow fell, and the Dene put on their snowshoes. Hearne and his Cree had none, and they began to fall behind the others. On September 20, it seemed that Hearne and the Cree would starve or freeze to death before they could ever get back to Prince of Wales Fort. Then, by sheer good luck, they ran into a party of a dozen or so Chipewyan Dene. Hearne would write later, "we encountered the famous Captain Matonabbee."

Matonabbee was a remarkable man. He was born about 1737 at Prince of Wales Fort. His father was a Dene hunter employed by then-governor Richard Norton, and his mother a captive with a band of Cree who came to the post to trade. The men at the post purchased her freedom. Matonabbee's father died when the boy was quite young, so Richard Norton took him in. When Norton went back to England, his immediate successor showed no interest in Matonabbee, and some of his father's relatives took him away to live in the traditional ways of his people. Later, another governor came to the post and took Matonabbee into his employ.

Matonabbee could speak Cree and Chipewyan, and some English. He was almost six feet tall—large for a Dene—and from Hearne's description, a muscular and handsome man. He did not have the three or four black streaks Dene men usually tattooed on their cheeks. He liked Spanish wine, which he did not drink to excess, and he did not drink strong liquor.

As a young man Matonabbee had served as the Hudson Bay Company's ambassador to the Dene and Cree, who were constantly at war. He had shown great courage in travelling deep into the lands of people who were his own nation's enemies, and on more than one occasion had boldly faced down men who wanted to kill him. Matonabbee's peace mission was remarkably successful. He brought about an end to the fighting, secured the release of some prisoners and increased the flow of furs to the Company posts. It is clear from Hearne's writing that he was very impressed with the Dene leader:

> He could by no means be impressed with a belief of any part of our religion, nor of the religion of the Southern Indians, who have as firm a belief in a future state as any people under the Sun. He had so much natural good sense and liberality of sentiment, however, as not to think that he had a right to ridicule any particular sect on account of their religious opinions. On the contrary, he declared, that he held them all equally in esteem, but was determined, as he came into the world, so he would go out of it, without professing any religion at all. Notwithstanding his aversion from religion, I have met with few Christians who possessed more good moral qualities, or fewer bad ones.

Matonabbee could not have come into Hearne's life at a more dramatic moment, for the other natives were obviously content to let him die. He gave Hearne a warm suit of otter fur, and told his wives to make clothes for the two Cree. He gave other women the task of making snowshoes for all three men. The hunters in Matonabbee's party brought back meat, and Matonabbee held a feast, with singing and dancing.

When Matonabbee learned of Hearne's intent to find the copper mine, he volunteered to guide the Englishman himself, with

Governor Norton's approval. He said Hearne's previous attempts had failed only partly because of the incompetence of his guides. The main reason, he said, was that he had not taken women along. "There is no such thing as travelling any distance in this country, or for any length of time, without their assistance," he said.

After a hard return journey, Hearne arrived at Prince of Wales on November 25, 1770. He had been away for almost nine months on a "fruitless, or at least unsuccessful, journey." After two failed missions, numerous hardships and a close brush with death, many other men would have given up. Hearne, however, was anxious to go again.

Governor Norton readily agreed to let Matonabbee take Hearne to the "metal river." When Matonabbee explained that women were absolutely essential to the success of the expedition, Norton did not argue. But he insisted that Hearne take along two of the local Cree. This, Hearne stubbornly refused to do. The Cree he'd had along on the other trips had been a hindrance. There might currently be peace between the Cree and Dene nations, but out on the trail the Dene had resented the Cree who travelled with Hearne, and that made the Englishman's situation awkward. However, by sticking to his guns on this matter, Hearne "offended Mr. Norton to such a degree, that neither time nor absence could ever afterwards eradicate his dislike of me; so that at my return he used every means in his power to treat me ill, and render my life unhappy." Nonetheless, Hearne continued, "whatever our private animosities might have been, [Norton] did not suffer them to interfere with public business: and I was fitted out with ammunition, and every other article which Matonabbee thought could be wanted." Norton also gave Hearne a quadrant to replace his broken one, though this device was antiquated and inferior.

On December 7, just twelve days after stumbling in from his second defeat, Hearne walked out of Prince of Wales again, this time with Matonabbee and a handful of Dene; no Cree and no other Englishmen. Three weeks of tough travelling northwest took them to the lake where Matonabbee had left his people, including four of his five wives, seven children and two adopted children. He had taken one wife with him to Prince of Wales, but her illness on the return journey slowed then considerably. Then food ran out, an emergency cache Matonabbee had left was found pillaged, and game was scarce. Hearne reported going three days on nothing but water and a puff of his pipe. His loneliness at Christmas was revealed when he wrote of his longing for the festivities that would be taking place in Europe.

Hearne was getting a first-hand course in survivalist living and basic Dene philosophy. Women were meant for labour, which left the men free to hunt. Men ate first, because the women licked their fingers during cooking. If anything was left after the men had eaten, the women got it. When there was food, you ate until you could eat no more. Matonabbee himself once became ill because of overeating and had to be carried on a sledge. When there was no food, you bore hunger stoically—even cheerfully. Modern-day scholars studying Hearne's chronicle have determined that he was not just an outsider travelling with the natives, but was more or less accepted as being adopted into the band. It seems he even had at least one Dene "wife."

Living with the Dene, and understanding their language, Hearne came to understand the people in a manner in which no Englishman previously could. If their ways seemed brutal to the whites, it was because they lived in a brutal environment. Hearne even observed a dark humour in the Dene during a crossing of 14-mile-wide Partridge Lake in the teeth of icy Arctic winds.

> Several of the women were much frozen, none of them more disagreeably so than one of Matonabbee's wives, whose thighs and buttocks were in a manner incrusted with frost; and when thawed, several blisters arose, nearly as large as sheep's bladders. The pain the poor woman suffered on this occasion was greatly aggravated by the laughter and jeering of her companions, who said she was rightly served for belting her clothes so high. I must acknowledge that I was not in the number of those who pitied her, as I thought she took too much pains to shew a clean heel and good leg; her garters being always in sight, which, though by no means considered her as bordering on indecency, is by far too airy to withstand the rigorous cold of a severe winter in a high northern latitude. I doubt not that the laughter of her companions was excited by similar ideas.

Hearne took daily readings with his quadrant. He also filled pages with information on the country, the wildlife, and especially the people. Ironically, he was among the first to note the adverse effect that trade with the white men was having on the Natives.

> What then, do the industrious gatherers of fur gain for their trouble? The real wants of these people are few, and easily supplied; a hatchet, an ice-chisel, a file, and a knife, are all that is requited to enable them, with a little industry, to procure a comfortable livelihood; and those who

> endeavour to possess more, are always the most unhappy.... It is undoubtedly the duty of every one of the company's servants to encourage a spirit of industry among the natives ... and I can truly say that this has ever been the grand object of my attention. But I must at the same time confess that such conduct is by no means for the real benefit of the poor Indians; it being well-known that those who have the least intercourse with the factories (trading posts) are by far the happiest.

Hearne's first two guides had attempted—half-heartedly— to take him directly to the place where the copper mine might be. Matonabbee knew better. It is not certain what his exact route was. But using Hearne's information, though it is sometimes confusing, historians have produced what is probably a fairly accurate map.

Through the coldest months Matonabbee moved westward, keeping his people in the shelter of the taiga. Sometime in early April, about 600 miles west of Prince of Wales, he halted his band of perhaps seventy men, women and children at a place the Dene called Thelewey-aza-yeth (Lake of the Little Fish Hill; possibly modern-day Spearfish Lake), where they prepared for the crossing of the barren grounds.

The men hunted deer. The women dried, pounded and packed the meat. The men cut birch saplings that would later be used as tent poles, and for the frameworks of canoes and snowshoes. These were tied into bundles that would be hauled by dogs. The men also cut a quantity of birch bark for making canoes.

The band then turned north. On the edge of the barrens, about 85 miles from Thelewey-aza-yeth, they stopped at a place Matonabbee called "Clowey Lake." Here they met another group of some two hundred Dene. Once again Hearne found himself surrounded by Natives who saw him as a good prospect for robbery. This time, however, Matonabbee intervened. When men demanded that Hearne, as a Hudson's Bay Company trader, provide them with tobacco and gunpowder, Matonabbee gave them some of his own supplies. But for all his virtues, Matonabbee was a very proud man, and a series of incidents that led to his pride being sorely wounded almost ended the expedition.

It was common for men to buy and sell wives, to hold wrestling matches in which wives were the stakes, or for physically strong men to take wives away from smaller, weaker men. Matonabbee, a tall and powerfully built man, added to his harem by taking the pretty young wife of a smaller man, actually stabbing the unfortunate husband three times—though not fatally. A week after Matonabbee's people left Clowey Lake, the girl ran away in the night, evidently to return to her husband. Matonabbee could not understand why the woman would prefer her first husband, a man of no importance, to so renowned a personage as himself. Then, to add insult to injury, a man from whom Matonabbee had bought a wife came forward and demanded extra payment for her; a kettle, some tools and ammunition. If Matonabbee refused to pay, he would have to wrestle the man.

This other man was a giant, standing over six-foot-four. He dwarfed even the great Matonabbee. Matonabbee knew if he wrestled this man, he would be humiliated in front of people who held him in high regard. Hearne, recalling how Matonabbee had obtained the pretty young wife from the other man by means of his knife, advised his friend against bloodshed. Matonabbee relented and gave the other man the goods he had demanded. But to Matonabbee, this meant a significant loss of face— and in front of the Englishman! It was too much!

Matonabbee refused to go farther, saying he would go and live with the Athabasca Cree, who knew how to show respect to a man such as him. He assured Hearne that he would have safe conduct back to Prince of Wales.

Hearne was alarmed. He couldn't even consider having his expedition sabotaged for a third time, so he gave the injured leader time to cool down, noting in his journal:

> I used every argument of which I was master in favour of proceeding on the journey; assuring him not only of the future esteem of the present governor of Prince of Wales Fort, but also of that of all his successors as long as he lived; and that even the HBC themselves would be ready to acknowledge his assiduity and perseverance in conducting a business which had so much the appearance of proving advantageous to them.

Matonabbee finally agreed to continue north. Accompanied by another band of men they went just 7 miles before stopping for the night. Hearne soon learned there was trouble of a far more horrific nature afoot. Besides building canoes, he had also seen Dene men making shields. Hearne asked what they were for. Matonabbee told him they were to ward off Inuit arrows. They were nearing the "metal river" he said, and the Dene knew that Inuit often went there to hunt and fish. Matonabbee and the other Dene men intended to kill any Eskimos they found. Their justification was that the Inuit used witchcraft to kill Dene people.

Hearne was appalled when he heard this. He had met Inuit, and knew them to be an inoffensive and peaceful people. He tried to talk the Dene out of committing what he saw as cold-blooded murder. The Natives scorned him as a coward.

> As I knew that my personal safety depended on the favourable opinion they entertained of me, I was obliged to change my tone … I never afterwards ventured to interfere with their war plans, for to have done so would have been the height of folly for a man in my position.

At some point Matonabbee's band left behind the children and all but a few women. Matonabbee's route took Hearne north through Eileen Lake, Artillery Lake and Clinton-Colden Lake. At the Conge-catha-wha-chaga River (Burnside River), on June 22, they encountered people Hearne called "Copper Indians," who were actually the Yellowknife, a sub-branch of the Dene. These people, whom Matonabbee evidently knew well, had never seen a white man before, and so they flocked around Hearne to examine him "from top to toe as a European naturalist would a non-descript animal." He described the encounter in his journal:

> They found and pronounced me to be a perfect human being, except in the colour of my hair and eyes. The former, they said, was like the stained hair of a buffalo's tail; the latter, being light, were like those of a gull. The whiteness of my skin was, in their opinion, no ornament, as they said it resembled meat which had been sodden in water till all the blood was extracted.

When the Yellowknife learned of Matonabbee's intention of making war on the Inuit, they expressed a desire to join in the bloodletting. To Hearne's surprise, Matonabbee's men began to rob the Yellowknife men of their bows and arrows, and women. Hearne protested to Matonabbee that such robbery left the other men with no way of getting food. Matonabbee told his men to give the Yellowknife men fair exchange for the things they took, but he did nothing about the abduction of Yellowknife women. To do so would have lowered him in the eyes of his people.

After laying in a supply of deer meat for the women, who were not to accompany them further north, the men moved out on July 2. Their path lay across the desolate Stony Mountains. Unusually bad weather made the crossing a cruel ordeal. Howling winds forced them to crawl instead of walk. When they weren't drenched by icy cold rain, they were smothered by heavy, wet snow. Their clothes were constantly sodden, they could not make a fire, and they had only crevices in the rocks to crawl into for shelter. Some of the warriors turned back, complaining that making war on the Inuit wasn't worth such a journey.

The weather finally broke, and the men continued north, stopping only to hunt. Mosquitoes made sleep almost impossible. Then there was an encounter with a band of Yellowknife who not only refused to share food with them, but also would have robbed Hearne of his clothing and everything he owned, if they'd been permitted. When Matonabbee realized what was going on, he and his warriors robbed the Yellowknife men instead.

On July 14 1771, Hearne reached the river that he called the Coppermine, about 40 miles above its mouth on the Arctic Ocean. He could see at once that it was too narrow, and too full of shoals and rapids to be navigable. There was very little firewood available and Hearne knew they could not build a trading post there.

The next day Hearne did surveys until bad weather made that work impossible. Then the scouts Matonabbee had sent out returned with the news that Inuit were camped not far down the river. Whether he liked it or not, Hearne had to accompany the raiders.

The war party soon found the Inuit camp. They watched the unsuspecting people from concealment, and prepared for battle. They painted magic signs on their shields, painted their faces black or red, tied back their hair and—in spite of the mosquitoes—stripped off their clothes. Just after one o'clock on the morning of the seventeenth, when the Inuit were all asleep in their tents, the warriors struck. Hearne watched in horror as he stood "neuter in the rear."

What followed was not a battle, but a savage massacre. About twenty men, women and children, dragged naked from their tents, were butchered without a chance to resist. Hearne recorded his account of the attack:

> The shrieks and groans of the poor expiring victims were truly dreadful. My horror was much increased at seeing a young girl of about eighteen years attacked so near me that, when the first spear was thrust into her side, she fell at my feet and twisted herself around my legs, so that it was with some difficulty I could disengage myself from her dying grasp. Two Indian men were pursuing this unfortunate victim, and I solicited very hard for her life. The murderers made no reply until they had stuck both their spears through her body and transfixed her to the ground. Then they looked me sternly in the face and began to ridicule me by asking if I desired an Eskimo wife:

> meanwhile paying not the slightest heed to the shrieks and agony of the poor wretch who was still twining around their spears like an eel.

The victors mutilated the bodies, plundered the tents, and threw anything they could not use into the river. Minutes later they detected a second Inuit camp on the other side of the river. All but one of the people in that camp escaped alive, but they lost all of their belongings to the marauders. The warriors sat down to a meal of fresh salmon, and then asked Hearne how they could assist him with his survey. Hearne named the place where the slaughter had occurred Bloody Falls. Years later, he said, he could not think of the dreadful events of that day without shedding tears. Yet he did not doubt that Matonabbee had done something he thought absolutely necessary.

The men walked down to the coast, and Hearne looked out upon what is now called Coronation Gulf. He surveyed the river mouth, noted the tidal marks, and erected a mark, taking possession of the coast for the Hudson's Bay Company. He was the first known European to set foot on that Arctic shore. But after the bloody events of the early morning, Hearne took no joy in his accomplishment.

An elderly Yellowknife man guided Hearne and the Dene to the rich "copper mine" the Hudson's Bay Company was so interested in; it lay about 30 miles to the southeast. But Hearne was in for a huge disappointment.

> This mine, if it deserve that appellation, is no more than an entire jumble of rocks and gravel, which has been rent many ways by an earthquake. Through these ruins there

> runs a small river; but no part of it, at the time I was there, was more than knee-deep.

This, then, was the legendary river. Hearne made a thorough search, and found only one lump of copper, which weighed about four pounds. He believed the area once had plenty of copper, but it had been picked over by the Natives. Considering the latitude he was at, he knew there was no Northwest Passage out of Hudson Bay.

Hearne believed his entire mission had been a failure. Now he faced a long and difficult journey back. Matonabbee and the other Dene were anxious to return to the place where they had left their families. Going back through the rugged Stony Mountains, Matonabbee set a gruelling pace of up to 40 miles a day, slowing down for nothing and no one. By the time they reached the women's tents, Hearne was limping badly. He had bruised his toenails among the rocks so that some of them had turned black and fallen off: "I left the print of my feet in blood at almost every step I took." He greatly feared that if he could not keep up with the others, he would be left behind. But once they had made camp, the men decided to rest for a couple of days. This gave Hearne a chance to doctor his feet, and he was quickly back to normal.

As Matonabbee's people moved south, Hearne continued to write down his observations about their ways, and about the land around him. On December 21, 1774, he became the first white man to see Great Slave Lake. The people crossed the lake, moving among the many islands, which were well-populated with beaver. Hearne noted that though they were now in that period when the sun never rose above the horizon, the hunters worked by the illumination of the Northern Lights. He said the light was bright enough for him to read and write by.

On June 30, 1772, Samuel Hearne arrived back at Prince of Wales Fort. From the time of his first start in 1769 he had been roaming a howling wilderness for two years, seven months and twenty-four days. He had travelled close to 5,000 miles. In spite of his objections, some of the young men from the post carried him in on their shoulders.

Hearne had not found a fabulous copper mine, and he had not found the Northwest Passage, but he had proven that a European could live on the barren grounds if he adapted to the Native ways; a lesson that would be lost on the British for a long time to come. His calculations would cause Captain Cook to concentrate his search for a Pacific entrance to the Northwest Passage above the latitude of 60° north. Hearne's studies of Arctic and sub-arctic fauna would also keep naturalists busy for years. And his recommendations would convince the governors of the Hudson's Bay Company to move inland from the bay to establish new posts that were more accessible to many of the Natives. Hearne would found the first of them, Cumberland House, north of The Pas in what is now Saskatchewan. It was here that Hearne came up with the idea for the York boat, a light vessel that would be the work horse of the fur trade for more than a hundred years.

Moses Norton died of an abdominal ailment on December 23, 1773. On January 17, 1776, Samuel Hearne became governor at Prince of Wales. Soon after, Hearne took the late governor's sixteen-year-old daughter Mary as his "country wife." This was not an unusual practice, and girls much younger than Mary Norton became partners to men much older than thirty-one-year-old Hearne. Hearne took charge of Prince of Wales just in time for the American Revolutionary War.

Prince of Wales was a massive stone fortification, supposedly impregnable. But as an experienced military man, Samuel Hearne had known from the time he first set foot inside that it would be impossible to defend in the face of any serious attack. The post's forty-two cannons looked formidable enough, but they were old. Moreover, the forty-odd Englishmen employed at the post were not trained soldiers, let alone gunners. And even if they had been veterans of many battles, they were far too few to man the ramparts. Prince of Wales had no protective moat, nor even an uphill slope an enemy would have to climb. Worst of all, there was no well inside the walls.

In 1778, France entered the war as an ally of the rebelling American colonies. On August 8, 1782, three French warships approached Prince of Wales across the choppy waters of Hudson Bay. Hearne knew at a glance what kind of firepower they carried: 146 big guns! Many of his own thirty-nine men were away hunting ducks. Hearne could only look on while the French landed four hundred men. As an admirer of Voltaire, Hearne was not about to get men senselessly killed "for the sake of honour," and he surrendered without firing a shot.

The French commander took Hearne and the rest of the Englishmen aboard his vessels as prisoners. The troops sacked and partially destroyed the post, but the commander gallantly allowed Hearne to keep his journals. The Englishmen were eventually allowed to return to Britain. The Hudson's Bay Company agreed that Hearne had done the prudent thing in capitulating, but some of his countrymen thought he should have put up at least a token fight.

In 1782, Hearne sailed back to Hudson Bay to build a new, smaller post called Churchill a few miles from the ruins Prince of

Wales. However, a smallpox epidemic had taken a frightful toll on native lives. Other Natives, no longer able to trade for gunpowder and ammunition, had starved because they had lost their old hunting skills. Mary Norton, whom Hearn was obliged to leave behind when he was taken prisoner, was one of the dead. The great Matonabbee, when he'd learned of the surrender of the fort in which he'd been born, hanged himself.

Hearne's last few years in the bay were not happy ones. The Canadian traders of the upstart North West Company had made inroads into Cree and Dene country. The French destruction of Hudson's Bay Company posts had given these interlopers in Rupert's Land a wide-open field. Many of the surviving natives now did their trading with those competitors. The governors in London—none of whom had ever set foot on the shores of Hudson Bay—were critical of Hearne's management. They accused him of being too generous with the natives, and too lenient with company employees who dabbled in a little illicit fur trading. In 1787, feeling bitter and in poor health, Hearne gave up command of Churchill and returned to England.

In retirement in London, Hearne was much sought after by scientists and naturalists interested in his notes and personal accounts concerning the geography and wildlife of the northern lands. He was reconciled with the Hudson's Bay Company, and was valuable to the governors as an adviser. His journals were never meant to be read by the public, but so great was interest in the wild country he had travelled that Hearne went to work on the manuscript titled *A Journey From Prince of Wales Fort, in Hudson's Bay, to the Northern Ocean, in the years 1769, 1770, 1771, and 1772.* This book, full of factual stories of adventure, as well as vivid descriptions of Native ways of life, was tremendously successful and made Hearne famous. However, the explorer did not live to enjoy his success. In November 1792, in London, Hearne died of dropsy at the age of forty-seven. His *Journey* was not published until three years after his death, and was soon translated into German, Dutch and French. One critic praised the book as "a valuable addition to the discoveries which the enterprising spirit of our countrymen lends them to make."

Peter Pond

Furs and Murder

Peter Pond is one of the least-known explorers in Canadian history. He was a man of incredible energy and possessed remarkable skills at organization. No one could doubt his courage, and he would open key areas of the Canadian wilderness to the fur trade, pushing farther north and west than any other trader in the 1770s and 1780s. But he was also an eccentric with a hair-trigger temper. When he finally left Canada for good, it was under a cloud of suspicion that he was involved in murder.

Not much is known about Pond's early life. According to his own account, Pond was born in Milford, Connecticut, in 1739 or 1740, to Peter and Mary Pond. The elder Peter Pond was a shoemaker. Pond wrote that for five generations his family were all "waryars [warriors] Ither by Sea or Land."

In April 1756, during the Seven Years War, sixteen-year-old Peter disobeyed his parents and joined a Connecticut regiment, hoping for battle and adventure. He was proud of his regimental coat, but soon learned he did not care for army life. The food was bad, men died from dysentery, and the troops were often in a rebellious mood.

Pond first saw action in the attack on the French fort at Ticonderoga in 1758. This was his first venture into "Cannaday." In 1759, after being promoted to sergeant, Pond was with an army that went "a ganst Niagaray" (against Fort Niagara). The strategic fort was captured, and Pond noted in his journal: "I Got But One Slite wound Dureing the seage."

After the Niagara campaign Pond returned to Milford. He mixed with the French soldiers who were being kept there as prisoners of war, and learned to speak French. His superiors were impressed enough that they offered him an officer's commission. Meanwhile, the French fortress at Quebec City fell to General James Wolfe in 1759. The "ondley plase the french had in possession in Canaday" Pond wrote, was Montreal. He was with a column of soldiers that marched north to join the siege, but probably arrived a day or so after Montreal surrendered on September 8, 1760.

Canada had fallen to the British, and twenty-year-old Pond realized "thare was no bisnes left for me" in the former French colony. He took a turn at being a sailor, and made a voyage to the West Indies. When he returned to Milford, Pond found out that his mother had died and his father had gone on a fur-trading expedition to Detroit. For family reasons, Pond stayed in Milford for three years. In 1762, he married Susanna Newell, with whom he would have two children. He wrote later that it was the longest period in his adult life that he had stayed in one place.

The fur trade in the Detroit region was disrupted by Pontiac's War in 1763, and Pond's father returned to Milford. He died there in 1764, leaving behind considerable debts. It may have been for this reason that Peter Pond looked to the fur trade as a means of making money. He would have to satisfy his father's creditors before he could even think about making a fortune for himself.

In 1765, Pond went to Detroit, which at that time was very much a raw frontier community. Violence was not uncommon. Pond spent six years there, engaged in the fur trade. Little is known of his activities during that period, except for one fatal incident. Pond wrote of a fellow trader who would "abuse me in a shameful manner." Not one to be bullied by any man, Pond challenged his tormentor to a duel and shot him dead. He then reported the affair to whatever authorities were on hand, but he said "thare was none to prosacute me." It would not be the last time Peter Pond walked away from a killing.

Pond made another voyage to the West Indies, probably in 1772. He evidently decided there was more money to be made in the woods than aboard a sailing ship, because in 1773 he was back in Montreal, purchasing trade goods for an expedition to Michilimackinac (now Mackinaw City, Michigan), a rugged but strategically located post on the Straits of Mackinac that join Lake Michigan to Lake Huron. By this time Pond was an experienced trader, and was certainly a cut above the riff-raff who poured out of posts like Detroit to debauch the Natives with rotgut liquor, and then squandered their earnings in taverns and brothels. Pond had integrity and skill as a trader. In addition to having a working knowledge of French—which many of the Natives spoke because of their dealings with French traders—he had also picked up some of the Native dialects. Pond had entered a partnership with New York businessman Felix Graham. Then while in Montreal, Pond met James McGill, one of the most important men in the early days of the Canadian-based fur trade. He arranged with McGill to have his goods sent to Michilimackinac by canoe.

Michilimackinac was the staging point for traders throughout what was then called the Northwest Territory. Every summer these rugged men—British, Scots, French Canadians and colonial Americans— poured into the post to load up their canoes with supplies and trade goods. Then they would push off for a winter of trading; to the west in the Lake Superior country, south down Lake Michigan to Green Bay, and beyond that to the headwaters of the Mississippi River. Pond recorded his observations of life at Michilimackinac and his journal became an important source for historians attempting to reconstruct the eighteenth-century frontier community. Pond also travelled among the local Natives, observing their ways and writing about what he saw. It was a practice he would follow throughout his career, and his descriptions have provided vital insights for anthropologists.

In Michilimackinac, Pond organized his trading expedition. According to his journal, he bought a "small fleat" of twelve canoes that he loaded with 4,600 pounds of goods valued at 1,200 English pounds. This was a considerable investment for the men who were Pond's financial backers; not something to be entrusted to a man without a proven record for reliability. Pond hired men to do the packing and the paddling. Then he set out on Lake Michigan for Green Bay.

From 1773 to 1775 Pond traded in the territory now occupied by the states of Minnesota and Wisconsin. He dealt with people of various tribes, including the Menominee, Winnebago, Sauk and Fox. To dispose of the bulk of his goods and bring in the largest harvest of furs in the shortest time, Pond dispatched eleven of his men to various locations. He portaged from the St. Lawrence drainage system to that of the Mississippi, and competed with traders who had come up the great river from New Orleans. "All my Outfits had Dun well," he wrote later. Pond had done so well, in fact, that he could afford to buy out his partner, Graham, who had made the journey to Michilimackinac with a cargo of new trade goods.

For a man who prided himself on being from a family of "waryers," Pond demonstrated that he could also be an effective peacemaker. War had broken out between the Sioux and the Ojibwas. Fur traders hated "Indian wars" because more fighting meant less collecting by the Natives for the trade. Moreover, white traders caught in the wrong place at the wrong time were liable to be killed.

In the summer of 1774, the commander of the British garrison at Michilimackinac, Arent Schuyler DePeyster, sent several traders bearing gifts of wampum belts to the chiefs of the warring nations. Pond was given the delicate task of carrying the wampum to the Sioux, many of whom had never seen a white man before—and bringing their leaders back to Michilimackinac the following spring for a peace council. Pond travelled to Sioux country and spent the winter trading and talking. Though he wrote little about this diplomatic mission in his journal, Pond must have been an effective speaker. In the spring of 1775, eleven Sioux chiefs accompanied him to Michilimackinac. There, DePeyster sat as chairman at a grand council that put a stop to the Sioux-Ojibwa war for ten years. By the time the war resumed, Peter Pond had moved on to other ventures.

In 1775 Pond learned that traders from Montreal and the Hudson's Bay Company were penetrating into the Saskatchewan Valley in search of higher quality beaver pelts. Though other furs such as fox, wolf and marten were valuable, beaver had always been the staple of the fur trade. As each Native community trapped the local beaver population to the point of extinction, the traders were forced to move ever farther afield to find new sources.

Around this time, Pond entered into a new partnership with Alexander Henry, a man who had lived with the Natives and was himself a renowned trader and pathfinder. Pond left Michilimackinac with two canoes and a few men, and headed west. He took the Sault Ste. Marie–Lake Superior–Grand Portage route that would eventually become the main fur trade highway to the West. On August 18, 1775, he joined Henry—who had set out earlier with eight canoes—in a Cree village on Lake Winnipeg at the mouth of the Winnipeg River. They were proceeding together along the east shore of the lake, when a severe storm struck, causing them to lose a canoe and four men.

On September 7, Pond and Henry were overtaken by Thomas and Joseph Frobisher, and Charles Paterson. The whole party now consisted of thirty canoes and 130 men. On October 1, they reached the mouth of the Saskatchewan River, where they discovered that the smaller lakes had already frozen over and two feet of snow lay on the ground. This early arrival of winter was alarming because the country through which they were travelling was uninhabited. If ice barred their way, the entire party would perish. The men bent their backs at the paddles day and night to outrace the freeze-up. On October 26 they arrived at Cumberland House, a Hudson's Bay Company post run by Matthew Cocking. Of course, the Hudson's Bay Company considered all independent traders in Rupert's Land to be trespassers, but Cocking treated the unwanted guests hospitably.

At Cumberland House the thirty-canoe flotilla broke up, the various contingents heading for specific locations where they could intercept Natives heading in to trade at the Hudson's Bay post. Pond took his canoes south through Little Lake Winnipeg (Lake Winnipegosis) and up the Mossy River to Fort Dauphin on

Dauphin Lake. There, at the edge of the prairies, he could trade with Assiniboine hunters for buffalo meat, while siphoning off the flow of furs originally destined for Cumberland House. He found he was able to strike good bargains with Natives who were glad they did not have to travel all the way to the Hudson's Bay post.

In the summer of 1776, Pond took a rich haul of furs to Michilimackinac. Upon his return, he realized that the post at the Straits of Mackinac was not suitable as a base for the more distant western trade, and he was instrumental in having Grand Portage and later Fort William (Thunder Bay, Ontario) replace it as major supply depots. This happened at just the right time, as word had reached the frontier about the rebellion in the Thirteen Colonies to the east, and there was fear that Michilimackinac might fall to the American rebels. If this happened, American supply sources, such as New York and Albany, would be cut off to independent traders, and men like Pond would have to depend entirely on Montreal.

Many of the independent traders were content to spend just a few years in the business and then get out with their swag. But a quiet life at home, living a life of ease on a tidy fortune did not appeal to Pond. He had to keep pushing into new, uncharted territory. He was an accomplished map-maker, and created some of the earliest maps of the Canadian West.

There was also a dark side to the seemingly boundless energy that drove Pond. He was impatient and arrogant, and he seemed to believe he could best gain the Natives' respect by bullying them. Witnesses once saw him strike a Chipewyan hunter with the flat of his sword. When the man protested at being abused in such a manner, Pond bellowed that "the country and the Indians belonged to him, and he would do with them as he pleased." Pond could be just as rough with rival traders.

Pond spent the winters of 1776–77 and 1777–78 trading in the Saskatchewan country. He did extremely well, but once again the same old problem arose: a diminishing supply of beaver. Other traders, such as the Frobisher brothers, were looking farther north toward Athabasca country. They had heard of this territory from the natives, but no white man had yet set foot there. The traders had seen samples of the thick, rich furs that came out of that very cold land, and they were anxious to travel there. However, it was also very far away, and none of the whites knew exactly where it was. The Frobisher brothers made an attempt to reach it in 1776, but made it only as far as Île-à-la-Crosse before severe weather halted them.

Some of the more prescient of the independent traders, such as Pond, had come to realize that much more could be accomplished through cooperation among the traders than through endless rivalry. By sharing their resources and pooling their manpower, they would be better equipped to mount expeditions farther afield than any one of them could do alone. They would also strengthen their position against the mighty Hudson's Bay Company.

In 1778, several traders, mostly those connected with the Frobisher brothers and Simon McTavish, a Montreal merchant who was emerging as a force to be reckoned with in the fur trade, decided to work together toward a common goal: the Athabasca country. They put all the provisions and trade goods they could spare into a joint stock, and then gave it to Peter Pond, with instructions to find the way to Lake Athabasca.

Pond set out with four canoes and a few men, and he achieved his goal. Unfortunately, no record of the expedition has survived, aside from remarks in the journals of a few of Pond's contemporaries. Pond's own memoir, written when he was in his sixties, was lost for many years. When it was finally discovered, its narrative ended at the year 1775. Allegedly some of the pages had been torn out. All we know of Pond's expedition is that he followed the route blazed by the Frobishers as far as it went, and that beyond Île-à-la-Crosse he was travelling in unknown territory. In all likelihood his party paddled up the La Loche River, crossed the lake of the same name, and arrived at what would come to be known as the Methye Portage (also called the La Loche Portage). This 12-mile-wide land barrier was fairly flat for most of the way, except for a steep drop of 690 feet to the Clearwater River. According to a report Pond made later, it took his party eight days to complete the portage. The path that Pond trod would become a well-worn highway of the fur trade, but he was the first white man to travel it.

Pond followed the Clearwater to the Athabasca River, which he descended to a point about 40 miles from Lake Athabasca. There he saw "a vast concourse" of Crees and Chipewyans who were en route to the Hudson's Bay Company post at Prince of Wales Fort (Churchill, Manitoba). These people annually made the long and dangerous journey to the post, and they were delighted when Pond and his men appeared, seemingly out of nowhere.

Pond set up camp, and as always he was a hard bargainer. He demanded much more for his merchandise than the Natives would have been charged at Prince of Wales, but the Natives were more than willing to meet his terms because he had spared them the gruelling trip to the bay. They even provided Pond and his men with food over the winter, and provisions for the journey south in the spring.

Pond had no trouble disposing of all his trade goods. The people were so anxious to have the white man's wares that, according to one account, Pond traded the very clothes off his back. He had more furs than he could transport in his canoes, and he had to leave the surplus in one of his winter huts. When he eventually came back for them, he found the bundles of valuable pelts untouched; as safe as if they had been in a bank vault.

While Peter Pond was wheeling and dealing with the Natives in the far north, down on the Saskatchewan River, his partners were waiting anxiously. Rumours of disaster abounded. The men of the Pond expedition had starved to death! Pond had penetrated so far into the wild northern country that he would never be heard from again! Then on July 2, 1779, Pond arrived at Cumberland House with one of the richest cargoes of furs the traders had ever seen. It was not just that Pond had so *many* pelts, but the thick dark lustre of the furs that made the haul so impressive. By discovering the way into the Athabasca country, Pond had opened up a fur trader's motherlode.

Further explorations by Pond and others revealed Lake Athabasca to be at the hub of several major river systems: the Slave, the Athabasca, the Peace and the Fond du Lac. These waterways carried trade to and from the Rocky Mountains, the Arctic tundra, the Prairies and Hudson Bay. Pond also learned from Natives of the existence of Great Slave and Great Bear lakes, and of another mighty river to the west, for which he produced a map, showing the river's approximate location. Pond's information would be of vital importance to Alexander Mackenzie, who explored that river and for whom it was named. Ironically, Mackenzie, whose exploits owed much to Pond, would be among his detractors. Some historians have suggested that Mackenzie was jealous of Pond's accomplishments.

The great distances involved in the northern fur trade posed many problems. Food was the most basic one. Cargo space in a canoe was very limited, and if the craft was loaded with enough provisions for a long expedition, there wouldn't be much room left for trade goods or bales of pelts. Moreover, due to the very short travelling season, the men did not have time to hunt or fish. Pond solved the problem with the introduction of a traditional Native food made of dried meat mixed with fat. Pemmican (the Cree word for "grease") was packed into rawhide bags and was so resistant to spoilage, it could keep for years. It was highly nutritious; one pound of pemmican was equal to four pounds of fresh meat. Pemmican was also versatile; it could be tossed into boiling water to make a soup, pressed into cakes and warmed over a fire, or eaten cold right out of the bag. The whites sweetened it by adding berries and nuts. Considered the precursor to modern military field meals, pemmican became the staple food of the traders and voyageurs of the Canadian fur trade.

The expansion of the fur trade had made such things as transportation and the marketing of goods even more complex. It was clear that a permanent partnership was necessary for planning and coordinating trading ventures. In 1779, a coalition of trading partners that included the Frobisher brothers, McTavish and McGill became the North West Company, with its headquarters in Montreal. This organization seriously challenged the Hudson's Bay Company's domination of the Canadian fur trade. Pond, who held one share in the new company, was placed in charge of the lucrative Athabasca district. Pond's energy and gift for organization certainly stood him in good stead in establishing a post in the territory, but his explosive temper would cause Pond to leave yet another dead man behind him.

In spite of the formation of the North West Company, there were still many independent traders in the northwest, and they quickly moved into the Athabasca country. Representing their interests in the shadow of the larger North West Company was a Swiss-born trader named Jean-Étienne Waddens. In 1781–82, Pond and Waddens wintered at Lac La Ronge. Alexander Mackenzie wrote, "two men of more opposite characters could not perhaps have been found. In short from various causes their situations became very uncomfortable to each other and mutual ill-will was the natural consequence."

One night in March 1782, Waddens' employee, Joseph Faignant de Berthier, heard two shots in the room next to his. He found Waddens unconscious on the floor, having been shot in the thigh. He never regained consciousness to reveal his assailant, and died the next day from blood loss. De Berthier said he saw Peter Pond and one of his men leaving Waddens' room immediately after the shooting. Mackenzie's journal says Pond was sent to Montreal for trial, but if there was a trial, the records have been lost. Pond was either acquitted, or the case was dismissed for lack of evidence or because authorities in Montreal decided they had no jurisdiction over the far West. It wasn't long before Pond was back in Athabasca, looking after the interests of the North West Company.

Around this time a smallpox epidemic swept across the north, killing thousands of helpless Natives, and disrupting the fur trade. There were still many independent traders in the area competing with the North West Company. Waddens' death had hurt small trader's interests, and resentment was beginning to grow toward the North West Company.

One of those dissatisfied with the way the North West Company operated was a trader named John Ross. He and a few other small traders were considering forming their own company to more seriously compete with the North West Company. At first Peter Pond considered throwing in his lot with them. He was extremely disappointed that he, the discoverer of the Athabasca country, had been allowed only one share of the North West Company, while men who had accomplished less received multiple shares. In the end, however, Pond remained with the North West Company, and in 1786 found himself in the Athabasca country in stiff competition with Ross. The following year word reached the outside world that Ross had been "shot in a scuffle with Pond's men."

Apparently Ross had interfered when Pond was involved in a transaction with a Native. One story has it that there was a struggle during which Ross was shot. Another says that a man named Peshe shot Ross on Pond's orders. Peshe was described as "a little crack brained and as variable as the wind." He and another man were sent to Montreal for trial, and were acquitted. No charges were ever brought against Pond, but suspicion tarnished his name and reputation. Meanwhile, the small traders and the North West Company merged to avoid further violence.

In the restructured company Pond still held only one share. He was now in his mid-forties; quite old for a trader working in the wilderness. The two murders had made Pond into something of a pariah in his community. Nonetheless, he wanted to spend his final years in the northwest exploring. In the summer of 1787, he evidently visited Great Slave Lake, and may have found the entrance of the Mackenzie River. When he returned to Athabasca, Pond said he hoped to follow the great river to its mouth, to see if it emptied into the Pacific, and might therefore be a link in a possible Northwest Passage.

That same year, however, Mackenzie arrived as Pond's successor in the Athabasca country. To Pond's further chagrin, the young Scot held a full share in the company, just as the veteran trader did. Mackenzie was fired-up by Pond's idea to follow the big river to its mouth. It would be he, and not Pond, who accomplished this feat. In 1789, Mackenzie was able to go straight to the river's entrance on Great Slave Lake to begin his epic journey. There is no doubt, however, that Pond's work made Mackenzie's expedition possible.

In the spring of 1788, Pond went to Montreal. He would never see the northwest again. He remained in Montreal for two years, making maps. He presented one to Lord Dorchester (Guy Carleton) at Quebec City. Another was intended as a gift for the empress of Russia, though she never did receive it. Pond produced yet another map for the United States' Congress. Pond's maps were of great importance at the time, and even though they had errors, they were mistakes that were typical of the period. Ironically, one of Pond's early maps suggested that the Mackenzie River flowed to the Arctic Ocean. Pond changed his mind after learning of Captain James Cook's discoveries on the west coast, and thought it emptied into the Pacific. It remained for Mackenzie to prove that Pond had been right in the first place, though Mackenzie was reluctant to give Pond credit. Mackenzie got the glory and a knighthood, while Pond faded into obscurity. In 1790, an embittered Pond sold his share for eight hundred pounds to William McGillivray, an ambitious trader who wanted a partnership in the company. Pond moved back to Milford, Connecticut. He was offered a position with an American "Company of the N.W." whose founders dreamed of repeating what the North West Company had done. There is no record of Pond's response to the proposal. In 1792, after American armies had suffered two humiliating defeats by Natives on the western frontier, Peter Pond was instructed by the American government to go to Niagara and Detroit to negotiate a peace with the tribes. It is not known if Pond actually made the trip.

Peter Pond spent his last years in Milford. If he had made a fortune in the fur trade, the money was all gone by the time he died impoverished in 1807. A lake in Saskatchewan as well as a National Historic Site in that province have both been named after him.

Was Peter Pond guilty of murder? Unless some long-buried evidence should turn up, no one will ever know for sure. As with so many other "villains" in history, we have only the testimonies of his adversaries by which to judge him. Yet, in spite of his shortcomings, Peter Pond should be recognized for the vital role he played in the fur trade.

David Thompson

The Man Who Mapped the West

In his long and eventful life, David Thompson was a fur trader, an explorer, a surveyor, a justice of the peace, a businessman and an author. He rose from humble beginnings to become the man who was perhaps the greatest map-maker in Canadian history. Travelling under conditions that were often harsh and primitive, he saw more of Canada than most Canadians, who have the benefit of modern transportation at their disposal. Yet, this man, who did so much to shape Canada, spent his final years in neglect and poverty, and died in virtual obscurity.

David Thompson the boy would hardly have inspired anyone to believe he was destined for greatness. He was born in Westminster, England, on April 30, 1770, to impoverished Welsh parents and lost his father before he was two years old. When Thompson was seven, his mother put him into the Grey Coat Hospital, a charitable institution where poor children were cared for and educated. In addition to reading, writing and mathematics, Thompson received basic training in navigation. He was also given religious instruction, which stayed with him for the rest of his life. No matter what challenges he faced, Thompson always remained a devout Christian.

Thompson was not a handsome child. He was small, squat, pug-nosed, and his dark hair stood out against his sallow skin. But he was also bright eyed and an eager learner. He enjoyed the works of Daniel Defoe and Jonathan Swift, and he loved to take "strolls to Spring Gardens and other places, where all was beauty to the eye and verdure to the feet."

Thompson's world was suddenly turned upside down in December 1783, when a representative of the Hudson's Bay Company arrived at the Grey Coat Hospital looking for boys to apprentice as clerks. The school was always willing to send older boys off to employment in order to make room for younger children, so David, he and another lad were signed over to the Hudson's Bay Company, whether they liked it or not. The other boy ran away, but Thompson resigned himself to his fate. On May 20, 1784, the fourteen-year-old left the only real home he had ever known to begin a seven-year apprenticeship. He was soon on board the Company ship *Prince Rupert,* bound for a strange new world.

Thompson was assigned to Fort Churchill on the west coast of Hudson Bay where Samuel Hearn was governor. When the boy was not busy with clerical duties, he was put to work copying sections of Hearne's book, *A Journey From Prince of Wales Fort.* Thompson did not like Hearne, who had bluntly told the youth he was not a Christian and preferred the philosophy of Voltaire to the teachings of the Bible. Nonetheless Thompson was fascinated by the stories in Hearne's journal. They stirred his imagination and sense of adventure even more than his favourite novels by Defoe and Swift.

Company superiors in London had instructed Hearne to keep

young Thompson away from the "common men," meaning the fort's servants. Many of these men were illiterate, and their jobs were to hunt geese, cut firewood and generally perform manual labour. But Hearne could not watch the boy all the time, and Thompson did not care to spend his free time cooped up indoors. So he mixed with the commoners and learned to hunt, shoot and use snowshoes. He was a smart and curious boy, who had an interest in everything, from polar bears and migratory birds to the manner in which mosquitoes fed on blood. Thompson eagerly read all the books on natural science and other subjects that the officers of the post lent him.

In September 1785, Hearne sent Thompson to York Factory. The youth would be travelling with two male Natives who were employed as packet carriers, delivering mail from one Hudson's Bay post to another. A Company sloop took the trio about 35 miles down the coast, and then put them ashore to travel the rest of the way by land.

Someone had given the Natives a gallon of liquor. As soon as they came ashore they began drinking. Soon they were staggering drunk, and finally they passed out, leaving Thompson alone with his thoughts. This experience had a strong impact on Thompson, making him a staunch opponent of alcohol use in the fur trade. Later in his career, he would smash kegs of rum and brandy rather than deal the liquor to the Natives.

The natives awoke early the following morning, none the worse for their overindulgence, and resumed their journey. Natives on the move, Thompson observed, were hard travellers who did not waste time. Besides the correspondence entrusted to them, each man carried only a blanket and a musket. They had no provisions and lived off the land. They walked at a brisk pace, and

Thompson had to keep up as they followed a muddy trail along the shore until evening. When they finally stopped, the Natives shot a goose and three ducks, which they cleaned and cooked for their only meal of the day. They followed the same routine for the eight days it took them to reach York Factory. For delivering Thompson safe and sound—though hungry and exhausted—the Natives were rewarded with three gallons of brandy and four pounds of tobacco.

The governor at York was Humphrey Marten, a vile-tempered man who was hated by every Company employee in the bay. Even Hearne considered him insufferable. Trade at York declined under his administration because he mistreated the Natives. It must have shocked Thompson to learn that the governor—in spite of official Company policy—kept two or three Native girls as bed partners.

Marten's instructions were to put Thompson to work writing accounts, teach him to transact business, and keep him away from the common men for the good of his "morals and behaviour." But Marten didn't have the time or patience to train a young clerk, so instead he sent the lad out to one of York's hunting camps.

With cargo space in the annual ship from England extremely limited, the Company restricted the food it sent to the bay to items like flour and tea. The people in the bay were expected to stock their own larders with meat and fish, which is why each post maintained its own hunting camps. The men who lived in these camps slept in tents or crude wooden sheds, even during the dead of winter. During the cold months they endured frostbite, while during the brief summer the men in the bush were tormented by mosquitoes. Thompson would write that even smoke didn't drive the hordes of bloodsuckers away, instead the mosquitoes seemed to like it.

Working with the hunters proved to be excellent training and conditioning for Thompson. He learned to net ptarmigans and catch trout. The hunters also showed him how to snare rabbits and trap foxes, wolverines and martens. Most importantly, he became hardened to the rigours of outdoor life in the subarctic.

That spring when the Natives came to the post to trade, they brought a disappointing harvest of pelts. Marten suspected the Natives had been trading with "the Canadians from Montreal" and had brought only the leftovers to the post on the bay. These rivals in the fur trade were the men of the upstart North West Company; men who would go down in history and legend as the Nor'Westers.

The North West Company was a partnership of trading firms that officially came together in 1779, with its headquarters in Montreal. It was run by businessmen who did not believe the London-based Hudson's Bay Company had a God-given right to every animal pelt in Canada. They established posts in the Canadian interior, which meant the Natives did not have to travel all the way to Hudson Bay to trade. The Nor'Westers sent their pelts to Montreal via Lake Superior, using the water route blazed by Étienne Brûlé and Samuel de Champlain.

The North West Company's main disadvantage, however, was its distance from England. Fur ships from Montreal had twice as far to travel as vessels from ports in Hudson Bay. The Nor'Westers tried to legally challenge the Hudson's Bay Company's virtual ownership of the great bay, but the charter approved by King Charles II was iron clad. However, there was little the supposedly all-powerful Company could do to prevent the Nor'Westers from establishing posts in Rupert's Land.

The Hudson's Bay Company had established three inland posts of its own: Cumberland House on Pine Island Lake (now

Cumberland Lake) that was part of the Saskatchewan River system, Hudson House and Manchester House, both on the north branch of the Saskatchewan. It was plain, though, that the Company would need a post on the south branch of the Saskatchewan to stop the flow of furs into Nor'Wester posts. The man chosen to be governor at the new post was Mitchell Oman. He was a very capable man, but he was illiterate. Oman needed a clerk to keep the account books, so Marten gave him David Thompson, who was about to turn sixteen.

In the summer of 1786, Thompson made a back-breaking journey across country with thirteen other men to a spot near the site of present day Batoche on the South Saskatchewan River. There they established South Branch House, which was only eighty yards from a North West Company post. Though the Hudson's Bay men and the Nor'Westers were rivals, they visited back and forth, and relations were cordial.

That winter Thompson finally had an opportunity to learn the fur-trade business. He met Cree and Assiniboine people, and gained a working knowledge of the Cree language. As the most junior member of the staff, he had no say in the matter of trading alcohol to the Natives. However, he did deplore the fact that the rum the Hudson's Bay Company traded was much stronger than the liquor the Nor'Westers traded.

In the spring of 1787, Thompson was sent to Cumberland House. The governor there, George Hudson, was a former resident of Great Coat Hospital. Hudson had been in charge of Cumberland House for six years, and the long period of virtual isolation in the wilderness had made him morose and lethargic. He did not even speak to his men except when it was necessary. There were no books in his post; not even a Bible. An example of the dangers of long isolation, Hudson made a strong impression on young Thompson.

Like the other men assigned to Cumberland, Thompson found it a dreary place, largely because Hudson did nothing to provide distractions for his staff in their free time. Thompson enjoyed fishing in his spare time, but aside from that the only distraction was a checkerboard. Thompson often played checkers, and when he could not find a fellow employee who wanted a game, he would play against himself. It was on one such occasion that he had a very strange experience:

> I was sitting at a small table with the chequer board before me, when the devil sat down opposite to me. His features and color were those of a Spaniard, he had two short black horns on his forehead which pointed forwards; his head and body down to his waist (I saw no more) was covered with glossy black curling hair, his countenance mild and grave; we began playing, played several games and he lost every game, kept his temper but looked more grave; at length he got up, or rather disappeared.
>
> My eyes were open. It was broad daylight, I looked around, all was silence and solitude, was it a dream or reality? I could not decide. Young and thoughtless as I was, it made a deep impression on my mind. I made no vow, but took a resolution from that very hour never to play a game of chance, or skill or anything that had the appearance of them and I kept it.

After a tedious winter at Cumberland House, Thompson was relieved when William Tomison came through with canoes from

York. Three of the men who had started out with Tomison had died, so he took Thompson along with him as a paddler. He had heard good reports about the young man, and was impressed when he learned Thompson could speak Cree.

The Hudson's Bay Company wanted to undercut the North West Company by contacting more distant tribes, particularly the Peigans, the Bloods and the Blackfeet. These allied subgroups all spoke Blackfoot. Tomison thought that if Thompson could learn Cree, he could also learn Blackfoot. He sent Thompson and six other men, their horses loaded with trade goods, out to live among the Peigans.

The men spent a month travelling west, and were actually within sight of the Rocky Mountains when, somewhere near the Bow River, they met a band of Peigans. There were some anxious moments, as few of these Natives had ever seen white men before. They had a reputation for being aggressive, and for ferociously defending their home country against trespassers. The mounted Peigan party outnumbered the bay men two to one, and they were armed with bows and arrows. As it turned out, the white men had nothing to fear. A Peigan elder named Saukamappee approached them and extended his hand in greeting. He spoke Cree, and invited the strangers to eat with them. Thompson quickly learned from talking to the man that the Peigans were very interested in the white men's trade goods, especially guns and ammunition.

The white men spent that winter with the Peigans. Thompson lodged with Saukamappee and spent long hours listening as the old man explained tribal ways and customs. Thompson learned more about the Natives and the land during that winter than he would have in a lifetime working in a trading post.

Afterwards, Thompson returned to the Saskatchewan River,

where he spent the winter of 1788–89 at Manchester House working for Tomison. It was during this time that Thompson had a fateful accident that would change his life. On December 23, Thompson fell down a riverbank and fractured his right leg. It was so badly swollen that Tomison could not set it properly. Although Tomison provided the best care he possibly could in what were rather primitive conditions, the fracture healed slowly and Thompson spent many weeks in constant pain.

In the spring Thompson was taken back to Cumberland House, where Malcolm Ross was now in charge. By late August he could move around with the aid of crutches, but was still unable to do any work. David Thompson hated to be idle, and he was not looking forward to another long winter of limited activity. Then, on October 7, three canoes arrived from York Factory, carrying Hudson, Oman, and the individual who would open the door to an exciting new world for Thompson: Philip Turnor.

Turnor was a Hudson's Bay Company surveyor, who was just returning from a trip to London. Turnor had already travelled extensively in Rupert's Land, surveying the trading posts, taking readings for latitude and longitude, and determining distances between the settlements. He had produced the first maps that were ever drawn of some of the isolated regions of Rupert's Land. Now he had the task of finding and charting a route from the Saskatchewan River to Lake Athabasca. Peter Pond had opened up the Athabasca country for the Canadians in Montreal, and the Hudson's Bay Company now wanted to move in there to get at the high-quality furs.

Thompson listened in fascination as Turnor discussed his plans with the senior men at Cumberland. For all his experiences in the wilderness, Thompson was still only an apprentice whom the Company expected would one day manage a trading post. But Thompson began to see a different future for himself.

He was intrigued by the brass instruments that were the tools of Turnor's profession: a telescope, a chronometer, a sextant, a thermometer, a compass and several watches. At every opportunity Thompson asked the surveyor questions about these devices and about his Athabasca expedition. Turnor liked the bright and inquisitive nineteen-year-old, and no doubt Oman spoke well of the lad. Turnor knew that as the fur trade expanded into the vast uncharted wilderness, the Company was going to need more surveyors and map-makers if it was to seriously compete with the aggressive Nor'Westers. Thompson's still-mending leg kept him from most of his usual duties, so Turnor took him on as a student and taught him all he knew. As Thompson wrote later: "This was a fortunate arrival for me, as Mr. Turner [*sic*] was well versed in mathematics, was one of the compilers of the nautical almanacs, and a practical astronomer. Under him I regained my mathematical education … and thus learned practical astronomy under an excellent master of the science."

Even after he was fit enough to return to work, Thompson continued to study. He learned how to determine latitude, and the more difficult and time-consuming art of determining longitude. Using Turnor's equipment he took readings, and he learned how to use a thick reference book called *The Nautical Almanac*. He learned to identify certain stars, the planets and the moons of Jupiter, all important points of light in the night sky. Thompson would sit up well into the night, making calculations by candlelight. Finally, he decided that running a trading post was not for him; instead he wanted to accompany Turnor on the expedition to Athabasca.

With the spring of 1790 approaching, Turnor had yet to make

final decisions on who would go with him. George Hudson was to have been his chief assistant, but in April Hudson died. Thompson thought himself capable of replacing Hudson, but Turnor did not agree. He felt Thompson was still too weak from his long recuperation to endure the rigours of a trek into the bush. Moreover, Thompson had developed an infection in his right eye that impaired his vision. (He would eventually lose the sight of that eye completely.) Turnor chose a young man named Peter Fidler as his assistant and began to train him. Ross was also chosen. Thompson was sent back to York Factory to complete his apprenticeship. The young man took this as a blow to his pride, and for the rest of his life he held a grudge against Ross and Fidler.

Thompson was not about to let the valuable instruction he'd received from Turnor go to waste, however. From York Factory he sent a letter to London requesting a sextant, a magnifying glass, a pair of parallel glasses and a set of nautical almanacs. Thompson explained that he wanted these items in lieu of his clothing allowance and would repay the Company the difference if the equipment proved more costly than the clothes. He offered the Company his services as a surveyor. In the same ship that carried Thompson's letter was another one from Turnor, highly recommending young David Thompson.

While Thompson awaited a reply, he worked as a clerk under Governor Joseph Colen. In his free time he used a borrowed sextant, compass and watch to make observations, which he recorded in a journal. He would eventually pass all of this information on to London.

When the supply ship of 1791 arrived at York, it brought the equipment Thompson had requested. In an uncharacteristic act of generosity, the Company directors were giving Thompson the instruments as a *present!* He was still entitled to the usual endowment of clothing. There was also a letter offering him a contract to work as a trader and surveyor for three years at fifteen pounds a year. In fact, the gentlemen in London were very interested in receiving whatever work Thompson could send them:

> We have received the Copy of your Observations, which together with Mr. Turnor's are put into the hands of Mr. Wm Dalrymple, from whom we doubt not to have a good account of them, shall be glad to receive your Obs. Of the Lakes and Rivers from York to Cumberland House every information that can tend to form a good Survey and Map of the Country Inland will always be particularly acceptable to us.

This was thrilling news for Thompson, but it also marked the beginning of a long period of frustration. Thompson wanted to explore, and for quite some time he was given little opportunity to do so. For the next year he remained stuck in York Factory, working as a trader. Then, in 1792, he was put in charge of a trading expedition north of the Saskatchewan River. Thompson surveyed and made maps everywhere he went, but this work was secondary to trading. Finally, in the fall of 1792, Thompson was given the kind of assignment he'd been yearning for.

The Nor'Westers had been getting bolder in their incursions into Rupert's Land. They were going into the Natives' winter camps even before spring thaw and scooping up furs that might otherwise have been taken to Hudson's Bay posts. Governors Tomison and Colen decided on a plan to outflank the impudent Canadians. Turnor had already done some surveying in the

Athabasca country. Now the Bay men wanted David Thompson to follow up on Turnor's work and find a shorter route into that fur-rich territory.

Taking seven men and two canoes, Thompson traveled 250 miles up the Nelson River to Sipiwesk Lake, in what is now Manitoba, where they spent a hard winter. At the end of May, Thompson continued north with three men, one of them a Cree guide. After a week's travel they met two Chipewyans who agreed to join them as guides. As they continued north, they passed North West Company posts. Thompson noted their positions for his maps. At one location on the Churchill River, they saw a Nor'Wester post that appeared to have been ransacked by Chipewyans. The guides were fearful of going on, but Thompson convinced them to continue. The following day the guides led them to a dead end, and Thompson had no choice but to turn back.

When Thompson reported back to Colen and Tomison, he considered his trip a success, even if it had been cut short. He had found three of the trespassing Nor'Westers' posts, and he believed he had found a possible shortcut to Athabasca via the Burntwood River, Duck Portage and the Churchill River. He wanted to go back and explore more new country. Instead, he was sent to Buckingham House, a new post on the North Saskatchewan.

In 1794 the Hudson's Bay Company renewed Thompson's contract and raised his pay to sixty pounds a year. That was more than seasoned traders like Malcolm Ross were earning. Thompson was certainly grateful, but he was disappointed that the letter from London said nothing about his future as a Company surveyor. He had to be content the following year with opening a new post on the Churchill River. His frustration increased when he found himself in competition not only with Nor'Westers who erected a post thirty yards away from his, but also with another group of Hudson's Bay men who set up shop in the same vicinity.

It wasn't until 1796 that Thompson got another opportunity to continue his search for a shorter route into the Athabasca country. He set off in a large canoe that he built himself with only two young Chipewyan guides and only the barest necessities for survival.

Thompson went up the Reindeer River to Reindeer Lake, and then followed the Paint River through swampy, mosquito-infested country to Manitou Lake. He was now in country that no white man had seen, and which was rarely even visited by Natives. Thompson found the head of the Black River and followed it about 160 miles down to Lake Athabasca. He had finally found the route his superiors wanted. Thompson, however, almost didn't make it back alive to tell them.

For the trip back up the turbulent Black River, Thompson and the Chipewyans had to make many portages and sometimes line the canoe through dangerous, rocky stretches. "Lining" meant pulling the canoe upstream with ropes. They were in the process of lining their craft through one difficult rapid just above a waterfall when the canoe was suddenly swept sideways across the current. Thompson described what happened in his journal:

> To prevent the canoe upsetting … I sprang to the bow of the canoe, took out my clasp knife, cut the line from the canoe … by this time I was on the head of the fall. All I could do was to place the canoe to go down bow foremost. In an instant the canoe was precipitated down the fall (12 feet), and buried under the waves. I was struck out of the canoe and when I arose among the waves the canoe came on me and buried [me] beneath it …

Thompson pushed his feet against the stones on the river bottom and shot upward. When he broke the surface, he was right beside the canoe and grabbed it before the current could carry it away. Fortunately the force of the water was pushing it toward shallows.

Thompson dragged himself from the river with the skin almost completely torn from the bottom of his left foot. His body was covered with cuts and bruises. His Native companions recovered his gun, sextant box and the paddles, but their powder, ammunition and fishing nets were lost. So were their blankets and spare clothing. They had no food, and no way of getting any. Amazingly, Thompson had managed to hold onto his knife, and they used it to tear up their tent to make crude blankets and bandages for Thompson's foot.

The accident was followed by a two-week nightmare of cold and hunger. Their clothes were torn to shreds as they hauled the canoe through rock-strewn rapids. They found crowberries, but they were bland tasting and provided little nutrition. Once they found three baby gulls in a nest, which they killed and ate, but the morsels only sharpened their hunger. The next day one of the natives climbed a tree and stole two baby eagles from a nest, while Thompson and the other guide threw rocks to keep the adult birds away. They divided the fat and the flesh into three equal shares. One of the Natives rubbed the fat on his body, but Thompson and the other man ate their fat, saving the meat for the next day. They did not know that the fat from fish-eating birds is dangerous to humans. Thompson and his Native guide awoke that night violently ill from dysentery. The sickness lasted several days and left the two so exhausted they were about ready to give up and die. Thompson even used charcoal and birchbark to write a statement so that the surviving guide would not be accused of murder. By sheer good fortune they met a party of Chipewyans who nursed the sick men back to health and provided them with some food, clothing, shot and powder.

When Thompson finally made his report to Ross, the governor was not pleased with the route he had found. The Black River had barely been navigable for Thompson's three-man canoe! How were canoes laden with men and trade goods supposed to manage it? Moreover, the route had too many lengthy portages to be at all practical. It seems that Thompson had been so wrapped up in surveying this virgin waterway, he'd given no thought to such obviously important matters.

While Thompson had been off exploring, Ross had decided to retire, and sent the standard one year's notice to London. He discussed the matter of his replacement with Colen and Tomison, and all three agreed that David Thompson was the logical choice. Thompson was made supervisor of inland trade in the Northern District.

This was a tremendous show of the trust and confidence the three veteran traders had in Thompson, even if his journey to Athabasca had been somewhat of a fool's errand. But Thompson was not at all happy with the promotion, because he knew what it meant: years of working in trading posts, with no time for exploring and surveying.

In the autumn, the Bay men went to Reindeer Lake where they built a rough post called Bedford House, and spent a miserable winter. It was probably about this time that Thompson first considered the unthinkable: quitting the Hudson's Bay Company and joining the North West Company. Thompson often went out to hunt and fish, and on one of his forays he had a chance encounter with a party of Nor'Westers led by Alexander Fraser. Just what Thompson and Fraser discussed at this and subsequent meetings was never recorded, but it seems Thompson came away with a better opinion of the "Canadians" (actually a mix of French Canadians, Scots, Englishmen and Americans) than he had held previously. They certainly enjoyed more freedom than the employees of the Hudson's Bay Company. Furthermore, Fraser told Thompson the North West Company could use a man with his skills.

It was a difficult decision for Thompson to reach. The Hudson's Bay Company had been good to him. If he left, he would be turning his back on friends who would see his defection to the other camp as treason. His awkward situation meant that he would not even be able to give the customary one year's notice, which the Company would take as an ungrateful and dishonourable act. But Thompson wanted to survey, and the Hudson's Bay Company wanted him to be a businessman.

Thompson and Ross were still at New Bedford House on May 21, 1797, when he broke the stunning news. Ross wrote in a report that was sent to London: "Mr. David Thompson acquainted me with his time being out with your Honours' (his contract had expired) and Thought himself a free born Subject and at liberty to choose any Service he thought to be more to his advantage and was to Quite [quit] your honours service and Enter the Canadian Company's Service." Because of Thompson's decision, Ross had to postpone his retirement for a year.

Two days later Thompson left New Bedford House in the company of two French Canadians and two Natives to start a 75-mile walk to the nearest North West Company post. That first night in camp he wrote in his journal: "This day left the Service of the

Hudson's Bay Co and entered that of the Company of Merchants from Canada, May God Almighty prosper me."

Thompson made the long journey south to the Nor'Westers' annual rendezvous at Grand Portage in what is now Minnesota. There he learned that the North West Company did indeed need a man of his talents. In fact, they had a major project for him; surveying the international border between the new republic of the United States of America and the domain of British North America.

One of the clauses of the Treaty of Paris that ended the American War of Independence established a boundary between the former Thirteen Colonies and the colonies that had chosen to remain British. The line ran roughly through the middle of the Great Lakes, and then it followed the Pigeon River from Lake Superior to Lake of the Woods. It continued west along the forty-ninth parallel until (people thought at that time) it met the headwaters of the Mississippi River. In accordance with the Jay Treaty of 1794, all British trading posts on American soil had to be abandoned. The North West Company desperately wanted the border surveyed. They already knew Grand Portage was on the American side of the line. They needed to know which other posts were as well. They also wanted to locate the source of the Mississippi River, and for Thompson to explore the upper Missouri country, which was thought to be south of the forty-ninth parallel and therefore not British territory. The Nor'Westers had heard that the Mandan people living there had high-quality furs and thought they could persuade them to go north of the border to trade. If Thompson had felt any regrets over leaving the Hudson's Bay Company, they were quickly banished. He was soon on his way west with a brigade of hommes du nord, the toughest and most experienced of the French Canadian voyageurs.

Travelling by canoe, on horseback, and even by dogsled, Thompson spent the next ten months completing the tasks set out for him by his new employers. He charted every mile he covered. He visited Lakes Winnipeg, Manitoba and Winnipegosis. He determined the positions and lengths of rivers, and took readings at every Nor'Wester post to pinpoint its exact location. He also met native tribes he had never met before: Ojibwas, Nipissings, Iroquois and Algonquins. Many of these groups had migrated west because the beaver in their own lands had been trapped out. Thompson travelled in sub-zero weather to reach Mandan country. He was off by only a few miles when he concluded that Turtle Lake (Minnesota) was the source of the Mississippi River. The information he gathered on the headwaters of this great river was the most accurate to that date, and showed them to be well south of the forty-ninth parallel. The maps that he made—considering the technology of the time—were remarkably accurate. He did make errors in judging distance, and that may have been because of his partial blindness.

Once Thompson had done all that had been asked of him, he could have returned to the relative comfort of Grand Portage. Instead he struck out on his own initiative to map the south shore of Lake Superior, working his way some 700 meandering miles to the falls at Sault Ste. Marie. While in Sault Ste. Marie, Thompson met two distinguished men who were on their way from Montreal to the rendezvous at Grand Portage:

> I had the pleasure of meeting Sir Alexander Mackenzie, the celebrated traveller who was the first to follow down the great stream of water flowing northward from the Slave Lake into the Arctic Sea, and which great river bears

> his name … the next day the Honourable William McGillivray arrived. These gentlemen were the agents and principal partners of the North West Company; they requested me to continue the survey of the lake round the east and north sides to the Grand Portage …

By the time Thompson arrived back in Grand Portage on June 7, 1798, he had travelled almost 4,000 miles. Alexander Mackenzie was certainly impressed with Thompson, stating, "He has performed more in ten months than I expected could be done in two years." For David Thompson it was just the beginning.

Thompson had established himself as an explorer and surveyor, and was about to experience another significant change in his life. In September 1798, while working near the headwaters of the Churchill River, Thompson stopped at the North West Company post of Île-à-la-Crosse. This post had once been managed by a Scott named Patrick Small, who had taken a Cree wife and fathered three children. Small made a tidy fortune in the fur trade, and then returned to Britain, leaving his "country wife" and children to fend for themselves. One of the children was a daughter named Charlotte. She was bright, attractive, and only thirteen years old when Thompson, age twenty-nine, met her. It was a case of love at first sight for both. Native girls and girls of mixed blood customarily married as young as thirteen or fourteen. Many white traders—like Charlotte's father—took advantage of these young women; "marrying" them, and then abandoning them. But not David Thompson! He married Charlotte on June 10, 1799, in a traditional Cree wedding, and he accepted her as a partner for life. At the first opportunity, he exchanged vows with her in a Christian ceremony. They would be together for fifty-eight years and have seven sons and six daughters.

Years of competition between the Hudson's Bay Company and the North West Company had ravaged the beaver population in the West. The Nor'Westers, always trying to stay a jump ahead of the Bay men, began looking toward the Rocky Mountains. So far only Mackenzie had crossed the Rockies. But the route he had used, via the Peace River, was not at all navigable. In 1806 David Thompson, who was now a full partner in the company, was given the job of finding a pass through the mountains that would be practical for trade. There was also concern about a recent American expedition led by Meriwether Lewis and William Clark. The Columbia River had been only partially explored, and the Nor'Westers wanted to find out if it might be a potential highway for trade.

Thompson's base of operations was Rocky Mountain House at the confluence of the North Saskatchewan and Clearwater rivers in what is now Alberta. He wintered there with Charlotte and their three children. Thompson soon learned, however, that the local Peigans had no intention of letting him explore the mountains. The Peigans had obtained guns and ammunition from both the North West Company and the Hudson's Bay Company, and had used the weapons to dominate their neighbours to the west, the Kootenays. The Peigans did not want to lose their profitable position as middlemen in the fur trade. They did not want the Kootenays to have access to guns. Peigan scouts patrolled the North Saskatchewan River to discourage traders from trying to move west. Warriors would stop at Rocky Mountain House periodically to warn Thompson against any westward expeditions. Nonetheless, Thompson began to assemble men, horses and supplies. He sent a Métis named Jaco Finlay to follow the North Saskatchewan River into the mountains and blaze a trail to a river they believed to be on the other side of the Rockies.

Then an unfortunate incident to the south turned out to be a lucky break for the Nor'Westers. In the summer of 1806, on the Upper Missouri, a party of Americans who had formerly been part of the Lewis-and-Clark expedition clashed with a band of Southern Peigans and killed two warriors. The news spread north from village to village until it reached the Peigans who were watching Rocky Mountain House. In the course of the story being told and re-told, the number of Americans involved had grown from just a few men to forty or fifty well-armed interlopers. The Peigans brooded over the outrage until the snows melted enough to permit travel. Then they formed a large war party and rode off to the Upper Missouri country to seek revenge. The way was now clear for Thompson to explore westward. He set off on May 10, 1807, and his party included his wife and three children, the youngest of whom was still a baby.

The explorers followed the North Saskatchewan to the Kootenay Plains, a game-rich region of woodlands and meadows well within the first range of mountains. For much of the way the men had to tow the canoes through frigid water that numbed their legs. A day and a half past the Kootenay Plains, though it was early June, they found the way blocked by deep snow and were held up for three weeks.

Thompson was at the entrance of a pass that would later be named for Joseph Howse of the Hudson's Bay Company (between Mount Conway and Howse Peak in what is now Banff National Park). Not until June 22 were Thompson and a voyageur named Bercier able to ride up on horseback to inspect the pass. The 12-mile ascent took four hours. The men were following a poorly blazed trail left by Finlay. Then they came to a vast marshy area where the waters from many springs bubbled up from the ground and mixed with the runoff from the melting snow. This water fed a tiny rill that slid away to the *west!* At that lonely spot Thompson was standing on the Continental Divide. For years he had paddled canoes in waters that eventually flowed into the Arctic or Atlantic oceans. Now he was at the edge of the Pacific watershed. Thompson wrote in his journal: "May God in his Mercy give us to see where its waters flow into the Ocean, and return in safety."

The whole party began the ascent on June 25. It took them five days to make the descent on the western side. They had to follow a raging torrent now called the Blaeberry River, which twisted and turned in its 40-mile rush to the valley floor, forcing them to cross and re-cross , while urging along cranky, uncooperative pack horses.

On June 30 Thompson discovered that the Blaeberry was a tributary of a much larger river. Because of the river's northward flow, and because he knew they were about 500 miles from the Pacific coast, he did not realize he had reached the Columbia River, whose mouth was about a thousand miles away. Thinking it an entirely different stream, Thompson called it the "Kootenae" River. He led his party south about 70 miles to a place near Lake Windemere and there he established Kootenay House. By this time they were almost out of food, and hunting was poor. Several of the party became ill after eating rancid flesh from a dead horse. Eventually they were able to trade for food with local Kootenay hunters.

The Kootenays lived in considerable fear of the Peigans, and the slightest rumour that these enemies might be approaching caused them alarm. Thompson knew that sooner or later the Peigans would show up, and would not be pleased at the sight of a post in Kootenay country. He had his men build a strong palisade. On August 27, twelve Peigan men and two women arrived. The men said they were very happy to see the new post, but Thompson didn't believe them.

Soon other Peigans arrived. They asked for rum, which Thompson would not have given them even if he had any. Seeing the stout wall around the post, the Peigans did not attack. But they did harass the Kootenays and stole some of their horses. Thompson learned that even though the Peigans were extremely angry about the post on Kootenay land, the chiefs did not want a quarrel with the whites. Many of the young warriors, however, were spoiling for a fight. Thompson warned them of "a warm reception, however numerous they might be." The Peigans remained in the area making a nuisance of themselves for three weeks, but because the hunting was poor, they finally moved on.

For the next three years Thompson was obliged to work as a trader. He had been placed in charge of the Columbia Department. In 1809, he established Saleesh House near the site of Thompson, Montana, to trade with the Flathead tribe. Surveying was still his first love, but he wanted to earn enough money to provide his children with a good education. Also, as he approached the age of forty, he found the rigours of life on the trail harder on his body. But that didn't mean Thompson spent all his time in the trading posts. Still thinking the Columbia River was the Kootenay, he followed it to its source (now called Columbia Lake). He also mapped the wild Pend Oreille River as he investigated whether it could be used in trade, and made a trip of some 1,500 miles to Rainy Lake House to exchange furs for trade goods.

The trouble with the Peigans that had started in 1807 did not blow over. In 1810, they were still seething over the posts the

Nor'Westers had built on the western slopes of the Rockies. They had also suffered a defeat in battle at the hands of the Salish, who'd obtained guns from the whites. To make matters worse, three Nor'Westers had fought on the side of the Salish. This would have a direct effect on Thompson's activities and his reputation.

In April 1810, Thompson left Saleesh House to make the long journey to Rainy Lake. He left his wife and children at Bas-de-la-Rivière (Fort Alexander, Manitoba). He had planned to go all the way to Montreal to make arrangements for a leave of absence that was long overdue. Instead, he found a letter from his superiors waiting for him at Rainy Lake House. What was in that letter remains a matter of considerable debate. Some historians believe Thompson was instructed to locate the Columbia River and survey it as quickly as possible. The American business giant, John Jacob Astor, had formed the Pacific Fur Trading Company, and was sending a ship from New York to the mouth of the Columbia by way of Cape Horn. The North West Company, it is believed, wanted Thompson to get there first. It has also been suggested that Thompson was instructed to get to the Columbia and *confront* Astor's men. Thompson's own journal sheds little light on the matter.

As far as the North West Company was concerned, the Americans had no business on the Columbia. That territory, the Nor'Westers argued, and already been claimed by Britain. The agreement on the forty-ninth parallel as the international border, they said, did not include the Rocky Mountains. Astor made an offer to the Montreal men, suggesting a partnership. While the Canadians argued over the pros and cons of such a deal, Astor went ahead with his own plans. He dispatched an overland expedition to the Columbia, and sent the ship *Tonquin* from New York. Whatever Thompson's instructions were, it was important that he get to the Columbia with all possible speed. But something mysterious happened on the way.

Nor'Wester Alexander Henry, who would also earn fame as an explorer, was sent out to re-open Rocky Mountain House, which had been unoccupied for several years. When he arrived there on October 5, he was surprised to find David Thompson's canoe men there, but not Thompson. The men said they had not seen Thompson since September 15 when he'd parted company from them upriver, apparently to go hunting. They were supposed to meet him at Rocky Mountain House, but had seen no sign of him. Meanwhile, they had been warned that a Peigan war party was waiting upstream to ambush any whites who tried to enter into the mountains.

Of course, Henry was afraid something had happened to Thompson, particularly since his cousin, William Henry, was with Thompson. But he had to deal with the Peigans first. On October 11 he sent them an invitation to come to the post to drink. He let them drink themselves into a stupor, and early the following morning sent the canoe men on their way upriver to Howse Pass.

That very evening three canoes arrived from downriver. In one of them was William Henry. He said he had left Thompson 50 miles downstream at the confluence of the North Saskatchewan and Brazeau rivers. He had orders for Thompson's men to join him there, because the explorer had decided on another route. This was perplexing! How had Thompson got from upstream to downstream without coming to Rocky Mountain House? What had he been doing for the past four weeks? Thompson's own journal—in which he wrote faithfully for many years—is strangely silent during this time. It hints at a fight with the Peigans, but doesn't clearly say so.

The day after William Henry arrived at Rocky Mountain

House, Alexander Henry sent a message to bring the men back from Howse Pass. Then he went down river to meet Thompson. Henry, who was as avid a journal keeper as Thompson, wrote: "At noon we embarked and at 4 p.m. reached Mr. Thompson's camp, on the N. side, where tall pines stood so thickly that I could not see his tent until I came within 10 yards of it. He was starving and waiting for his people — both his own canoes and those men who were coming down with the horses." Presumably Thompson had not hunted because the sound of a gun might attract the attention of the Peigans.

Why had Thompson separated from his men, especially when, as leader, he was expected to stay with them? Why had he taken a cross-country route instead of staying on the river? Why had he stayed in that camp for so many weeks? Why had he sent William Henry to Rocky Mountain House instead of going there himself?

Thompson's behaviour has led some historians to the conclusion that when he became aware of the Peigan threat, he showed cowardice by taking a detour and hiding for almost a month. However, there is another possible explanation, and this one is based on information Alexander Henry received from William, his cousin. William Henry said that when he and Thompson had left the canoe brigade they were accompanied by two Iroquois hunters. They went in a southwesterly direction following an old trail often used by natives, much of which passed through thick forest. Thompson believed they would emerge somewhere near Rocky Mountain House. Instead, they became lost. When they finally struck the Brazeau River they were well west of the post. Then they found their way blocked by Peigans.

Thompson was aware that the Peigans were in an ugly mood. He wrote in his journal that "they were determined to wreak their vengeance on the white men who crossed the mountains to the west side and furnished arms and ammunition to their enemies." Thompson and his companions saw a Peigan camp, though they themselves managed to keep out of sight.

Never before had David Thompson become lost in the wild, and he quite likely reproached himself for taking that trail. But he had also never lost a man under his command, and he wasn't about to do so now. It could very well be that he avoided contact with the Peigans not out of fear, but common sense. His party of four would not have stood a chance against a numerically superior war party. Moreover, if there were a fight in which Peigans were killed, it could spark a war in which the Peigans and their Blackfoot allies would ride out against all of the white traders. Though it would cost him precious time, he quite likely knew it would be preferable to avoid the Peigans altogether and find a different route across the mountains. The great mystery is why Thompson never fully explained his actions to his colleagues or left a detailed, written account.

The detour Thompson had chosen followed the Athabasca River, and the trail he blazed would one day be the Nor'Westers principal highway of commerce through the mountains. But for the men who made that first pioneering journey it was a tough trek indeed. It took them almost four weeks to hack through thick brush. When they reached frozen swampland the going was easier, but the temperature plummeted to as low as -34.4° C. They had to hunt frequently to keep up their food supplies, and game was scarce. They even had to eat some of their horses. Finally, Thompson was forced to send some of his men back to Rocky Mountain House. Others took that as an opportunity to desert. Back at the post they told Alexander Henry that the condition of the men still with Thompson was "pitiful."

The sub-zero temperatures continued and snow fell heavily. Thompson had to transfer their supplies from horses to dogsleds. Even the sleds became bogged down, obliging Thompson to unload surplus goods and leave William Henry behind to guard them. The horses were useless in the snow, so Thompson turned them loose and the men had to carry the loads on their backs. On January 8, 1811, Thompson wrote: "Broke my Snow Shoes. Du Nord beat a Dog senseless -& the Sled we made got broke & was with the Dog thrown aside." The next day Du Nord refused to carry his pack. Thompson ordered him back to Rocky Mountain House, but allowed him to remain with the group once he expressed remorse.

On January 10 they reached the Continental Divide. The snow was so deep, the men pushed a twenty-foot pole down through it and it still did not touch the ground. When they built a campfire, it sank into the snow and went out. The next day they began their descent down the western slope of the mountain, but the snow was wet and sticky, making travel extremely difficult. "The Courage of part of me Men is sinking fast," Thompson wrote.

On January 18 Thompson's party reached the Columbia River. He knew now that the stream he had called the Kootenay was in fact the Columbia. This was a moment of triumph for him. He had found the great river that had eluded explorers like Alexander Mackenzie and Simon Fraser. This was the highway to the Pacific the Nor'Westers had dreamed of. But before Thompson could travel down to its mouth, he would have to go *upstream* to get more men and supplies. After a few days of tramping the weary men refused to go any farther. They wanted to camp and wait for spring thaw. In his journal Thompson described them as "useless as old Women" and added that he was "heartily tired of such worthless fellows." Near the mouth of the Canoe River the men constructed a hut and went to work building a canoe out of cedar boards.

It was April 17 before the men could move again. Snow was still deep and the river still frozen, so they towed the canoe. After nine days they reached navigable water. Thompson and his men portaged from the Columbia to McGillivray's River, and then canoed 270 miles to a point where they stored their boat and obtained horses. They rode 75 miles to Saleesh House on the Clark Fork River. Finding the post deserted, they built another canoe and went downriver to Kullyspell House on Pend Oreille Lake. It too had been abandoned. Thompson sent two Native scouts to Spokane House, about 65 miles away, to tell the Nor'Westers where he was. Two days later men and horses arrived at Kullyspell.

A ten-man party, including Thompson, rode to a spot on the Columbia River now called Kettle Falls, about 40 miles south of the forty-ninth parallel. They built a canoe, and on July 3 began the journey to the river mouth. This section of the great river was uncharted. As they journeyed downstream, Thompson stopped at every Native village they passed to meet the people and give them gifts of trade goods; things they could get in abundance if they brought furs to the posts he would establish. These people—Yakimas, Nespalem, Wennatchees and Methows—had never seen white people before. At the confluence of the Columbia and Snake rivers, Thompson erected a post with a sign on it claiming the territory for Britain and announcing the intention of the North West Company to build a post there.

The trip down the Columbia was an adventure in itself. The surrounding countryside changed from barrens to richly forested mountains. For most of its course the river was about a thousand yards wide. But at one 2-mile section the water was forced through a channel only 60 yards wide. The men portaged past this gorge of white water fury, and Thompson later wrote, "Imagination can hardly form an idea of the working of this immense body of water under such compression, raging and hissing as if alive."

On July 15 Thompson and his men came within sight of the sea. They washed, shaved, put on their best clothes, and then continued on. They knew the Americans were already there, and that afternoon they saw Fort Astoria, with the Stars and Stripes flying above it. Duncan McDougall, the man in charge, was a former Nor'Wester.

Thompson seems to have been under the impression that John Jacob Astor and the North West Company had finalized an agreement. It is not clear if the men in Fort Astoria told him that it was not the case. The Americans received Thompson and his men hospitably, but at least one of them, Alexander Ross (who later joined the North West Company when it acquired Fort Astoria), looked upon Thompson as a rival. Ross noted somewhat peevishly in his journal: "M'Dougall received him like a brother; nothing was too good for Mr. Thompson; he had access everywhere; saw and examined everything; and whatever he asked for he got, as if he had been one of ourselves."

Thompson stayed at Fort Astoria for a week, and then headed back up the Columbia to do some surveys so he would have completely charted the river from its source to the sea. He retraced his steps through Athabasca Pass to pick up William Henry and the goods he had left there. He spent the winter of 1811–12 west of the Rockies engaged in trade. By the summer of 1812 Thompson was in Fort William (now Thunder Bay), the Nor'Wester post on Lake Superior that had replaced Grand Portage.

David Thompson was now ready to settle down. He had not seen "civilization" since he'd left London as a boy. When the fur canoes departed for Montreal in mid-August, Thompson went with them. By now a state of war existed between the United States and Britain, but the swift seizure of the American fort at Michilimackinac by a combined force of British troops, Canadian militia and Native allies kept the route from the West to Canada open.

The North West Company was grateful for the work Thompson had done for them, and he was granted an annuity plus a full share of the profits for three years. During that period he was to compile his observations and draw maps. After that he would officially retire, and be granted a seven-year allowance of a one-hundredth share of the company's profits.

Thompson and his family settled in the village of Terrebonne, about 30 miles northeast of Montreal. It was there that Thompson produced his magnificent "Map of the North-West Territory of the Province of Canada." This "Great Map," as it came to be called, measures 10 feet by 6.5 feet. It shows, in detail, the region between Hudson Bay and the Pacific Ocean, and from the Great Lakes and the Columbia River in the south to Lake Athabasca in the north. It also shows the locations of seventy-eight North West Company trading posts. When Thompson first arrived at York Factory in 1784, that territory on a map was almost completely blank. Thompson was the man mostly responsible for filling in the empty spaces. He had, after all, travelled some 50,000 miles across that land. The map is considered one of Thompson's greatest accomplishments, and it was copied many times over. So accurate were Thompson's observations, that a century later his map was still being used. The original map hung in the Great Hall at Fort William until 1821, when the Hudson's Bay Company finally took over the North West Company. The map then disappeared for many years, before it was found again. It now hangs in the Public Archives of Ontario in Toronto.

After he had completed the map, Thompson moved his family to Williamston in Glengarry County, Upper Canada (Ontario). Several other retired Nor'Westers lived in the same community, and Thompson liked having old friends for neighbours. He bought a large house and eighty acres of land. From 1816 to 1826 he was an "Astronomer and Surveyor" for the British Boundary Commission. When the War of 1812 ended on Christmas Eve, 1814, there were once again boundary disputes to settle. Over that period Thompson was part of the British team that worked with an American counterpart, mapping the border from St. Regis, Lower Canada, to Lake of the Woods. Relations between the British and Americans were cool at times, but Thompson won the respect of all. In the hot summer of 1819 while working on Middle Sister Island in the eastern end of Lake Erie, Thomson and several other men came down with "swamp fever" (probably malaria). Thompson was bedridden for ten days, but survived. Three of his colleagues died.

As the surveyors made their way through the upper lakes they had to endure bad food, poor accommodations, mosquitoes, fog, illness and smoke from forest fires. Some men hired for the job quit after a few days. Thompson stayed on the job through all conditions, and one summer took along his teenaged son Samuel. Sometimes there were disputes over the ownership of certain islands, and the boundary commissioners had to make some trade-offs. Of course, not everybody was happy with the compromises, so Thompson and his fellow surveyors came under sharp criticism from some quarters. In 1826 at Lake of the Woods, which is now shared by Ontario, Manitoba and Minnesota, the British and American surveying teams ran into a serious disagreement. They could not resolve it, and everybody went home. That border dispute between Canada and the United States would not be settled for another century.

Thompson returned to Williamston where he expected to live the rest of his life in financial security. He served as a justice of the peace, and enjoyed dinner parties at the homes of fellow Nor'Westers. He occasionally went to Montreal where he was a welcome guest at the mansion of William McGillivray. A guest who once met Thompson at a dinner there wrote:

> His speech betrayed the Welshman—he has a very powerful mind, and a singular faculty of picture-making. He can create a wilderness and people it with warring savages, or climb the Rocky Mountains with you in a snowstorm, so clearly and palpably, that only shut your eyes and you hear the crack of the rifle, or feel the snowflakes melt on your cheeks as he talks.

But the man who had mapped the Canadian West did not enjoy a comfortable old age. When the North West Company went bankrupt and was absorbed by the Hudson's Bay Company, Thompson lost his pension. He had invested in several businesses, trying to get his sons established, and all of those ventures failed. His sons also ran up enormous debts, which Thompson paid off. He became estranged from his eldest son, Samuel. A project to provide cordwood for the British garrison at Montreal turned into a financial disaster.

Thompson also loaned large sums of money to other people,

who failed to repay him. Meanwhile, Thompson was running into debt and creditors were hounding him. Eventually, he was forced to sell his Williamston property and move into cheap rented quarters in Montreal. As his fortunes continued to slide, he and his family were forced to move to even shabbier accommodations.

Thompson worked on a variety of surveying projects for the government and for private companies. But the money he earned was not enough to make up for his losses. Even with these jobs he ran into difficulties because individuals he had angered with his decisions as a border surveyor came forward to discredit him. Thompson swallowed his pride and sought employment with the Hudson's Bay Company. But his old employers had long memories, and turned him down. He tried to have a book of his maps published, but to no avail. In fact, the Hudson's Bay Company did publish the maps Thompson had made while he was in their employ, but they failed to give him credit.

Thompson was forced to put two of his teenaged daughters into domestic service because he could no longer afford to care for them. To pay for food, he sold some of his clothing and his precious surveying tools. Finally, he and Charlotte had to move in with their daughter Elizabeth and her husband.

Thompson had already begun to write his autobiographical *Narrative.* Now dependent on the charity of his daughter, he tried to continue with the work, but the vision in his one good eye was failing. He hoped the story of his life and adventures would be published and bring him financial relief. Like his Great Map, Thompson's book is considered one of his greatest accomplishments. Unfortunately, he didn't live to see it published. David Thompson died in dire poverty on February 10, 1857, in Longueuil, Lower Canada. He was buried in Mount Royal Cemetery, Montreal, in an unmarked grave. Three months later Charlotte was buried next to him.

Thompson's death went almost completely unnoticed. None of the geographical features he had discovered and charted bore his name. His fellow explorer Simon Fraser had named a river in British Columbia after him, but few people actually knew why that river was called the Thompson. The great explorer didn't begin to get his just due in Canadian history until the late nineteenth century, when a clerk with the Geological Survey of Canada became curious about the creator of the excellent maps of the Canadian West he had seen. Joseph Burr Tyrell would almost single-handedly rescue David Thompson from obscurity. He located Thompson's journals and his *Narrative.* He edited the manuscript and had it published in 1916 as *David Thompson's Narrative of His Exploration in Western America.* Thanks to Tyrell, Thompson is now recognized as a giant among Canadian explorers, and a monument marks his grave. According to Tyrell, Thompson was "The greatest land geographer who ever lived."

Captain George Vancouver

Surveyor of the Pacific Coast

The very first charts showing sections of the Atlantic coast of Canada were made around the turn of the sixteenth century. Generations of explorers and adventurers gradually pushed the map westward, filling in the spaces occupied by the St. Lawrence River, the Great Lakes, the prairies and the Arctic tundra. But almost three hundred years after John Cabot explored the waters of Newfoundland, almost nothing was known of the North American continent's west coast. Francis Drake might have sighted Vancouver Island in 1579 during his circumnavigation of the globe. The Spanish, who had colonized most of South and Central America, Mexico, and much of what is now United States territory, including California, had mapped all of the coastal regions of their New World empire, but were very secretive about their charts. Moreover, there was considerable dispute over whether Spain was legally entitled to all the territory she claimed. Britain, laid her own claim to some of America's west coast, but that territory was half a world away from the British Isles. For an expedition to sail there, thoroughly map the coast then return home would take years. The commander of such an undertaking would have to be a superb seaman, a skilled geographer, and a strong leader of men. The Royal Navy had such an officer in George Vancouver.

George Vancouver was born at King's Lynn, England, in 1757 and joined the Royal Navy at the age of fourteen. Young Vancouver had the good fortune to be appointed to the *Resolution* under the command of Captain James Cook, perhaps the greatest navigator and marine geographer of his time. Cook was also among the most enlightened officers in the Royal Navy, and initiated changes in sailors' diet and hygiene that drastically reduced cases of scurvy and other diseases aboard ship. Captain Cook took notice of Vancouver and made him a midshipman-in-training. The youth also received instruction from the ship's noted astronomer, William Wales. Vancouver learned from the best, and to the end of his life, James Cook was his idol.

Vancouver sailed under Captain Cook for eight years and was with him on his second and third great voyages of discovery. On these long expeditions Vancouver sailed inside the Antarctic Circle and visited such exotic locations as New Zealand and Tahiti. He saw the coast of Alaska from the Bering Sea, and on March 29, 1778, at Nootka Sound, Vancouver and two shipmates became the first Europeans known to have set foot in what is now British Columbia. On February 13, 1779, while ashore at the Sandwich Islands (Hawaii), Vancouver was injured and was very nearly killed in a clash between the English and the Natives. The following day, Cook himself was slain during a confrontation on the beach.

After his return to England following the last tragic voyage with Cook, twenty-three-year-old George Vancouver passed his examinations and received his first officer's commission in the Royal Navy, with the rank of fourth lieutenant. Late in 1780 he was appointed to the sloop *Martin* and spent over a year escorting convoys and patrolling the North Sea. In 1782 the *Martin* was sent to Port Royal, Jamaica. France and Spain were supporting the American rebellion against Britain, so the *Martin* cruised the Caribbean in search of French and Spanish ships. Vancouver participated in a sea battle that resulted in the capture of a Spanish vessel. He later transferred to the seventy-four-gun ship of the line *Fame,* where he was in charge of a battery of guns. The worst enemy of a British sailor in the tropics was disease. Not every British captain subscribed to James Cook's theories of diet and sanitation. Vancouver was appalled at the high death rate aboard the *Fame* due to scurvy and other illnesses.

The war ended with Britain's defeat, and in the summer of 1783 Vancouver found himself in England on inactive service and half pay, along with thousands of other naval officers. But with his excellent record and good connections, by late 1784 he was aboard the fifty-gun *Europa,* once again heading for the Caribbean. Naval duty in the southern waters in peacetime was a dull routine of patrols and chasing down smugglers. But ambitious young officers like Vancouver eagerly sought duty there because the death rate from disease was so high, there was a good chance of promotion through attrition. Vancouver did indeed benefit from this grim reality.

In 1786, Commodore Sir Alan Gardner became commander-in-chief at Port Royal when the previous commander died. Gardner was an energetic and progressive officer in the mould of Captain Cook, and he took a quick liking to Lieutenant George Vancouver. As disease carried young officers away, he promoted

Vancouver from fourth to first lieutenant. Among other duties, Vancouver was given the task of helping sailing master Joseph Whidbey survey the harbour of Kingston, Jamaica. The chart Whidbey and Vancouver made can still be seen in the Admiralty library in London. Soon after the trip, Gardner was made a member of the Board of the Admiralty.

In 1789, after five years aboard the *Europa,* Vancouver was once again ashore. But he would not be without a ship for long. His friendship with Gardner, supported by the skills he had learned under Cook and demonstrated in the Caribbean, were about to launch him into the project that would secure his place in Canadian history.

Captain Cook's voyages had raised considerable interest in the Pacific. Whalers were drawn to the South Pacific, and European settlement in Australia was just beginning. Britain's particular interest lay with the northwest coast of North America. Former officers from Cook's crews had started an extremely lucrative business, selling sea otter furs to China. The British government thought the fur trade on that part of the continent was worth developing.

The Spanish, however, believed the entire west coast of the Americas was theirs. They were worried about the Russians, who were staking claims in Alaska; the British, who in spite of the loss of the Thirteen Colonies still dominated a major portion of the continent; and the newly independent Americans, who were already looking westward from the eastern seaboard. In 1789, the Spanish government sent Captain Esteban José Martinez north from Mexico to establish a post at Nootka Sound on the west coast of what is now called Vancouver Island. (Europeans did not yet know that it was separated from the mainland.) Ostensibly the post was thought to be for trade. In fact, it was established to block potential threats to the Spanish colony of California. When Martinez found British merchant vessels there, he seized them and sent them to Mexico. He also formally took possession of Nootka Sound for Spain. The Englishmen were eventually released and their ships returned to them, but Britain was outraged at this "insult to the flag."

The British government said it did not recognize Spain's claim to anything north of San Francisco, and demanded compensation for the illegal seizure of British ships and subjects. The British made it clear to the Spanish that they were prepared to go to war to settle the matter. Spain quickly sought an alliance with France, in case the Nootka Crisis turned into a shooting war. King Louis XVI would have gladly joined forces with Spain against Britain, but his country was on the brink of revolution and in no position to go to war with Britain. The Spanish knew they would not stand much chance fighting alone against the British, so they agreed to settle the matter diplomatically. The Nootka Sound Convention required Spain to make restitution for the seizures, and recognized the rights of both nations to trade in the region. Spain still did not give up her claims to all of the west coast. In order to avoid a war, Britain said it was willing to discuss the matter in future negotiations. Meanwhile, the government decided to send out an officer to firmly establish Britain's claim. George Vancouver was selected for the job.

Actually, the first man chosen for command was Captain Henry Roberts, and Vancouver was to be his second in command. But a change of orders sent Roberts to the Caribbean. Vancouver was promoted to master and commander—quite likely through the Gardner's influence—and put in charge of the newly constructed

340-ton *Discovery,* a ship especially fitted out for surveying. She carried 101 men, including cooks, servants and marines. Vancouver was to plant the flag, survey and map the coast from California to Alaska, and determine once and for all if there was a commercially viable Northwest Passage. Accompanying the *Discovery* was the 130-ton brig *Chatham,* with a crew of forty-five commanded by Lieutenant William R. Broughton.

Because this was to be largely a scientific expedition, Sir Joseph Banks, the autocratic president of the very influential Royal Society took great interest in it. In fact, he had considerable authority over the preparations for the voyage. Banks held a baronetcy and was a personal friend of King George III. He was an excellent person to have as an ally, but he was also a man whom one crossed at one's peril. James Cook had once objected to what he considered Banks' interference with his preparations for a voyage. George Vancouver would have a similar problem with Banks.

Banks sent Vancouver a naval surgeon named Archibald Menzies to be the expedition's doctor and botanist. He arranged for a greenhouse to be built on the quarterdeck of the *Discovery* for any samples of flora Menzies would want to take back to England. Vancouver had nothing personal against Menzies, but he did object to Banks making such decisions about the expedition. Therefore, his reception of Menzies was cool. Menzies was soon writing to Banks, while the *Discovery* was being outfitted and provisioned, complaining that he did not like the messing (dining) arrangements Vancouver had made for him. Vancouver would one day have reason to regret getting off on the wrong foot with Menzies. On the other hand, Vancouver was delighted to have along his old mentor Joseph Whidbey as master sailor.

The *Discovery* and the *Chatham* sailed from Falmouth on

April 1, 1791. Going by way of the Cape of Good Hope, the Indian Ocean, Australia, New Zealand, Tahiti and the Sandwich Islands, it would take them more than a year to reach their destination. This was Vancouver's first command, and he was determined to carry it out to the best of his ability. As a former protégé of Captain Cook, Vancouver ran a tight, disciplined ship and he expected Broughton to do the same with the *Chatham.* When several of the men became involved in a drunken brawl during a stopover at Tenerife in the Canary Islands, Vancouver had them lashed. By the standards of the time, Vancouver was not a brutal commander. To have shown leniency would have cost him the respect of the crew and his junior officers. Vancouver balanced his authority with the kind of tact and wisdom he had observed in Cook. Yet, the day would come when Vancouver would be accused of unnecessary harshness.

For a large number of men crowded aboard a wooden sailing ship on a long voyage, life was uncomfortable and monotonous. There was no privacy. Nerves became frayed. Petty squabbles could bloom into major disputes if not checked. For health reasons, Vancouver regularly had the quarters below decks fumigated with smudge pots and scrubbed with vinegar. He also ordered clothing and bedding to be washed whenever fresh water could be spared. Many of the men resented these chores.

At times Vancouver gave vent to sudden outbursts of temper. While no one knew it at the time, there is speculation that George Vancouver may have been afflicted with a hyperthyroid condition now known as Graves' disease that periodically made him irritable and difficult to work with. This problem worsened as the months passed.

When the ships reached Tahiti, only men on duty were allowed to go ashore to get water and trade with the natives for food. This too caused resentment. But Vancouver was well aware of the trouble sailors on shore leave could stir up among natives. Those who did go ashore were under strict orders not to abuse or cheat the Tahitians in any way, or they would suffer severe penalties. By the time the English left, Vancouver had won the respect and admiration of the island people. However, aboard the *Discovery,* one young seaman's resentment toward the captain was festering into hatred.

Thomas Pitt was sixteen years old when he signed aboard the *Discovery.* He was the unruly son of an aristocrat, the Baron of Camelford, and had been sent to sea at the age of seven in the hope that the Navy would tame him. It didn't. When he joined the *Discovery*'s crew, all of the midshipman positions had been taken and he had to sign on as an able seaman, something that offended his aristocratic pedigree. When Pitt looked at Vancouver he saw—despite the captain's uniform—a man of common birth. In Tahiti Pitt was caught trying to trade an item stolen from the ship for the sexual favours of a native girl. Theft aboard ship was a flogging offense, and in trying to solicit a native woman Pitt had disobeyed one of Vancouver's strictest orders. Vancouver knew the story of HMS *Bounty* and the infamous Captain William Bligh, and he was sure liaisons with native women were at the root of that notorious mutiny. Undoubtedly he punished Pitt for the violations, but whether he actually had the son of a baron flogged would later be a matter of great controversy.

At Hawaii Vancouver followed a policy of caution with the natives. Of course, he remembered Cook's bloody fate, but he also knew the Hawaiians were more warlike than the Tahitians. His officers felt that Vancouver's concerns were based on "ill founded suspicion." Nonetheless, when Vancouver learned of a power struggle going on amongst various chieftains, he refused to trade firearms to the contending factions.

On April 18, 1792, Vancouver sighted the North American coast at 39.7° north, about 110 miles north of San Francisco Bay. He at once began the survey that was his principal mission. And, of course, he would look for anything that might hold any promise of being the opening of a Northwest Passage. Vancouver has been unfairly criticized for his failure to explore the Columbia River. In fact, it was not really a failure. As he slowly made his way up the northwest coast of what is now the United States, Vancouver could see the Rocky Mountains to the east. Any river entering the ocean, he reasoned, had to come through those mountains, and was therefore not a likely candidate for a Northwest Passage. Vancouver's priority, therefore, was to proceed with the survey, as ordered. Unfortunately, he has been made a scapegoat for the fact that the United States, and not Great Britain, claimed the Columbia River country.

The project Vancouver had been assigned was huge to start with. Many surveyors of the time made rudimentary maps that were somewhat useful but not exactly accurate. Vancouver was not a man for half measures. He would take many compass bearings and other observations to be sure he had a position exactly right. Before making the California landfall, he and the midshipmen took eighty-five sets of lunar observations to establish the starting point for the survey. As a result of the meticulous manner in which he carried out his orders, the map Vancouver drew was not far off the ones produced today with twenty-first century technology.

Charting the coasts of what are now the states of Oregon and Washington was relatively easy, but when Vancouver reached the

Strait of Juan de Fuca, he realized he had a very challenging task ahead of him. This strait is actually a channel separating Vancouver Island from Washington's Olympic Peninsula, and leads to Puget Sound and the Strait of Georgia, which separates Vancouver Island from the Canadian mainland. The water here is rough, and frequently shrouded in fog.

Vancouver established a base camp and observatory at a place on the mainland he called Port Discovery (Point Grenville, Washington). From here he began to explore the intricate waterways. He discovered Puget Sound, which he named for one of his officers, and surveyed all of it in just a month. The main reason the *Discovery* had been accompanied by the much smaller *Chatham* was that the little tender could enter narrow, shallow waters that the *Discovery* was too large to navigate safely. However, Vancouver found conditions in the Strait of Juan de Fuca and Puget Sound could be hazardous even for the *Chatham.* Tidal and wind conditions posed problems, and in some places the water was too deep for the use of an anchor. He had to fall back on the ships' pinnaces, cutters and launches. Using such small, open craft was labourious and dangerous, and the boats would eventually prove vulnerable in another way.

As Vancouver filled in his map bit by bit, he continued to name prominent geographical features after officers in his crew and Royal Navy officers he admired: Mount Baker, Mount Rainier, Hood Canal, Whidbey Island, to name a few. Most of these names, or remnants of them, remain in use today.

Vancouver passed the delta of the Fraser River, but because it was not navigable, he did not bother to explore it. He also charted the Burrard Inlet, where the city that would one day bear his name would grow.

The Englishmen found the coast of what is now British Columbia to be very irregular, with many inlets and fiords, and the waters strewn with islands. Every foot of it had to be explored, so the going was slow. The captain personally participated in as much of the work as he could, but the sheer magnitude of it required him to delegate some of the surveying to junior officers. One of these young men, midshipman Thomas Manby, who was in charge of a boat, accidentally took a wrong channel and caused a delay in the surveying. Vancouver, who was exhausted from his labours and (unbeknownst to his men) feeling the effects of his illness, gave Manby a severe dressing down, using exceptionally strong language. Humiliated, Manby wrote in his journal, "His salutation I can never forget, his language I will never forgive unless he withdraws his words by satisfactory apology." Of course, no apology was forthcoming. Even though Vancouver later promoted the midshipman to master's mate of the *Chatham,* Manby still held a grudge.

On June 22, 1792, Vancouver was returning from his exploration of Howe Sound, when he saw two strange ships anchored near Burrard Inlet. These were the Spanish survey ships *Sutil* and *Mexicana.* From their officers Vancouver learned that Don Juan Francisco de la Bodega y Quadra, who was a naval commander and the representative of the Spanish government, was waiting for him at Nootka Sound.

Vancouver had not yet received specific instructions regarding his meeting with Quadra and how to settle the problem caused by the Spanish seizures. Those orders were aboard a supply ship that was supposed to rendezvous with him, but which had not yet arrived. So he decided to continue with the survey. Vancouver proposed to the Spanish captains that both parties cooperate in the surveying work. The Spanish agreed, and for a time the collaboration went well. Then the Spanish officers became miffed when the English insisted on surveying an inlet they had already visited. Vancouver told them he had every confidence in their work, but his instructions compelled him to have his own people cover every bit of coastline. Quite likely Vancouver the perfectionist was not impressed with what he would have considered the lackadaisical methods of the Spanish surveyors. Relations between the two parties remained cordial, but the cooperative effort came to an end. The Spanish simply could not match the British standards or keep up with the British crews.

During that summer Vancouver reached the northern end of the island that would be named after him, establishing its insularity. He was the first European known to guide a ship the full length of the Georgia Strait. He charted the only safe navigable passage from the strait to the open sea—a route that is still used today. There were some very close calls, however. In the shoal-ridden waters both the *Discovery* and the *Chatham* had run aground. But thanks to calm seas and good luck, the expedition did not end in disaster.

By August Vancouver had pushed as far as Burke Channel at 52° north. There he learned from the captain of a British trading vessel that his supply ship, the *Daedalus,* was at Nootka Sound. Having accomplished more in one summer than his Spanish counterparts would do in three, Vancouver gave up surveying for that season and sailed for Nootka Sound.

Quadra was a gracious host who entertained Vancouver and his officers in grand style, including multi-course dinners served on silver dishes. He and Vancouver struck up a genuine, warm friendship. Vancouver suggested they name the large island they were on Vancouver and Quadra's Island. Quadra agreed, and the name was officially used until the middle of the nineteenth century when, for the sake of convenience, it was shortened to simply Vancouver Island. Despite the congeniality, the two commanders did not reach complete agreement on a settlement regarding Nootka Sound, each having received conflicting instructions from their superiors. Quadra agreed to reparations for the seized ships and conceded that a small plot of land at Nootka was British property. Vancouver believed the whole sound was British. They agreed to refer the matter to their respective governments and await further instructions. During the following three years of the survey, Vancouver received no further word from London on the matter, and the Spanish eventually withdrew from Nootka. In politely turning down Quadra's request that he recognize Spain's claim to Nootka, Vancouver had unknowingly played a part in what would be the first step in the break-up of Spain's American empire.

In early October with winter approaching, Vancouver sailed south for Monterey, then the capital of Spanish California. Once again Quadra and other Spanish officials entertained the English officers regally. The ordinary seamen were also given leave to enjoy the pleasures of the Spanish town. Five men took this as an opportunity to desert. In the Royal Navy desertion was a crime second in seriousness only to mutiny, and Vancouver could not ignore it. Only one of the deserters was captured before the English were to sail. The deserter was put in irons and, once at sea, was punished with six dozen lashes—twice! Shocking as that may seem today, in the eighteenth century it was commonplace, and some commanders were known to mete out punishments of one hundred lashes or more. This was the most severe punishment Vancouver ordered during the entire expedition. Nonetheless,

Archibald Menzies considered it excessive. The other deserters were eventually captured by the Spanish and held in jail until they could be turned over to the English. Unsurprisingly, there were no more desertions during the voyage.

Vancouver sailed for Hawaii and spent the winter surveying the islands. He established a good relationship with Kamehameha, the king of the largest island, but he remained suspicious of Hawaiians in general. The captain gave orders restricting the activities of the men when they went ashore. He also forbade midshipmen to go ashore except in the company of an officer. Once again, this bred resentment. But Vancouver had good cause for his actions, and it involved more than the death of Captain Cook.

Kamehameha explained to Vancouver that Captain Cook—however inadvertently —had violated a Hawaiian taboo by taking wood from a sacred place, and that action had inflamed the islanders against him. Vancouver accepted that story as a way of making peace with the king. But that hadn't been the only English blood shed in Hawaii.

En route to the rendezvous with Vancouver at Nootka, the *Daedalus* had stopped at Hawaii, where the commander, Lieutenant Hergest, and two other men had been murdered. Kamehameha said the Englishmen had committed no offence, and that the killing was a random act of violence carried out by a group of renegades living on the island of Oahu. Vancouver wanted to impress upon the islanders that they could not murder British subjects with impunity, so he went to Oahu and told the local king he wanted the guilty parties to be tried and punished. Three of the four men identified as the killers were apprehended; the fourth took to the hills. The accused were tried in a court presided over by their king and Vancouver, and were convicted and condemned.

Their own chief executed them with a pistol.

By May 1793, Vancouver was back on the west coast continuing his survey. He explored Dean Channel, and missed meeting the explorer Alexander Mackenzie by just a few weeks. Mackenzie came down the Bella Coola River and reached the sea just a few miles from where Vancouver had been anchored, thus becoming the first European to reach the Pacific overland.

The Englishmen's relations with the west coast natives so far had been friendly. As always, Vancouver sternly warned his men against abusing or cheating the local people. It was quite surprising then, when his small boats suddenly became targets of attack by Natives in canoes. The first few assaults were easily turned away when the Englishmen discharged their guns over the warriors' heads. But then there was a deadly clash in which Vancouver was personally involved. This time a volley of lead fired over their heads did not discourage the attackers. In the fight that followed eight to ten warriors were killed by gunfire, and one Englishman was wounded by a spear.

At first Vancouver thought the Natives had considered the pinnaces, cutters and launches as easy targets for pirate raids. He later decided that American traders, who were becoming more and more numerous, were largely responsible for the sudden hostility of the Natives. Some of these traders did indeed treat the indigenous people badly. Moreover, they traded them poor quality guns that tended to blow up when fired. The Natives were evidently taking revenge on all white men. Vancouver condemned the trafficking of firearms to Native peoples in the Americas, the Pacific islands, or anywhere else.

After charting the western coasts of the Queen Charlotte Islands, Vancouver again ended the work for the season and turned south. In San Francisco and Monterey the English found that the friendly atmosphere of the previous year was gone. The governor, José Joaquín de Arrillaga, had been outraged when he'd learned how hospitably the English had been entertained. Spain and England were traditional enemies! He gave orders that only minimal assistance was to be given to English ships entering California ports, that only senior officers were permitted ashore—and only under Spanish armed escort—and that the English were to depart as soon as they had taken on food and water.

Vancouver was not happy with this state of affairs, but there was nothing he could do about it without creating a new international crisis. Of course, the men resented this treatment, feeling their captain had failed to stand up to the Spanish. Menzies wrote that Vancouver "treated the matter too lightly, he even permitted the limits of the ground he was to walk over to be pointed out to him, and a guard accompanied him to prevent their being encroached upon."

In a letter that Vancouver said was written in "a sneering, forbidding and ungracious stile," Arrillaga denied the English permission to stop at any other California port once they left Monterey. But Vancouver put in at Santa Barbara anyway. The commandant there, Don Felipe Goycochea, had received Arrillaga's instructions but chose to ignore them. He was gracious with the English officers, and allowed the seamen to come ashore as long as they behaved themselves. After paying a similar visit to San Diego, Vancouver once again sailed for Hawaii.

Vancouver's mistrust of the Hawaiians had waned somewhat, but he nonetheless ordered the same precautions he had the year before. Kamehameha himself warned Vancouver that he had enemies who might try to bring disgrace to him by harming the English visitors.

Even so, the men aboard the ships were just as rankled by the restrictions as they had been a year earlier.

Since Captain Cook's "discovery" of what he called the Sandwich Islands in 1778, an increasing number of European and American traders had been doing business there. King Kamehameha had been extending his control over the lesser kings of the smaller islands, but Vancouver foresaw problems. Sooner or later one of the "civilized" nations would seize Hawaii and have a strategic link in trade between North America and Asia. Vancouver convinced Kamahameha that it was in his best interest to formally and legally cede the islands to Great Britain. That would give the British an indisputable first claim. On February 25, 1794, aboard the *Discovery,* the king officially placed his domain under British protection and declared his people subjects of King George III. For a number of reasons, the British government never formally annexed Hawaii into the empire, but Vancouver's actions quite likely discouraged France, Spain or perhaps even Russia from seizing the islands.

Meanwhile, Vancouver had to deal with a problem in his own ranks. He had come to the end of his patience with Thomas Pitt. The obnoxious young aristocrat had added to his list of violations. He had been caught trading illegally with Natives. Next, in a show of horseplay, he and another man had broken the binnacle glass, which housed the ship's compass. Then he had been caught sleeping while on watch. For the latter offence Vancouver had Pitt manacled and tossed in the brig along with common sailors. In Hawaii Vancouver sent the supply ship *Daedalus* back to England with dispatches. He decided to dismiss Pitt from service and send him home as further punishment. When the *Daedalus* reached Australia, Pitt learned that his father had died and he was now the

Baron of Camelford—a peer of the realm with connections and influence. By the time Pitt reached England in September 1796, he was seething for revenge on Captain George Vancouver.

In March 1794, Vancouver sailed from Hawaii to complete the survey. He went straight to Cook Inlet, Alaska, and worked his way down the coast to where he had left off the previous year. He tried to be personally involved in the work as much as possible, but illness left him confined to his cabin for days at a time. On several occasions the surveyors had trouble with Natives. Since the Englishmen had done nothing to offend the local people, Vancouver reasoned that the hostility had been the result of experiences with unscrupulous white traders. The survey was completed on August 19, and Vancouver allowed the men to celebrate with "an additional allowance of grog." Two days later the *Discovery* and the *Chatham* set sail for Nootka, where Vancouver was saddened to learn his good friend Quadra had died in March. After a stopover at Monterey—where the ill-mannered Arrillaga had been replaced—Vancouver sailed for England via Cape Horn at the southern tip of South America, thus making his voyage a circumnavigation of the globe. After a series of delays, they reached Ireland on September 13, 1795. A month later Vancouver was in London.

Captain George Vancouver had successfully completed the most ambitious marine surveying project ever undertaken up to that time. He had been away over four and a half years, and had sailed approximately 65,000 miles, to which he could add some 10,000 miles in excursions by small boats. He and his men had, in painstaking detail, mapped the west coast of North America from 30° north to 60° north. Vancouver had proven beyond any doubt that the Northwest Passage did not exist in latitudes that would permit commercial traffic. He had claimed new lands for Britain, and for good measure he had charted the Hawaiian Islands and provided Britain with the opportunity to add them to the empire. En route to North America he had even mapped three hundred previously uncharted miles of Australia's south coast. In an age when the death rate for men at sea was high, Vancouver had lost only six men; one to disease, one to accidental poisoning, one by apparent suicide and three to drowning. Captain Vancouver should have returned home to a hero's welcome and a knighthood; instead, he found himself in the midst of scandal and acrimony.

Though Vancouver and Menzies had managed to work together, their relationship was strained. Menzies complained to his good friend Sir Joseph Banks, who was in a position to undermine recognition of Vancouver's accomplishments, as well as to promote innuendo regarding the captain's character. Added to this were Thomas Manby's charges that Vancouver was a harsh and cruel commander. "Haughty, proud, mean and insolent" were the words Manby used to describe Vancouver. The worst, however, was to come from Thomas Pitt, now Lord Camelford. Pitt had not yet arrived back in England, but the story that Vancouver had ordered him flogged had reached London and created a scandal. If Vancouver did indeed have Pitt flogged, he would have seriously overstepped his authority. Even a captain could not have an aristocrat whipped like a common sailor. Vancouver neither confirmed nor denied having Pitt flogged. He said only that he had acted to preserve discipline on the ship, and that Pitt's own misconduct was the reason for his punishment. None of the journals kept by any of the men aboard the *Discovery* mention anything about a flogging.

When Pitt returned to London he sent Vancouver a note challenging him to a duel. Vancouver was by this time a very sick man. Duelling was out of the question. He replied to Pitt that he could submit the affair to any flag officer in the Royal Navy. If that officer judged that Vancouver had acted unjustly, then the captain would meet his lordship on the field of honour. That wasn't good enough for Pitt, and he wrote back, threatening Vancouver with physical violence.

On September 21, 1796, George Vancouver was walking along London's Conduit Street with his brother Charles, when they were confronted by Pitt and two of his cronies. Pitt immediately attacked George with his cane. Charles tried to protect his ailing brother, but some of the blows found their target. Some passersby intervened, and Pitt stalked off, announcing that he would do the same thing to Vancouver every time he saw him. A court placed Pitt on bond to keep the peace.

The newspaper stories about "The Caning on Conduit Street" made it appear that the two Vancouvers were the villains in the affair. A caricature of the event drawn by newspaper artist James Gilroy was both misleading to the public and humiliating to Vancouver. It presented him as being short, fat and pompous. Furthermore, words written on various objects in the cartoon suggested that Vancouver was a bully, a coward, an embezzler and a disgrace to the navy. The Royal Navy now considered Captain Vancouver an embarrassment.

Vancouver never faced a court martial or a court of inquiry, but it seems there was an investigation into his conduct as a commanding officer. The fact that he was not charged indicates that the investigators were satisfied that he did not act with undue severity. But the incident with Lord Camelford helped to colour his undeserved future reputation as a brutal commander.

Vancouver spent his last months writing his journals for the Admiralty. He died at the age of forty on May 12, 1798, with the work unfinished. His brother John completed the last one hundred pages of the three-volume work, and the published version received high praise from reviewers. Lord Thomas Pitt of Camelford, a violent troublemaker to the end, was killed in a duel in 1804. One of Captain Cook's biographers would state later that of all the officers who trained under the great man, only Vancouver was in the same class as his old commander as a marine surveyor.

Bibliography

Anderson, Bern. *Surveyor of the Sea: The Life and Voyages of Captain George Vancouver.* Toronto: University of Toronto Press, 1960.

Armstrong, Joe C. W. *Champlain.* Toronto: Macmillan of Canada, 1987.

Butts, Ed, and Harold Horwood. *Pirates & Outlaws of Canada 1610–1932.* Toronto: Doubleday Canada, 1984.

Cook, Ramsay. *The Voyages of Jacques Cartier.* Toronto: University of Toronto Press, 1993.

Cranston, J. Herbert. *Etienne Brule: Immortal Scoundrel.* Toronto: Ryerson Press, 1949.

Firstbrook, Peter. *The Voyage of the* Matthew: *John Cabot and the Discovery of North America.* Toronto: McClelland & Stewart, 1997.

Francis, Daniel. *Battle for the West: Fur Traders and the Birth of Canada.* Edmonton: Hurtig Publishers, 1982.

Hearne, Samuel (Farley Mowatt, ed.). *Coppermine Journey: An Account of Great Adventure Selected from the Journals of Samuel Hearne.* Toronto: McClelland & Stewart, 1958.

Innis, Harold, A. *The Fur Trade in Canada.* Toronto: University of Toronto Press, 1956.

———. *Peter Pond: Fur Trader and Adventurer.* Toronto: Irwin & Gordon Ltd., 1930.

Jenish, D'Arcy. *Epic Wanderer: David Thompson and the Mapping of the Canadian West.* Toronto: Doubleday Canada, 2003.

Lehane, Brendan. *The Northwest Passage.* Alexandria, Virginia: Time-Life Books, 1981.

McDermott, James. *Martin Frobisher: Elizabethan Privateer.* New Haven and London: Yale University Press, 2001.

McGoogan, Ken. *Ancient Mariner: The Amazing Adventures of Samuel Hearne.* Toronto: Harper Collins, 2003.

Newman, Peter, C. *Company of Adventurers.* Markham, ON: Penguin Books Canada Ltd., 1985.

Rich, E. E. *The Fur Trade and the Northwest to 1857.* Toronto: McClelland & Stewart, 1967.

Rowe, Frederick W. *A History of Newfoundland and Labrador.* Toronto: McGraw-Hill Ryerson Ltd., 1980.

Smith, James K. *David Thompson.* Don Mills: Fitzhenry & Whiteside, 1975.

Thompson, David (Barbara Belyea, ed.). *Columbia Journals.* Montreal and Kingston: McGill-Queen's University Press, 2007.

Trudel, Marcel. *The Beginnings of New France: 1524–1663.* Toronto: McClelland & Stewart, 1973.

Vail, Philip. *The Magnificent Adventures of Henry Hudson.* New York: Dodd, Mead & Co., 1965.

Wagner, Henry R. *Peter Pond: Fur Trader & Explorer.* New Haven, Connecticut: Yale University Library, 1955.

Warkentin, Germaine. *Canadian Exploration Literature: An Anthology.* Don Mills, Ontario: Oxford University Press, 1993.

Library and Archives Canada, *The Dictionary of Canadian Biography*, www.biographi.ca.